To Dan

Your thoughts are
important – choose
carefully –

Barbara Jordan

# CONFESSIONS

*—of a—*

# REGRESSIONIST

*Is There a Life or Time
Other than the Present?*

## Barbara H. Pomar

iUniverse, Inc.
Bloomington

Confessions of a Regressionist
Is There a Life or Time Other than the Present?

iUniverse books may be ordered through booksellers or by contacting:

iUniverse
1663 Liberty Drive
Bloomington, IN 47403
www.iuniverse.com
1-800-Authors (1-800-288-4677)

ISBN: 978-1-4759-0740-7 (sc)
ISBN: 978-1-4759-0741-4 (hc)
ISBN: 978-1-4759-0742-1 (ebk)

Library of Congress Control Number: 2012905569

Printed in the United States of America

iUniverse rev. date: 07/31/2012

# Contents

For my husband, Craig Salsbury

# Preface

After more than three decades of leading regressions for individuals and presentations for groups, I still had questions about the nature of time and how the regression process works. Because 90 percent of my clients were accessing other lifetimes, I was convinced of the reality of past lives. Yet I was reading books and articles saying that "all time is now" and that "being in the moment" was the real goal.

My relatives who were active in various Christian churches believed fully that there was no such thing as a past life. Even so, my family members were tolerant of my belief, as I was of theirs. Some of my clients had the same disbelief. I explained that because we have genes of both mother and father, the memories of both families could be passed along genetically. Sometimes this satisfied the doubters—that is, until they reported a life in which they had died as a child before having children themselves. I had a feeling we were discussing different sides of the same coin, such as heads and tails. But where was the proof?

When I was enrolled in the doctorate program at American Pacific University in Hawaii, I decided to research the question and settle the debate: past lives vs. no past lives. The basic problem of studying beliefs is that they may not be founded in fact. A prominent person may think of or propose certain ideas and his/her followers take them as fact.

I needed to research the question of past lives, from historical and therapeutic points of view to current uses and various techniques of regression. Then I would research the views that claim there is no such thing as past life. I came upon dead ends that ended with quotations from inspired holy books. Some of the passages could be interpreted through opposing beliefs. I still had the feeling that there was truth behind the belief that there is no such thing as past lives. As Bruce Lipton was making news (although quietly) with theories about genetic memory, and many articles about quantum theories were headlining magazines, I was thinking there could be evidence in quantum theories that might support one belief or the other.

As a part of my dissertation study, I started reading about quantum theories by concentrating on various theories about time. My problem was that although physics had been a favorite subject of mine in the mid-1960s, I had not taken a major mathematics or physics class since then. After almost three years of reading, I felt there was an explanation that could reconcile the phenomenon of remission of physical and mental problems with regression therapy and the belief that there are no past lives.

As I was assembling the research, I found myself using my clients' stories as examples. Some stories are representative of groups of clients. Others are used with the written permission of the authors. I have not used identifying descriptions, as the stories, while unique, are typical of most clients.

# Acknowledgments

I want to acknowledge and thank my husband, Craig Salsbury, for his patience and for the good dinners he made me while I was immersed in this process. Gratitude goes to Brian Walsh for keeping me writing and directed toward the completion of this project. Mark Schlenz was a great guide, proofreader, and editor. I learned much not only from his grammatical notes but from his general comments as well. Ann West, my editor, was amazing in helping make a scholastic endeavor readable and ready for publishing. Her insights were invaluable. Karen Spaleta, a physics professor at the University of Fairbanks, was patient with my many questions about physics, and she helped me proofread the scientific aspects of this paper. I also am indebted to many friends who supported my research and put up with my absentmindedness when I would start thinking about *time* while on the golf course and forget where my ball was! Many thanks to all my clients over the years who permitted me to lead them on time journeys and who have taught me much along the way. My deepest gratitude goes to all my teachers—both officially in classrooms, unofficially in the school of life, and my clients.

Finally, I want to thank Spellman Evans Downer for permitting me to use one of his original oil paintings, *Koyukukiatatna*, for the cover of this book.

# Introduction

*Confessions of a Regressionist* may be read on several different levels. One level of reading might focus on the historical stories, as told by some of my clients. Some stories would make good bases for interesting historical novels. Another level might pursue interest in regression work, including past-life research, by following discussions about the various techniques of Morris Netherton, Roger Woolger, Helen Wambach, and Michael Newton, for example, and my comments about their usage. A third level might lead to the reasons that regression therapy is effective. Another level of reading might consider the controversy between many lifetimes and a single life. Or, one level could explore the scientific quantum theories behind time that affect regression work. *Confessions of a Regressionist* presents the idea that past-life theory can be used to good effect even by nonbelievers. I wanted to have context and background for the purpose and to use the fact that time has been different. It was one of the most common avenues into a no-time space. In the no-time space, the healing can occur.

Because the discussions about past lives and the view that there are no past lives usually have religious overtones, I wrote this book from a scientific point of view that at times acknowledges religious input. The reader is asked to keep an open mind and to not accept something because it is written, but to compare new ideas with previous thoughts and then continue to the finish before drawing any final conclusions. I was surprised at what I found during the research process, such as the early debates between mesmerism and meditation, the probable reason why Sigmund Freud gave up on hypnotism, the philosophical interpretations of concepts in physics, and the reality of time, among others.

I had to reread many books on quantum theories a few times before I could translate their contents into understandable, ordinary language. Often I reminded myself of the remark by Nobel laureate Richard Feynman: "No one understands the quantum theory" (quantum mechanics). Once I accepted that I was reading about philosophical interpretations of mathematics, I could better understand the ideas, and thus pass along my research and conclusions about time.

It appeared to me that time was nonexistent. The physicists were trying to explain how things really are and how, collectively, we have taken on a particular framework of reality. This may be a slow-reading section. From what I can tell, however, you already know this information; it just has to come to your mind again. The history of regression work goes back to the beginning of the twentieth century. Josef Breuer and Sigmund Freud were among the physicians who were convinced that the cause of neurosis, for example, was a past event in the early life of a patient.[1]

When I needed a topic for my dissertation at the American Pacific University, I chose to study *time,* which is crucial both to the field of physics and to regression work. Because physics had changed tremendously in the last few decades, I was almost certain I could find an answer in recent research to explain what was happening to my clients.

Not being a mathematician, I delayed accounting and statistics in my undergraduate degree until handheld calculators were permitted. I have no training in physics, other than a basic undergraduate course. Because my statements are written for the layperson with no background on the topic, they are my interpretations of the mathematics and physics principles. This could be a good thing, as my readers are also probably not trained in these subjects. Further, Karen Spaleta, a professor of physics at the University of Alaska, has reviewed my findings and agreed with the facts as presented. While doing regression research, I discovered that many sources were written in languages other than English. Thus, I depended on translations for the material in this book.

I would like to clear up some possibly confusing terminology at the outset. The medical professions use *subconscious* to refer to any mental activity that is below conscious awareness. The hypnotherapy professionals use *unconscious* to refer to the same thing. I will be using the term *unconscious*.

In the medical professions, most practitioners call their customers *patients*. Hypnotists and hypnotherapists refer to their customers as *clients*, as their therapeutic work involves a joint endeavor. The client hires the hypnotherapist to assist the client in changing or enhancing a situation. It is the client's responsibility to follow directions. Another possible confusion is in the use of time and tenses. During a regression session, past events are worked by using the present tense, because the clients are experiencing them or reviewing them now, in the present.

The term *regression* refers to traveling in time before the present moment, including before birth, in this life, or in other lives. In contrast, *progression* refers to travel into the future, including future lives. The word *regression* was first used by Freud. In my work and in discussions with other regressionists, I have found that when directed to regress to a specific cause for a current situation, clients often call to mind a future event. Therefore, I use the term *regression* as a noun or a verb that specifies another time frame other than the one experienced in my office at the time of the visit. *Regressionists* are those physicians, psychiatrists, psychologists, hypnotherapists, hypnotists, or others who access memories on a regular basis and use regression techniques in their practice. Specific terminology not explained in the text is explained in the notes.

In the first chapter, a client's session demonstrates the unexpected benefits of a regression session and connections with two recent researchers: Bruce Lipton's work in cellular memory and Hugh Everett's many worlds theory.

In the second chapter, in order to better understand regression work, the origins of hypnosis and mesmerism, including the initial work of Josef Breuer and Sigmund Freud are discussed. Hypnosis is linked to the work of James Braid and its beginnings with meditation. Mesmerism is discussed, including its use today as energy healing.

Further, the controversies around Franz Mesmer, Abbe Faria, and James Braid are reviewed. Mesmer developed his techniques within the traditions of magnetism. Faria and Braid independently found that the deep states of consciousness in which psychological healing takes place are the same levels that Indian holy men have achieved to change their physical and mental well-being. Thus, the meditation traditions of India have had an effect on the development of the hypnosis used today.

The physical and mental function of memory and the problems that are associated with accessing true memory are addressed in the third chapter. I conducted the original research for my master's thesis, *Past Life Therapy: Origins and Sources,* in 1995. I concluded that although most memories recalled during a past-life session are authentic, it is the impression the memories have on the client that provide the fodder for therapeutic work. Salient research pertaining to the dissertation follows and adds to my original research.

The fourth chapter explores regression work, including both hypnotic and nonhypnotic methods. This survey traces the history of regression from the sixteenth century to Freud and brings it forward to its current status. Regression is considered here as a means of obtaining information. Any therapeutic results of regression are thought of as accidental or a result of further work by a psychoanalyst or psychologist.

Chapter 5 examines the use of regression as a healing modality. The history of regression use in therapeutic situations surveys the work of Joseph Breuer to hypnotherapy techniques by Morris Netherton, Hans TenDam, Roger Woolger, and Tad James. Not all of the various regression techniques or authors are reviewed. The ones chosen are representative of various techniques. Illustrations of the progression of regression techniques are included. The case histories are drawn from my files, which I have kept since the mid-1980s, unless otherwise noted. Clients' actual names and identifying information have been changed or omitted.

Chapter 6 covers the newest area in regression work, the territory between death and birth, known as the life between lives. Although this area was hinted about in Alberto de Rochas's book

*Les Vies Successives*, published in 1911, it wasn't until Michael Newton published *Journey of Souls* in 1996 that it became generally incorporated into regressionists' available modalities.

A history of the study of time in physics is explored in chapters 7 and 8. Chapter 7 includes consideration of Isaac Newton's absolute time, Albert Einstein's relative time, and Roger Penrose's folding time—the outcome of special relativity theory. The time of quantum mechanics is reviewed in chapter 8. Traditionally, the terms *quantum mechanics* and *quantum theory* are used interchangeably. Hugh Everett's many worlds theory,[2] Julian Barbour's *Nows*,[3] and Roger Penrose's folding time[4] are also explored. Since new thoughts and theories are constantly being developed in these fields, I may not have the latest information at the time of printing.

The final sections pull all the strands together and weave a more complete tapestry within a larger context. What are the latest findings? Regression work, for current life as well as past and future lives, has many benefits and a significant place in various therapies. The ending considers how to use this information—now.

Chapter 9 presents the cases for the existence of past lives and the argument that the only time is now or that there is no such thing as past lives. In chapter 10, I answer the questions posed in the prior chapter. I tie in the understanding of time, as used in regression work, with the theories of time proposed by the latest significant physicists. Hopefully I can answer the question of how, if "all time is *now*," clients can go to a past event, change a decision or reframe an event, and change their present symptoms or conditions. Finally, in chapter 11, I carry the regression and physics work into the future.

By the end of the study, I expect to answer my central questions: Is there really such a thing as a past life? If so, what is it? If all time is really now, and there is no such thing as a past life, then what do regressionists really do? If these are polemic questions, then perhaps only individuals with assistance from their religious advisors can answer these questions. If there is a firm scientific rationale behind the questions, then I hope the field of quantum physics has the answers. Minimally, I will answer the question: What is the purpose for the regression work?

# Chapter 1

# When the Questions Started

"I don't believe in past lives!" My client was adamant. What had just happened had occurred in response to a question I had asked her unconscious mind. We were in the midst of a timeline regression session. She had traveled along both her mother's genetic line and her father's genetic line to neutralize a current problem, and some of her symptoms had subsided. I had just asked her unconscious mind if there was another event that had resulted in the current problem. Immediately she had responded, "It is in a past life." It was then that her conscious mind responded firmly, "I don't believe in past lives." She quickly came back to the present and terminated the session.

I have had other clients who, because of a strong religious belief, have stated they didn't believe in past lives. Usually, after I explain genetic memory à la Bruce Lipton and provide other possible explanations for the existence of past lives, they will go along with a trial explanation.[5]

Having talked with many people, my own family included, I feel there is a reason why so many are strongly against any notion of previous lives. Indeed, mathematically, no proof exists of a past or a future. If there is no past or no future, then how can there be past or future lifetimes? But then, what happens when regressionists lead a client to another lifetime and the current situation changes—sometimes in the same session, sometimes later? Those whom mainstream medical practitioners have not helped often benefit by regression. This transformation happens on a regular basis, and many therapists count on it to make a reasonable living.

Pam was on the telephone. She was in town with a medical problem that was chronic and had no current solution. Pam knew I was not a medical practitioner and did not request healing of any sort. She wanted to know only the origin of her situation and why she was having certain problems. She was comfortable with the prospects her doctors had explained. It seemed she had fallen after tripping over a threshold. Twisting her legs, she had hit her knees and fallen on her elbows. The doctors had found blood clots from her hips all the way down to her ankles. She was on medication not only to prevent a stroke but also for pain.

Because she would be in town only for a few days, we agreed to an extended session, so I could obtain background information as well as do a regular session with her. It is standard practice that before a regression the therapist elicits a history from the client, which includes contact information, past and current family members, the current environment (which may or may not have direct impact on the client's issues), and a brief medical history, including the history of the symptom. With this information, the regressionist can decide which technique would be the best to use for the specific client. Once I have this information, I can better assist clients in retrieving information, so they can answer their own questions.

Once Pam was in my office, I took a more complete history. Then I explained timeline therapy, as developed by Tad James. We would go above her own timeline and see if the cause was genetic, either in her mother's or father's genetic line. As memory is contained in each cell,[6] and as we are a combination of our mother's and father's genes, we also have their memories. We have our father's memory until conception and our mother's memory until our birth or shortly thereafter.[7] One benefit of the timeline therapy (TLT) is that the client does not have to reveal the content of memories to the regressionist for full therapeutic benefit. However, Pam was insistent: She wanted to know the cause, the *why*, of her condition.

I decided to use her timeline as a bridge into her past. Pam was familiar with past-life regression work, so we quickly got started.

With TLT, no formal induction is required, and the client's conscious mind is active while allowing the unconscious to guide the session. The following is a transcription of my notes with Pam.

Pomar: Go above your timeline. Turn toward the past, looking to the root cause of the deep clots, blood clots in the left leg. Was it before, during, or after birth?

Client: Before.

Pomar: Was it while you were inside Mother?

Client: No.

Pomar: Go to conception. Look down Father's genetic line. Was it Father's?

Client: No.

Pomar: Continue back above your timeline to the root cause of the deep clots, blood clots in the left leg. [pause] What are you wearing?

Client: The dress appears to be Egyptian.

Pomar: Where are you?

Client: On a slab of stone.

Pomar: What is happening?

Client: Something is being done to my legs. A cutting or mutilation, cutting off of circulation . . . a tourniquet. [grimacing and turning her head away]

Pomar: What is the next thing that happens?

Client: They move the tourniquet up my leg, causing limbs to die one part at a time. I have great pain.

Pomar: Go above. What are you learning?

Client: [shakes her head no]

[I am wondering what is in her mind. With TLT, clients are directed that they don't have to share or reveal details to the regressionist. My curiosity has to be kept in check.]

Pomar: Is this the first time? The beginning?

Client: (a long pause and then in another voice, similar but more directive than Pam's) Have to go back further.

Pomar: Go to the beginning of the root cause.

Client: I see cave drawings on cave walls. It is not like in North America, not like the book. [She was referring to a recent series of books on ancient North American Indian culture] There are skins are on the floor.

Pomar: What else are you aware of?

Client: Ceremonial lines drawn in a triangle. I am in a shelter made of skins. There is a crack in the walls. Someone is lying there.

Pomar: Who is it?

Client: Me. It is birth and death. I see a separation of colors. The baby is dark and covered with something. Mother has dark hair and is pale, like she has no blood left. She is bleeding to death. But there is joy in life.

Pomar: Where are you? What is the name of the nearest city, village? Go above the timeline, look down.

Client: Somewhere in the Middle East.

Pomar: What are you learning?

Client: Don't want to say . . .

[In timeline techniques, it is not necessary for the client to vocalize what she is learning.]

Pomar: Keep them in a safe place where you have other important lessons, so you may have access to them in case you might need them.

Client: (Another voice, similar to Pam's conscious voice) Have to go back. It has to do with Mother's genealogy. Father was a cousin. Bloodlines were not compatible.

[Her conscious mind is directing the action. As she is a meditator, she is accustomed to communicating with her unconscious and conscious minds. I wish all my clients had that faculty. It makes my job much easier. At this time, we start following her Mother's genetic line.]

Pomar: Go above the timeline, following Mother's genetic line.

Client: We are by the river. We are being attacked by another species. Mating was forced on us. [grimacing] Violence resulted in the mating. We were incompatible. I felt horror—profanity—at the rape.

[Was the DNA incompatible? I wonder. I really did want to go into this in more detail. A glance at the clock and the intuition that we are not even halfway through the story prompts me to move on. If there is time later, we could go back to this story and get the details.]

5

Pomar: Stay above the timeline. What are the positive lessons?

Client: You can choose. I can choose. I have a right to choose my mate. Some decisions are difficult. Some choices are difficult. Sometimes it might seem as if either choice is impossible or difficult. You can still choose.

Pomar: What could you do different?

Client: Choose another mate.

Pomar: Do it!

[I rarely tell a client what to do. I don't know what to expect when I do so. I immediately wonder why I did it and what the outcome will be. The timeline is an imaginary line of time that connects us with a past event. It is used as a bridge to a specific event. It stretches to an unlimited past as well as an unlimited future, as far as I can tell.]

Pomar: As you are above your timeline, go back to the cave. Look in the cave. What do you see?

Client: Mother is different, lighter color. Baby is lighter. Both live in joy.

Pomar: Go above to your higher self and ask what happened.

[The higher self is often considered to be the highest part of the nonphysical part of a person—the highest part of the soul and in constant contact with the Higher Self. At this point, I feel I need another opinion of what was going on.]

Client: It seemed that mother chose a different mate at the time of violence, closer to her own kind. The resultant DNA produced a more compatible mating and child.

Pomar: Go to the end of that life.

Client: I died young—an accident. An animal killed both me and my child.

[Did we jump timelines into a parallel timeline? Did it happen when she rechose her mate? I refocus my attention on the client's needs. We retrace our steps forward.]

Pomar: Go above your timeline, continue forward to the present. Go to Egypt when you were on the slab.

Client: I am still there.

Pomar: Ask why they are doing that to your legs.

Client: They are afraid of the Light. If they give me a horrible death, it will carry over to other lifetimes. They are evil. I didn't believe there was evil in the world. I didn't want to acknowledge it the first time. They want to make me afraid of death, the light. I am not the only one they are doing this to.

[This seems to be the event that caused her current problem and is a good place to change the current situation.]

Pomar: Take a saber sword in your hands and cut the ties, starting at the ankles.

Client: Why?

[The client's conscious is active. It is unusual for the client to question directions. It lets me know that regressions can be successful even when the client is conscious versus being in a deep hypnotic state.]

Pomar: If the blood is let go all at once, it might cause more damage as it hits the blockages, as the blood starts flowing down and up. Letting the blood flow gradually will be less damaging and more beneficial.

[I intuitively follow internal directions. I had learned it is important that the hypnotherapist project and think positive thoughts, never doubting a positive outcome. Often I feel I am guided while in this state. This time I saw the red eyes and had a very brief shot of fear. I surround myself with white light, saying a quiet prayer for protection and assistance. Then I follow the internal directions.]

Pomar: Feel the blood start flowing easily and effortlessly. Now cut the ties at the knees. [pause] The groin.

[I start feeling their eyes—small, red eyes. Not bloodshot. Red. They are communicating to me that they did not like my interference.]

Pomar: Feel the body, the unconscious mind, releasing what is needed to dissolve the blockages, the clots, easily and effortlessly. [pause] Go forward to just before death. Is there anything you want to say to the men who tied your legs?

Client: You knew what you were doing. You were following directions from someone else.

Pomar: Can you forgive them?

Client: Yes, I forgive them.

Pomar: What are you learning?

Client: There is evil in the world. I need to trust spirit. The first time, I felt the evil, but I didn't want to say it. I felt by saying it I was giving it power and acknowledging it.

Pomar: Go forward along your timeline to each time you had problems with circulation in your legs. Pick up what you are learning and collapse the event back to now.

Client: In the 1800s, I was a young tomboy. My sister was very feminine and did all the girl things. I loved to ride and play around the horses. This was a lifetime I didn't want to see. Later she pushed me in front of a wagon. My legs got crushed. She was sent away. She is my twin in this lifetime.

[Sometimes, clients need to relate what is going through their mind, but not necessarily in answer to my questions or directions. The client's unconscious is directing the session and will take the story where it needs to go. Earlier in the session, she had spoken of another partial regression about a life with her twin. This event was in her conscious mind. Also, during the intake interview, Pam had mentioned she suspected that her problem stemmed from a previous lifetime with her sister.]

Pomar: Go to the end of that lifetime. [pause] Is there anything you would like to say to your sister? [pause] See her in front of you? [pause] Let me know when you are done.

Client: [silence] It is done.

Pomar: Is there anyone else?

Client: No.

[This had taken more time than we had allowed. I quickly finished.]

Pomar: Process that lifetime and come forward. Collapse all other events to come back to now.

Pomar: Know that if you need to have more details about any of the lifetimes we touched on, all you need to do is to go into a meditative or self-hypnotic state and go above your timeline to that time.

I talked to Pam the next day, and she said she had had the best meditation in a long time. Although she was walking without her cane, with greatly diminished pain, she still had some discomfort. She felt the clots being released. Swelling had diminished in her legs. She was planning to resume her massage-healing practice. She felt that the reason for the blocks was to prevent her from doing what she knew she needed to accomplish in this life. If we had had more time, we would have processed the time before her current birth to find the reason for her entry into Earth at this particular time.

This experience verified to me the powerful benefits of regression work. But, how can these benefits be proven? The physical changes are evident, but why and how do they occur? Bruce Lipton, a cellular biologist who wrote *Biology of Belief* (2007), researched cellular memory. He came to the conclusion that memory lies not only in each and every cell of the person but within one's entire genetic line as well. Lipton goes on to say that memories are created by emotional impacts of an event, either witnessed or experienced, whether heard or read about. When the emotional impact of the memory of the event is neutralized, the event returns to a nonevent status.

Was this an instance of *cryptoamnesia*, when memories of forgotten passages from books or conversations are recalled? Pam answered that question without my asking. She said that the tent she saw in her earlier life was different from the tents in the Native American books popular at that time. I did not ask her to explain, for that was outside our current interest.

If time is linear, then how can a client travel back in time, change the impact of an event, and have her current life change? What does physics say about all this?

# Chapter 2

# In the Beginning
# There Was Meditation

To address the questions raised in the introduction, let us go back to the start of the session. Regression starts with a change in the state of awareness, such as hypnosis, a process tempered by the perception of time. "My session is over? It can't be. We just got started," my clients often complain when I start winding up the session. Meanwhile, the clock in my office says we have been working for over two hours.

Time is not a constant. Yet it *is* a standard of measurement for most people and projects. One of the places it is least consistent is the hypnotherapist's office. The clock states the actual time. Clients have visited another point in timespace[8] and returned. Their frequent perception is that minutes have passed during the hours of our session. Their bodies are less stressed, and often their perceptions have changed about a past event. The misperception of time is one of the indicators of having achieved a certain level of hypnosis.

To better understand what is involved in a session, I start by explaining two ideas: hypnosis that leads into regression, and the idea of time. Finally, I join both topics and address the questions raised by Pam's session. Although I used an informal induction (entering into another time frame without a formal introduction) with Pam, a formal induction (a set method of words, speech, or actions) is the hypnotic method approved by Division 30 of the American Psychological Association.[9] I have found that it is often

11

not necessary to use a formal induction to have the client skip into another timespace.

## Meditation

Meditation has been around for a long time, perhaps thousands of centuries. Its origin has been lost in oral traditions. Meditation, as commonly used, is a method of relaxing the body and focusing on a thought or simply on the breath. Many techniques are taught to achieve varying degrees of concentrated focus. It has been used in the practice of various religions—for instance, Hinduism. James Braid, in 1844, wrote a series of articles comparing hypnosis and meditation.[10] He mentions watching a Hindu holy man reduce his breath and vital signs to simulate death or hibernation. The holy man could do it for months at a time and be resuscitated with no physical damage. This can be compared with the use of hypnosis to reduce breathing and blood flow for painless surgery. In the twenty-first century, meditation is used to relax the body and mind to reduce stress and allow the body to heal itself. Special techniques to achieve other purposes are outside the scope of this book.

## Early Hypnosis

The state of consciousness that is now called the *hypnotic* state was first mentioned in Genesis 2:21 (Holy Bible Revised Standard Version): "So the Lord God caused a deep sleep to fall upon the man, and while he slept took one of his ribs and closed up its place with flesh."[11] Many ancient cultures used something similar to hypnosis. For example, the Egyptians described a practice similar to today's hypnosis on the Ebers papyrus in BC 1000.[12] Many native cultures have shamans or medicine men who use focused concentration, or their personal energy, a la Mesmer, for healing. In the Western written tradition, the next mention of someone causing that artificially created state for healing was in the mid-1700s. Franz

Anton Mesmer (1734-1815) went to a Jesuit University to study theology, switched to philosophy, and then turned to law. Finally, he graduated in medicine with a dissertation on the influences of planets on human diseases in 1766. In 1773, Mesmer started treating Fraulein Oesterlin, who had over fifteen symptoms.[13] He evolved a treatment based on the work of Father Maximilian Hell (1720-1792), an English physician who used magnets for healing, based on the work of Paracelsus (1493-1541). Mesmer thought he could use magnets to produce an artificial tide within Oesterlin that would improve her condition. After giving Oesterlin a preparation made from iron, Mesmer attached a magnet on her stomach and two others on her legs. Her symptoms lessened for several hours. Understanding that the magnets alone could not possibly cause the effects, he surmised the improvement must have come from a fluid that had accumulated within himself, which he called "animal magnetism."[14] Mesmer thought that his personal magnetism had been transferred to the patient and could thus heal nervous disorders, such as hysteria.

After Mesmer went to Paris in 1778, he often had up to two hundred patients in his office at home. They sat around a *baquet*, a large jar with holes in the rim. Iron rods poked out at right angles and different heights so they could be applied to parts of the body that were ailing. Also, a rope extended from the baquet to one person and then attached to another person and so on. Mesmer would vocally activate the liquid in the jar and direct it out to each connected person. Mirrors that reflected the fluid supposedly increased the magnetic influences, as did musical sounds from magnetized instruments, including a Benjamin Franklin glass piano that Mesmer played.[15]

The Academy of Science in France in 1784 investigated Mesmer's treatment and came to the conclusion that "imagination with magnetism produces convulsions, and the magnetism without imagination produces nothing." Mesmer left Paris. However, mesmerism was the only treatment for neurosis available at that time.[16]

In 1836, Antoine Despine (1777-1852) used animal magnetism, which came to be known as "uncovering hypnosis," with an eleven-year-old patient, Estelle. Despine would ask Estelle to lie down and would move his hands by using long strokes inches above her body. When Estelle was in the trance, Despine would give her suggestions about healing.[17] During her magnetic treatment, she would prescribe the nature of the treatment and tell when her situation would be cured.[18]

Marquis Armand-Marie-Jacques de Chastenet de Puysegur (1751-1825), along with his two younger brothers, was an early student of Mesmer. After returning home from a series of healing seminars by Mesmer, Puysegur started giving the laying-on-of-hands treatment called animal magnetism.[19] Puysegur did not use a baquet, but like Mesmer, he did give individual and group treatments at his home by a tree. In individuals, he would produce a magnetic sleep and lead them to produce the perfect crisis, similar to their original symptom. To accommodate a greater number of patients, primarily the peasants around his estate, he had them sit under a tree that had ropes hanging from the branches. Patients would wrap the ropes around ailing parts of their bodies and form a chain by holding thumbs. Puysegur direct the magnetism to flow from the tree into the ropes and through the ailing parts of their bodies. Energy continued flowing through the connected chain until Puysegur ordered the chain to be broken and patients to rub their hands. Some were touched by a rod, which put them into a perfect crisis (now called *abreaction*, which is any abnormal reaction, such as crying when sitting under a tree holding someone's thumb). Puysegur, or one of his assistants, would then treat those patients. To "disenchant" his patients (bring them back to full conscious awareness), Puysegur had them kiss the tree, after which they would have no memory of what had just happened.

During a private session with one of the workers on his estate, Victor Race, Puysegur was moving his hands over Race's body when he noticed that Race was in a peaceful sleep minus any of the usual abreactions. Race would responded to suggestions while in that state and also diagnose his own diseases, predict their course, and prescribe treatments. When it was requested, Race diagnosed for others.[20] Puysegur called this process *presensation*[21] and named the sleep-like trance *magnetic somnambulism*.[22]

After Napoleon's overthrow in 1815, most magnetizers, not knowing Mesmer, thought that mesmerizing was the work of Puysegur; but Puysegur always considered himself a disciple of Mesmer.[23] The main difference between Puysegur and Mesmer was that Mesmer believed it was animal magnetism, a magnetic fluid that flowed from him into his patient. In contrast, Puysegur believed a state, which he called *lucid sleep*, was the basis for the healings.

The *Mesmer pass* is rarely used today. Mesmerists have a client lie down, and they pass their hands about two inches over the body, from the top of the head down to the toes. Sometimes words are spoken aloud to ask the person to relax the body. The energy from the therapist's hands is thought to drain the energy from the person's body. After the session, the reverse is done, to leave the client fully energized. According to TenDam, the two main differences between hypnosis and magnetism are as follows: First, "hypnosis encourages the client's use of perception and imagination; magnetism uses the energy doors of the body."[24] Second, it is more difficult and time consuming to lead people into trance with magnetism than hypnosis.[25]

Interest in mesmerism renewed after the French Revolution (1788-1799). Abbe Jose Custodio de Faria (1756-1819), a Goan Catholic monk and the son of an Indian father, spent his childhood in Goa, in Portuguese India. In 1797, Faria went to Chateau d'If as punishment for his part in the French Revolution. While in solitary confinement, he trained himself in the uses of autosuggestion. He became a student of Mesmer in Paris after Mesmer's return at the end of the revolution.[26] In 1813, Faria disagreed with Mesmer and said it was the power of suggestion and autosuggestion that was effective in the healings. He believed that everything came from the subject, took place in one's own imagination, and was generated from within the person's mind, not from the power or animal magnetism of the conductor.[27] This was based on the Indian concept of sammohan bhavana shakti, a type of meditation using concentrated focus.[28] The method created expectancy followed by a command.[29] Faria would have his patients sit in a comfortable chair and stare at his open, raised hand while he commanding in a loud voice, "Sleep!"[30]

Faria demonstrated his technique before thousands. It would seem that the main difference between Faria and Mesmer was the explanation of what they did, not the methodology of their techniques.[31] During the late 1800s, Albert de Rochas used magnetism similar to mesmerism for age and past-life regressions.[32]

In other parts of the world, mesmerism evolved into magnetic healing, and it has been continuously practiced. The major difference between mesmerism and magnetic healing, then and today, is that mesmerists focus on mental diseases whereas magnetic healers work on physical ailments as well. Both imply that changes occur due to influences outside the patient, either from the healer or God. An inventor, scientist, and paranormal researcher named George Meek did a study in the 1990s on magnetic healing in various countries. He found such techniques were being used in Brazil and the Philippines, primarily as a method of moving energy through the body's electromagnetic system.[33] Once into a meditative state, the healers became aware of the energy of their client's body by using the Mesmer pass as a sensing step prior to actual transmission of energy and healing. At the same time, they remained in a constant state of meditation. The basic contrast is that the healer is the one in a meditative state, not the client or person who desires the healing.

Medical science has established that there are two nervous systems in the human body: the central nervous system (CNS) and the peripheral nervous system (PNS). The spinal cord and the brain make up the CNS. Its main job is to get the information from the body and send out instructions. The PNS consists of the nerves and the wiring. Both systems involve electric currents flowing over a network of nerves in somewhat the same way that electric current flows through the wires and printed circuit connections of your computer. Through Kirlian photography and other processes, scientists are studying the energy fields that make up the etheric body and the other (nonvisible) bodies. They have learned that at least one type of energy involved is magnetic by nature—an electromagnetism of a subtle type.

Meek found that each cell and each organ of a body is dependent upon a supply of magnetic energy. When the energy of the individual cells or a complete organ is deficient, that cell or organ cannot function properly. Since the whole body depends on the harmonious functioning of all parts, cells or organs that do not have sufficient energy to carry out their jobs sooner or later will cause the body to send out signals of pain or discomfort. These signals are a warning to the owner of the body that something has gone wrong in that area.

Healers using magnetism have the ability to sense the electromagnetic deficiencies in the body. Then, by using the techniques they have learned, they are able to recharge the weak cells, or organs, with energy. This energy can come from their own personal store of energy in the body, from the Earth's magnetic field, or from God.[34]

When I visited Manila, Philippines, in February 2010, I interviewed Pepito, a psychic surgeon[35] in Manila, Philippines, who was adamant that "the healing comes from God" and that he was the messenger of the energy from God. Years before, I had talked with Alex Orbito, a psychic surgeon who was visiting outside of Wilmington, Delaware, in 1986. Orbito said it was God who did the healing; he was just lending his hands so God could do what was needed.

The Dutch physician Andries Hoek (1807-1885) wrote an eighty-three-page case study describing his work with a woman called Rika from December 1850 to the end of 1853. Rika lived with Hoek and his family for eleven months of treatment and for two years afterward. Early during the magnetic treatment, she gave Hoek detailed instructions about the therapy. Later she told him when it would be finished. During the next two years, she provided Hoek with treatment strategies for his other patients as well.[36]

In the mid-1800s, James Braid (1795-1860), a Scottish surgeon and physician, also drew comparisons between his own practice of hypnosis and Hindu meditation, in *Magic, Mesmerism, Hypnotism, etc., Historically and Physiologically Considered* (1844-1845).[37] In 1842, Braid first used the term *hypnosis* to differentiate his approach from the mesmerists' thinking. He thought, as did Faria, that it was a state similar to a natural sleep. Less than a year later, he tried to change the term to *monoideism* (meaning "one idea") when he recognized that hypnosis was not always a sleep state. The term didn't take.[38]

In a letter written to the editor of *The Lancet* in 1845, Braid wrote: [that he]

[H]ad adopted the term "hypnotism" to prevent my being confounded with those who entertain those extreme notions, as well as to get rid of the erroneous theory about a magnetic fluid, or *exoteric influence of any description being the cause of the sleep.* I distinctly avowed that hypnotism laid no claim to produce any phenomena which were not quite reconcilable with well-established physiological and psychological principles; pointed out the various sources of fallacy which might have misled the mesmerists . . .

[Further, I have never been] a supporter of the *imagination theory*, i.e., that the induction of the sleep in the first instance is merely the result of imagination. My belief is quite the contrary. I attribute it to the induction of a habit of intense abstraction, or concentration of attention, and maintain that it is most readily induced by causing the patient to fix his thoughts and sight on an object and suppress his respiration.[39] [Italics are Braid's.]

Braid's induction consisted of asking his patients to fix their mental and visual attention on an object that was boring. When a patient becomes tired and unable to resist a "feeling of stupor . . . a state of somnolency is induced," he said.[40] Braid felt convinced that once the muscles and nerves became tired, the mesmerizer was able to direct the patient "to manifest mesmeric phenomena."[41]

In the mid-1800s, medical professionals were still using hypnosis in pain control and later as anesthesia in emergency operations, such as during the first war between India and Britain, in 1857. In 1845,

James Esdaile (1808-1859) pioneered the use of hypnosis in surgery at the Hooghly Hospital on a patient who was in great pain. He commented to one assistant that he had never seen mesmerism used but had read about the use of hypnosis in surgery and doubted he could succeed. Nevertheless, the surgery was a success.

Esdaile's method was to make the patient lie down in a dark room, wearing only a loincloth. For two to eight hours Esdaile would sit behind the patient, leaning over him almost head to head. He would repeatedly pass his hands in the shape of claws slowly over the patient's body within one inch of the surface, from the pit of the stomach to the back of the head, breathing gently on the head and eyes all the time. His right hand would be over the pit of the stomach for extended periods of time. Later, he trained his assistants in the technique, in order to conserve his own energy for surgery.[42] As chloroform became utilized, mesmerism's use as anesthesia declined.

Jean-Martin Charcot (1825-1893) studied under Mesmer and could reproduce all the symptoms of hysteria, which he thought came from an incurable structural inadequacy of the nervous system. Mesmer was highly dramatic, using wands and showman-like methods. Charcot was as dramatic as Mesmer, but his reputation as a neurologist gave credence to the use of hypnosis in the medical field.[43] It was only after the theatrics and animal magnetism were removed from the practice of hypnosis that physicians such as Ambroise-Auguste Liebault and Hippolyte Berheim in France, and James Esdaile (1808-1859), an English surgeon of the East India Company, began using hypnosis while working with patients, especially in surgery.[44] In the 1880s, mental-health professionals were not as highly regarded as surgical doctors. In 1986 John Ryan Haule wrote a paper on Charcot's student Pierre Janet (1859-1947). Janet was a medical professional and was the first to describe the relationships of the mystery of somnambulism to hypnosis. According to Haule:

> Somnambulism was understood to be a phenomenon whereby two or more states of consciousness, dissociated

by a cleft of amnesia, operate with seeming independence of one another. Hysteria was a pathological form of somnambulism in which dissociation appears autonomously for neurotic reasons, and in such a way as to adversely disturb the individual's everyday life. Hypnosis was "artificial somnambulism," dissociation induced by a therapist for experimental or therapeutic purposes, a deliberate imitation of hysteria.[45]

An example of somnambulis, known as *somnambulism*, is the deep state of sleepwalking. Most times, one is unaware of dreaming. This is Stage 6 on the Arons Depth Scale, the deepest stage in which surgery can take place.

Sigmund Freud (1856-1939) was another of Charcot's students at a school in Nancy, France, founded by Hippolyte Bernheim and Ambroise-Auguste Libeault. The school specialized in the use of suggestion, with or without hypnosis, for therapeutic purposes. On staff, too, was Joseph Breuer, who later worked with Freud. Freud also used hypnosis in the interview process when he was trying to find the origin of the patient's symptoms.

## Josef Breuer

Austrian physician Josef Breuer was the first to use the cathartic method primarily to cure hysteria, in 1880-1882. In this method—which got its name from Aristotle's ideas about the function of tragedy on stage—the therapist encourages the patient to express emotions (by crying, screaming, and raging). Aristotle considered catharsis to be the purification of the audience's emotions. Breuer and subsequent physicians assumed that the patient needed to express repressed emotions in order to be cured.

In 1880, twenty-one-year-old Bertha Pappenheim (known as Anna O. in basic psychology textbooks) came to Breuer for a nervous cough, facial spasms, hallucinations, and many other symptoms that Breuer diagnosed collectively as hysteria. Breuer visited Pappenheim daily and found that when she invented stories, which she told during her hallucinatory period during the day, a measure of relief would occur. On one occasion, she related the details of the first onset of a particular symptom, and to Breuer's great astonishment, that symptom completely disappeared. Together they developed a systematic procedure whereby the individual symptoms were gradually recalled in reverse chronological order, at which time they would, one by one, disappear. They vanished entirely following a reproduction of the original scene. Pappenheim noticed the results and continued repeating the history, from the beginning of the symptom. She started calling it the *talking cure.* [46]

For more than a year, Breuer saw Pappenheim for hours every day. In the evenings she recalled the day's events, and in morning sessions she under hypnotic regression.[47] Breuer's wife became bored with the constant conversation about his patient and was jealous of the time her husband spent with Bertha.

On June 7, 1882, Pappenheim reproduced under hypnosis the original event that had marked the onset of her illness in the summer of 1880 (a hallucination of snakes). According to Breuer's published account, this marked the conclusion of her treatment.[48] Because Pappenheim's symptoms had greatly diminished, Breuer abruptly brought the treatment to an end, telling her she was cured. But that evening, Pappenheim's family asked Breuer to return, because Pappenheim was demonstrating childbirth, the logical termination of a phantom pregnancy. Using hypnosis, Breuer calmed her down and left the house. The next day Breuer and his wife left on a second honeymoon. [49]

While Breuer was away, Pappenheim manifested other symptoms, such as convulsions. She was treated with morphine and became addicted. She was admitted to and spent several years in the Bellevue and Inzersdorf Sanatoriums before the doctors recommended surgery. Her mother was against the surgery and took her home to Vienna, where Pappenheim eventually recovered. By the end of her life, she had founded a periodical and several institutes to train students in social work.

When Breuer returned from his honeymoon, he discussed the Pappenheim case with Freud.[50]

# Sigmund Freud

By the time Freud started working with Breuer, from 1891 through 1892, Freud was a practicing neurologist and had studied with Charcot (who had learned mesmerism directly from Mesmer). However, in his writing, or at least what his translators wrote, Freud used what he called hypnosis, not mesmerism, in treating his hysteria patients. Since Mesmer and his students had been severely criticized about dramatic showman-like methods, Freud downplayed such dramatics with his patients.[51]

When Freud went into private practice, his main method was hypnotic suggestion, as well as "haphazard and unsystematic psychotherapeutic methods."[52] Freud admitted to two problems: One, he could not succeed in hypnotizing everyone. Two, he could not get all the patients he hypnotized into as deep a state of hypnosis as he wanted. He said that his great therapeutic successes using suggestions had been achieved only in his hospital practice, not with private patients.[53]

In *The History of the Psychoanalytic Movement and Other Papers* (1963), Freud wrote about his disinterest in the medical profession. Freud became a neurologist to help "nervous patients."[54] When Freud left the hospital, he opened a private medical practice to treat neurosis, or the nervous patient, using W. Erb's Electrotherapy as the main treatment[55] and producing cures along with physical treatments. The electrotherapy treatments, however, weren't successful. His main method of treating hysteria patients was hypnotic suggestion.[56]

Freud also used hypnosis for questioning the patient about the origin of the symptom. He felt the "physician . . . had a right to learn something of the origin of the phenomenon which he was striving to remove by the monotonous procedure of suggestion."[57] There doesn't seem to be much known about Freud's hypnotic techniques, nor has there been much written on his actual methods. He did put his hands on a patient's face to assist the patient in remembering and to remove the blocks to memories. Freud would suggest to the patient "that whatever resistance was being encountered would be overcome by this pressure, so that the patient would then perceive the idea or memory which was eluding him."[58] He also probably used the Mesmer pass, a sweep of hands and transfer of magnetic energy.

Freud and Breuer "guided the patient's attention directly to the traumatic scene in which the symptom had arised [*sic*]; we endeavored to find the psychic conflict and to free the repressed affect."[59] Freud called this process *regression*.[60] Eventually, Freud stopped using hypnosis for three reasons. The first two were due to his ongoing problems (he "could not succeed in hypnotizing every patient," and he "was not able to put individual patients into as deep a state of hypnosis" as he wanted).[61] The third was provoked by an incident with a patient. When he was using hypnosis to regress a female patient, she had spontaneously thrown her arms around his neck. Just at that time, his servant had unexpectedly entered the room.[62]

After Freud stopped using hypnosis, he asked his patients to lie on a couch. He sat behind them out of their sight, so they would not be influenced by his mannerisms or expressions. He also said that he couldn't look at the patients for very long, and it was a good time for a short nap while the patient kept talking.[63]

Freud agreed with Breuer that abreaction (having patients emotionally react to events they are recalling or reliving) was desirable and necessary for the client to improve. Charles Darwin disagreed with Freud.[64] Currently, *catharsis* and *abreaction* are used as synonyms and defined as the expression of emotions associated with forgotten memories. Darwin had stated that freely expressing emotions served only to intensify them and that when the outward expression of emotion was repressed, the emotions were softened. Freud had at one time claimed that the main therapeutic task of the therapist was to encourage the client into reproducing and vocalizing the impressions that had caused the hysterical symptom.[65] Later, Freud tempered his opinion on catharsis by saying that although catharsis had its advantages, it affected only the symptoms, not the underlying cause.[66] In 1986, W. P. Hull took Freud's premise one step further and said, "The experience must be relived by the patient in order to know, not just believe, what caused his/her feeling originally."[67]

However, Beck, Rush, Shaw, and Emery, in *Cognitive Therapy of Depression* (1983), mentioned that even though a client might feel better after an emotional expression, it had little lasting effect on the progress of therapy.[68] For Carl Jung and William McDougall, abreaction was not the concern so much as the integration of the separated mental processes of the psyche, or the combination of the separated parts of the psyche.[69]

During emotional release without the context of an understanding listener or supportive social situation, or in emotional release without attention to the psychological stability of the troubled persons, cathartic or abreactive measures can have certain risks.[70] One potential risk is that of actually reinforcing and intensifying disturbing symptoms or effecting only a temporary relief. It appears that emotional release as an element in a larger healing context may be eminently gainful. Conflict and discussion concerning the need for abreaction continue among therapists.

The medical profession and hypnotists continued using hypnosis for implanting and reinforcing suggestions. Public demonstrations of hypnosis for entertainment were becoming more and more common.

## Hypnosis in the Twentieth Century

In the 1930s, Johannes Schultz called his system of self-hypnosis *autogenic training* (AT). He had the patient sit or lie down, with eyes closed. He then gave instructions to increase feelings of heaviness and to let the feelings of heaviness relate to feelings of muscular relaxation. This self-relaxation produced a light state of hypnosis. The full instructions are in Kroger and Yapko's *Clinical and Experimental Hypnosis in Medicine, Dentistry, and Psychology.*[71]

Milton Erickson (1901-1980) developed a different form of hypnosis that used an informal permissive induction method. He had initially learned the direct-suggestion, autocratic method from one of his professors, Clark Hull.[72] From observing his clients, Erickson noticed that they would slide into a trance state while he spoke in a certain way and created metaphors based on stories drawn from his clients' own experiences. Erickson pioneered the use of reframing, directing the client to look at the situation from another perspective and to see another result, one with a more favorable outcome. When Erickson used ideomotor responses, the client's unconscious mind would speak directly to him, bypassing the conscious mind. These ideomotor actions are automatic responses of an individual muscle or a group of muscles to a question asked of the unconscious mind. The muscles have been previously designated by the regressionist and accepted by the client. Yes and no answers are then given.[73] His style is referred to as *Ericksonian hypnosis* and is the foundation of practices found in neurolinguistic programming (NLP).

Harry Arons, hypnotist and author of many books on the subject, pioneered hypnosis in the judicial system by investigating memory, age regression, induction techniques, and confabulation. He introduced a scale that is used in measuring the depth of trance, called the Arons Scale. The scale goes from Stage 1, a relaxed state in which it is difficult to move the eyelids, to Stage 6, anesthesia, in which the body does not experience pain; this could be used for surgery.

Dave Elmon (1900-1967) developed an induction in which it takes five minutes to reach the ideal somnambulistic state. This is the level that Freud and others deemed necessary for implantation of desired behavioral changes and is my favored induction technique when hypnosis is desired.

Ormond McGill (1913-2005) has been called the Dean of American Hypnotists for his extensive teaching and writing on hypnosis. See one of his case studies in the Regression section.

John Cerbone (a close associate of Ormond McGill) and Richard Nongard are best known for their work with instant inductions that take three to seven seconds. In their method, the therapist induces a trance by a mixture of boredom, confusion, loss of equilibrium, eye fixation, misdirection, shock, and overload.

In the mid-1950s, Morey Bernstein, a Colorado businessman, was using hypnosis as parlor entertainment. He repeatedly asked Virginia Tighe (Ruth Simons in the book *Bridey Murphy*) if she would volunteer for experiments, and finally she agreed to be hypnotized. After several tries with age regression, she accessed another lifetime as Bridey Murphy in Cork, Ireland.

On a side note, the Roman Catholic Church has made two declarations concerning hypnosis. The first was on July 28, 1847, when the Sacred Congregation of the Holy Office (Roman Curia) issued a decree declaring, "Having removed all misconception, foretelling of the future, explicit or implicit invocation of the devil, the use of animal magnetism (hypnosis) is indeed merely an act of making use of physical media that are otherwise licit and hence it is not morally forbidden, provided it does not tend toward an illicit end or toward anything depraved." Then, in 1957, Pope Pius XII stated that the use of hypnosis by health-care professionals for diagnosis and treatment was to be permitted.[74]

# Comments

Controversies between the competing theories of mesmerism and hypnotism have existed from the beginning. Despine and Hoek were using a form of lucid sleep, or meditation, in which patients prescribed their own treatment and expected date of recovery. Mesmer evolved his methods based on magnetizing healers from Paracelsus forward. Braid, and later Faria, adapted meditation into a form of self-hypnosis.

The basic difference between the two thought systems was Mesmer's claim that the personal power, or animal magnetism, of the mesmerizer was critical to the success of the cure. It was "done to" the patient. Braid and Faria agreed that it was instead the imagination within the mind of the patient that did the work. Mesmer was a fabulous showman and had terrific public relations. Puysegur continued public demonstrations similar to Mesmer's. Neither Faria, a friar, nor Braid, a physician who scientifically studied the phenomena of mesmerism, were gifted with the outgoing personality of Mesmer. This fact might have dampened the public's initial acceptance of their preferred methodologies.

There was also a difference between public demonstrations, such as with the baquet, and private sessions. In the private sessions, the patient would lie down and the mesmerizer would pass his hands over the patient's body with long strokes until the abreactions or catharsis would begin or the patient entered a deep sleep. This appears to be similar to the technique Freud used at the beginning. One of the main concepts of this approach was that the mesmerizers, not the patients, had control and used their own animal magnetism for the benefit of others.

Hypnotherapy can better trace its beginnings to meditation from India rather than from Mesmer's magnets. It would seem that Freud was acquainted with Faria's methods because of his study with Charcot. Freud's use of the word *hypnosis* instead of *mesmerism* indicates to me that he was also acquainted with Braid's work. The current practice of hypnosis has components similar to the beginnings of meditation: relaxation, specific breathing directions, and focus of attention.

Scientific studies continue, and the hypnotherapy profession is evolving. I talked frequently with Irene Foy in Tustin, California (1996-1997), who had successfully practiced hypnosis since the 1930s. She insisted that it took at least three hypnotic sessions to achieve the somnambulistic levels needed for successful hypnotic work. In 2007, I met with Robert Downing, a physician and hypnotist who had retired and was living in La Quinta, California. He also firmly stated that he needed three sessions for a successful trance. Now, with the Elmon induction, the Ericksonian method, and the Nongard and Cerbone instant inductions, the art of hypnosis is changing in surprising ways.

It appears that hypnosis can be divided into two types of systems. First, differences in the systems can be noted by the way the hypnotist looks at and treats his clients or subjects. Some hypnotists use methods that are autocratic. That is, they see themselves as boss and their subjects are supposed to follow orders. Weiss, in *Many Lives, Many Masters*, gives a good example of going from autocratic into democratic mode at the leadership of a client. Others use methods that are democratic; they see themselves as leaders and their clients as participants. Most hypnotherapists today are trained as democratic regressionists.

Second, differences can be seen in the purpose of the hypnosis. Some regressionists use uncovering methods and others use suggestive hypnosis. *Uncovering* is another word for regression, whereby the purpose is to uncover information that has been hidden in the unconscious. *Suggestive hypnosis* intends to implant posthypnotic phrases into the client's unconscious. These are to be available to the person's consciousness when the situation calls for the new information or behavior. Often, the regressionist will lead a client into another timespace to uncover the precipitating cause for an undesired behavior, such as smoking. Then later, or even in the same session, the hypnotist will take the client into a deeper level to implant suggestions that he or she become a nonsmoker.

# Chapter 3

# Memory: What Is Recalled?

When Freud stopped using hypnosis, he began asking clients to discuss the origins of their problems. He was following the method set by Josef Breuer while working with Pappenheim. As the information appeared to be coming from a patient's conscious mind, these therapists did not question the validity of the information.

However, today, my first-time clients frequently ask, "Where is this coming from? I must be making it up." Before we continue looking at the history of regression work, let us examine the basis of memory. That is, what are the clients remembering or making up? This is the question many research doctors are still asking.

Noted therapists—including Edith Fiore, Bruce Goldberg, Winifred Lucas, Raymond Moody, Brian Weiss, and Roger Woolger—indicate in their case studies that belief in reincarnation is not necessary by the client or therapist for past-life experiences to be effective in relieving a client's symptoms. Netherton wrote:

> After all, if the client (or the therapist) chooses to believe that it (the memory) was a product of a suddenly unleashed imagination; the client's therapy could proceed at that level. After all, what a person makes up about himself is bound to reveal a lot about the person, his obsessions, fears and self image.[75]

Other therapists say it is important to ascertain the truth so they can determine treatment plans for the effects of possible abuse or delusions. The court system says legal remedies are necessary, mainly to prevent what might be further abuse in this lifetime. In past-life therapy, just the same, we need to ask this question: who are we treating—the client or the system?

Sides of the conflict over the source of memories retrieved through regression have polarized. One side believes that memories, however retrieved or recalled, are the literal truth; the other believes that memories are unreliable, because they are easily fabricated and influenced. In discussing the sources of memories, I explore the mechanism of our memory system, along with its strengths and weaknesses. Each side of the debate is presented, including supporting evidence.

## Recalled Memory

Recalled material may come from three sources: personal memory that includes prenatal and past-life memories, the collective unconscious, and implanted memories. Personal memory incorporates the memories of the current life and prenatal memories, genetic memory (DNA), and memories of other personalities. Ellen Bass and Laura Davis proposed in their book *The Courage to Heal: Women Healing from Sexual Abuse* (1988) that memories, even suggestions or feelings of a memory, are the literal truth and real.[76] The only reason a person doesn't remember is that the memory has been repressed.

Karim Nader, psychology researcher, however, found that memory is malleable. Every time we recall a memory, we change it. And each time we retell an event, often at least one detail is different; thus, our original memory of the happening is no longer available. We remember instead our most recent *story* about the event. In addition, Nader showed in 2000 that experiencing a memory with the help of a regressionist can also cause one's memory to change.[77] The memory is often destabilized enough so that the therapist can help to reframe the event, resulting in an observable change in the current symptom.

The collective unconscious, as termed by Carl Jung—also called the *akashic records* by many Eastern traditions and the *morphic field* by Rupert Sheldrake—is a second source of memories. The memories could also come from formative causation, from the quantum field (see chapter 2 for details), from night dreams, or from metaphors and analogies.

The third source would be false memories, such as implanted memories, cryptoamnesia, and possession or attachment. Elizabeth Loftus wrote that memories are malleable, easily implanted, and are not all what they seem to be.[78] Cryptoamnesia is fabricating life from stories heard, articles read, or conversations heard that the unconscious puts together. One can also have memories that actually belong, instead, to an attached being (also see chapter 6).[79]

## Personal Memory

Alan Parkin, cognitive psychologist and coauthor of *The Neuropsychology of the Amnesic Syndrome*, reported in 1987 that memory consists of three stages. The first is the recording or encoding of the experience in memory. The facts of the event are tempered by the emotional state of the person and past emotions associated with similar events to produce an encoded memory. The second stage is the storing of the recorded memory of the experience. The last is the retrieval and use of the stored encoded information. What is stored or encoded in memory depends on the perception, including the current emotional state of the person, and what is encoded determines what will be received by the mind of the person. The ease of recall of an event increases in relationship to prior knowledge and occurrence of other events at the time of encoding. As the length of time between the event and the retrieval lengthens, the more difficult retrieval becomes.[80]

Personal memory consists of prenatal and postnatal experiences, genetic memories of both mother and father and their genetic lines,

31

and past-life memories. Prenatal memory has been the object of many studies, most centered on audio memory. As part of a twenty-year experiment by the BBC, psychologist Alexandra Lamont asked eleven expectant mothers to play their favorite song for a half hour daily during the last three months of their pregnancy. After birth, the mothers didn't play the song. One year later, Lamont visited the families and played a variety of songs. All the babies showed a statistical preference for their mother's particular song.[81] A research paper on fetal memory by P. G. Hepper for the Foetal Behavior Research Centre, School of Psychology, in the Queens University of Belfast, reported that fetal memories did in fact exist. The apparent purpose of fetal memory is to become accustomed to the mother's voice tone and patterns.[82]

Another possible source of personal memory concerns the RNA and DNA of genes. James D. Watson, a former physicist, and Frances H. C. Crick, a former ornithology student, described the double helix of DNA in 1953. DNA was found to have genetic memory, what was previously called nonlocal transfer of memories. Memory is transferred to the RNA, which in turn is transferred to associated proteins. The proteins subsequently affect the nerves into reactions.

These discoveries resulted in the prominent theory that genes control our lives.[83] Given that physical characteristics and some personality characteristics are transferred through generations, it is conceivable that memories could also be genetically transmitted. Extensive research has confirmed a nonlocal transfer of memories in experiments that lasted over fifty years and 110 generations of rats.[84]

In 1993, psychology researcher LaVonne Stiffler attempted to demonstrate Jung's synchronicity between adoptees and their adoptive families and the adoptees' birth families. These coincidences extended beyond physical characteristics normally connected with genetic transference to include choice of geographical locations, names, occupations, dreams, and intuition. A survey of seventy sets of parents and children who were separated by legal, secret adoption and reunited in adulthood resulted in narratives by birthparents, adoptees, and an adoptive parent. Sampling bias occurred, in that only those who had meaningful coincidences (whatever the participants determined such synchronicities to be) were asked to participate. There was no control group, so there is no way of knowing how prevalent coincidences are between birthparent and adoptive children in general.[85]

About 24 percent of the families related stories that could be attributed to genetic memory or prenatal experiences. Examples of characteristics that could have resulted from genetic transfer include the following: fifteen families (43 percent of those with experiences) shared similar occupations between the adoptee and someone in the birth family; eight families (23 percent) shared similar grooming patterns, such as hairstyle; eight families (23 percent) engaged in similar mating patterns, such as marrying a partner or into a family similar in some way to the birth family; and six families (17 percent) shared similar housekeeping characteristics, such as packrat tendencies or similar collections. In addition, prenatal experience could be inferred from naming pets or children after a mother or older sister, from fears related to specific prenatal trauma, or from similar hobbies in the birth family that were not available with the adoptive parents.[86]

Another notable finding in Stiffler's survey is the preponderance (33 percent) of coincidental dreams, intuition, and extrasensory perception between adoptees and parents. He suggested that this might exist especially between an adoptee and a birth mother, a relationship intensified by the genetic component.

In 1982, Bruce Lipton, a former tenured professor of cellular biology at the University of Wisconsin's School of Medicine, was teaching at an offshore medical college in the Caribbean. After a series of experiments, he found that memory resides not in the DNA of the nucleus, as schools taught at the time, but in each cell's membrane or skin. It is the membrane that transfers perceptions of its environment into the DNA, via the RNA, to the protein. Later, during stem-cell research at Stanford University in California, Lipton placed identical cells in different environments. In one environment, the cells produced fat cells. In another environment, the cells produced bone cells. Although the DNA remained consistent, the environment had effected the change. Because each cell mirrors the human body in function, and since the cell changes as the environment changes, he concluded that we are the byproduct of our environment, not our genes. [87]

Messages relayed to the cells are also affected by one's emotional reaction to the environment.[88] This is what Parkin was referring to (Personal Memory section, first paragraph); it is how memories are encoded by means of an emotional component. In Lipton's medical research, he found that memory, instead of being strictly located in the brain, is in every cell of the body. Memories are lodged in the cell's membrane when there is an emotional cause for learning a survival method. An example is keeping away from fire. You learned either by placing a hand on the fire or hot stove, or by approaching and hearing the emotional yelping of your mother commanding you to stop. The next time you got near a flame or the top of the stove, you flinched or stopped automatically.

Other experiments have also demonstrated that individuals are not always at the mercy of their genetic inheritance. Studies at Duke University, by Waterland and Jirtle, found that changing the diets of pregnant mice that displayed abnormal genes causing yellow coats and obesity could supersede the probability of passing these characteristics to their offspring. Their diets were high in the methyl group (folic acid, Vitamin B12, and choline, which can be found in health food stores). As a result, their offspring were thin and had normal appetites.[89]

Before considering memories of past lives, I will discuss alternate explanations of why you may feel you have lived before and in a particular way.

## Collective Unconscious

The psychologist Carl Jung stated that the collective unconscious is the part of the psyche that retains and transmits common physiological inheritances. Collective unconscious can also be described as the cumulative experiences of all previous generations. Archetypes found in the collective unconscious exemplify the predispositions to perceive the world in certain ways. Jung also stated that the "collective unconscious is common to all. It is the foundation of what the ancients called the 'sympathy of all things.'"[90]

According to philosopher William James, the unconscious is universal and is continuous in time and space with a person's consciousness, but it also operates outside the individual. The universal consciousness filters into one's personal consciousness through the brain. As the information comes into the brain, the person can be aware of the input. The brain organizes the material, files it in the proper order, and places the information in the unconscious. This expands automatically back into the universal consciousness, completing the cycle.[91] Some Eastern cultures refer to the akashic records as being the repository of all activities and memories that have occurred on Earth.

When a client is regressed, to this or another life, the client could be tapping into this universal or collective consciousness. The unconscious is creative and supplies material and energy for the conscious mind. In retrieving memories, the client's unconscious might supply a particular recall to fulfill one's own needs or the therapist's requests.[92]

# Formative Causation

Starting in 1920, William McDougall, a research psychologist, tested the hypothesis of *formative causation*, the propensity of learning to increase over generations. He conducted a thirty-two generation empirical experiment with rats that lasted for fifteen years. The rats were trained to go through a specific maze, and researchers noted the number of errors and the time it took them to complete the course. A control group was not trained. The results showed a marked tendency for the trained rats in successive generations to learn more quickly. This was indicated by the average number of errors made in the first group of eight generations (over fifty-six errors) as compared with the fourth group of eight generations (only twenty errors). Actual behavior also became more cautious and tentative in the later generations.[93] Formative causation has become a part of quantum theory.

McDougall tested rats in the untrained lines only occasionally. He noted "the disturbing fact that the groups of controls derived from the stock in the years 1926, 1927, 1930, and 1932 show a diminution in the average number of errors from 1927 to 1933."[94] He considered this result as probably fortuitous, but "it is just possible that the falling off in the average number of errors from 1927 to 1932 represents a real change in the constitution of the whole stock, an improvement of it (with respect to this particular faculty) whose nature I am unable to suggest."[95]

McDougall's earlier experiment was repeated by dividing the rats into groups of fast learners and slow learners, based on their learning scores (the number of errors). The results indicated that the fast learners tended to learn relatively quickly and the slow learners learned relatively slowly. However, in the slow learners, the performance of the later generations improved markedly in spite of repeated selection in favor of slow learning. The major problem with the experiment was the failure to test systematically the change in the rate of learning of rats whose parents had not been trained.[96]

McDougall's studies demonstrated possible genetic transfer of memory within the successive generations if there were no changes in the rate of learning of the untrained line of rats. It must be noted that DNA was not discovered until 1953, after which researchers observed the genetic transfer of other traits, including memory and learning. Surprisingly, the untrained line, the untested control group, seemed to demonstrate the greatest nonlocal predisposition for learning the task.

Psychologists Agar, Drummond, and Tiegs duplicated the experiment over a period of twenty years with fifty successive generations of untrained rats from a parallel line. The results showed a marked tendency for rats of both the trained and untrained lines to learn more quickly in subsequent generations.[97]

Biochemist and biologist Rupert Sheldrake's restatement of the theory of formative causation maintains that an organism's repetition of a particular behavior will increase the likelihood of similar organisms exhibiting the same behavior in the future. This concept is similar to Jung's archetypal memory of the collective unconscious. The unique form cannot be determined in advance of the first appearance, however. After the first appearance of the form, the action is repeated as a reaction to particular stimuli because the form of the first appearance influences the form of subsequent similar systems. The initial, first-appearance form cannot be duplicated or tested, because the first event influences all subsequent events. The initial event could be the result of chance, inherent creativity, or a transcendent creative agency.[98]

When asked about the Hundredth Monkey story, Sheldrake replied that he created the myth of the hundredth monkey to demonstrate formative causation. In his story, a team of biologists was studying a group of monkeys on an unnamed island in the South Pacific. The monkeys were eating bananas on the beach, resulting in sandy bananas. One young monkey dropped his banana in the water and enjoyed the taste. Other young monkeys did the same. Soon the adults were washing the bananas before eating. After the biologists made notes, they compared findings with biologists on other islands. The biologists on another island remarked that suddenly the monkeys were washing their bananas before eating. It was assumed that after the monkeys had repeated the new behavior a certain number of times, possibly one hundred, the action became part of their monkey consciousness.

If the formative causation, or collective unconscious, contains psychological inheritance, then what is known as past-life memories could be the physical and psychological memories accumulated by the human race throughout time, the universal past-life memories.[99] Empirical studies by Agar et al. (1954), McDougall (1927, 1938), Mishkind (1993), and Rosen (1991) indicate evidence of a morphic resonance supporting Sheldrake's theory of formative causation.[100]

Mishkind tested the theory of formative causation based on the physical quantum field theory (explained in chapters on time). The results indicated that individuals would tend to repeat a behavior if the same behavior had been repeated in the past. The formative causation theory poses that an organism's repetition of a particular behavior will increase the likelihood of a similar organism exhibiting the same behavior in the future.[101]

Sheldrake's *morphic resonance* is similar to energetic resonance in that the system or organism is acted on by an alternative force that coincides with its natural frequency, such as the tuning of a radio to the frequency of radio waves given out by transmitters. However, morphic resonance is not accounted for by any of the known types of resonance, nor does it involve a transmission of energy. Sheldrake's hypothesis of formative causation states that the consistency and repetitions of forms can be explained by the repeated association of the same type of morphogenetic field within a given type of physical-chemical system. The chemical and biological forms are repeated because of a causal influence from previous similar forms.[102]

The uncommon variable among genetic memory, collective unconscious, and formative causation is genetic memory, which is available only to direct descendants. The information in the collective unconscious and through formative causation is available to all, even the non-blood related. On one hand, life memories could be recalled by a great-great-grandson of his great-great-grandmother by tracing genetic memories. On the other hand, his wife would be using the collective unconscious to access her husband's relative's experiences. It could also be that the great-great-grandmother's soul returned to the same family via marriage, skipping one or two generations.

In the legal courtroom, genetic memory, collective unconscious, and formative causation are not considered personal memories. In the past-life therapy office, there is no functional difference. To gain and retain the trust of the client, the therapist needs to act as if anything the client reveals is *the truth* for the client. Treating the client in this manner can provide possible relief from symptoms or at the least a possible explanation of behaviors to assist in formulating a treatment plan.

# False Memories

Another source of possible memories could be false memories, such as implanted memories, cryptoamnesia, and possession or attachment. Psychologist Elizabeth Loftus wrote that memories are malleable, are easily implanted, and are not all what they seem to be. Memories can be implanted when the therapist asks leading questions of a client to elicit answers the therapist is seeking. As well, a story could be repeated and repeated with emotion and conviction, going into the deep memory of the individual so it seems as if it really has happened. A third possibility is when a person tries to please a questioner. The person responds to the voice, mannerisms, and speech of the questioner and replies with the expected information.[103]

A good example of possible cryptoamnesia is related in Michael Bernstein's *The Search for Bridey Murphy* (1965), a notable book on the *New York Times* nonfiction list. When regressed, Virginia Tighe (called Ruth Simmons in the book) reported a life as Bridey Murphy, who lived in Cork, Ireland, in 1798. She described a normal Irish life, her wedding to her husband, and the details of her death in 1864. Detractors proved her story was compiled from stories she probably heard from her neighbor, Bridie Murphy Corkell (1892-1957), who had moved from Ireland, according to the 1930 US census, and had lived across the street from Tighe's childhood home. Virginia gave such detailed and historically current information about her life and her society that it would have been unlikely for her to have fabricated it. However, the church in which she reported being married was not built until 1911.[104]

Another type of memory that is not the client's but that of another is memory of attachments. William Baldwin, certified hypnotherapist, wrote and talked about past lives of attached spirits influencing the lives of their hosts. These are usually souls or spirits of deceased persons who have not completed the dying process but wander around looking for another physical body for various reasons.[105] In my early experience with past-life work, I was occasionally questioned by a client about the purpose of the recalled past life that seemed to have nothing to do with the client's current life, other than providing a sense of general relief. One client, obviously distressed, said there was someone *there*, inside, who didn't belong. The client had mentioned psychic tendencies, so I inquired, "Where in the room is the one who didn't belong?" (I was careful to use the client's exact words, even if not grammatically correct.) The client responded that it was inside, pointing to her chest. I had been trained in house-clearing of negative energies, so I used that technique. The technique consisted of acknowledging their existence and the possibility that the intruders had not completed their dying experience. Then I quickly asked them to complete their dying process, and directed them into *the Light*,[106] to the other side. I asked them to fill the empty spot in my client with love, light, and peace. I soon learned to ask my clients if there was anyone there besides them, and I often got a positive answer. Past-life therapy or recall could start with the client's own memory after release of the attachments. I don't feel it is ethical to have my clients pay for another's therapy (see chapter 6, Regression as Therapy).

In discovering and ascertaining what is the true life (this or other) of the client, care—meticulous care—must be taken with the types of questioning. The best is the open, but not leading, question. Questions need to be asked in a way for the client to answer in the first person, present tense, and conclude by the regressionist accepting the answer. For clarification, the regressionist may say: "Then what happens?" or "Go back to (using the client's own words) . . . then what happens?"

In the case of Bridey Murphy, a deep level of hypnosis was used. The unconscious of the client might have wanted to please the hypnotist, thus coming up with a story. Sometimes, with a new client, the revelation of the first life can be a fabrication of the unconscious. Once the unconscious realizes and understands that the truth will be accepted, it gradually, and sometimes reluctantly, tells the story.

# Past Lives

Past-life memories are often a result of continuation of personal memory recall, thus the term *past lives* also refers to any life other than the current *Now*. Some regressionists use the same techniques to access the origin of an event or problem in the past as in the future. The cause of anxiety, which is the fear of an event in the future, is an example. Others use different techniques to access past and future events. Sometimes the origin is in a simultaneous lifetime (see sections on Regression and Time).

The word *hypnosis* was coined by James Braid to describe the process used by Franz Anton Mesmer and others with their patients. After further research, Braid found that what Mesmer and colleagues were doing had no connection to the sleep state. The state their patients had achieved was instead similar to meditation, that is, one-pointedness of the mind. Braid's attempt to call the process *monoideaism* was not successful, and the word *hypnosis* is still used erroneously today. So it is with the term *past lives*. The Association of Pastlife Research and Therapies (APRT) and its successor, the International Association of Pastlife Regression and Research Therapies (IARRT),[107] held conferences during the 1980s and 1990s. The regressionists conducted many discussions about changing the terminology of their therapies to reflect the various lifetimes that can be recalled. The term *past lives* won. During its formation, ARRT held discussions about using *past lives* as one word, *pastlives*. At that time, the emphasis was on past lives, because future lives, simultaneous or parallel lives, and "between" lives were not yet a part of many discussions. So the name of the organization included the word *past life*. However, as the members gradually began to explore the between and future lives, the terms *pastlives* and *past lives* were both used.

The term *past life* is usually connected with belief in *reincarnation* (formerly known as *metempsychosis* and *transmigration*), in which a person occupies a series of physical bodies in various, not always successive, time periods (see chapter 9). The earliest recorded teacher of metempsychosis, or soul recycling, was Pherecydes, a teacher of

Pythagoras who was also a teacher of Plato in the sixth century BC. [108] When I was in Tibet in June 2004, I talked with monks who had read the ancient Sanskrit texts; they said that the doctrine of soul return is thought to have developed in Greece before being imported in India.

Writings from the 1600s in England mention the term *reincarnation* in relation to the revolving of human souls.[109] Ian Stevenson's cross-cultural case studies of children's memories of a past life provide a research basis for confirming the theory of soul return in both genetic lines (related by blood) and nongenetic lineage (nonrelated).[110] Others researchers—such as Janet Cunningham, Edith Fiore, Marge Rieder, and Chet Snow—have also gathered case studies with historical data, including verification of the background of memories.[111]

In gathering information, Ian Stevenson, biochemist and professor of psychiatry at University of Virginia, studied children between the ages of three and six years of age who had been referred to him as having spontaneous recall of another lifetime. Eighty-four cases were selected cross-culturally, including children from Sri Lanka, Lebanon, Turkey, Thailand, and Burma. He interviewed each child, the parents, the relatives, and the neighbors. Then he verified the information of the child's previous life with interviews from surviving relatives and associates of the previous life. In many cases, he would take the child to identify significant people and places in the claimed past life.[112] The cases included in his study had a significant amount of correct correspondences between what the child stated and the past families' information. The main criticism of Stevenson's research is that he and his staff were biased to find proof of reincarnation.

In 1987, Mills, Haraldsson, and Keil started independent studies of 123 cases of children between the ages of three and seven in order to replicate Stevenson's earlier work. In 80 percent of the cases, a deceased person was found who apparently corresponded to some or all of the child's statements, at which time the case was considered solved. Of the ninety-nine solved cases, the person was unknown to the child's family in 51 percent, acquainted in 33 percent, and related in 16 percent. Of all of the 123 cases, only one case appeared to be either perpetuating a hoax or self-deceptive. In each case, the number of correct statements was compared with the total number of statements. In some cases, the incorrect statements were omitted.[113]

Researchers interviewed the children, their parents, the family, and friends of the deceased, and they compared interviewees' statements with those of the previous personality. Many of the statements were subjective. In several cases, the child who remembered a past life also had a phobia appropriately related to the previous personality's death. No data were kept about the remission or lessening of the phobias of the children after they had recalled the events that surrounded death.[114]

The case studies by Stevenson published between 1966 and 1985 and the case studies published by Mills, Haraldsson, and Keil in 1994 provide support for the existence of reincarnation. Researchers observed some carryover of physical, emotional, and personality traits from the previous lifetime. But they made no mention of the frequency of similar habits in the general or local population in order to compare these with random or chance occurrences. Due to the ages of the children, from three to six, one can almost eliminate cryptoamnesia as well as access to the collective unconscious because of the youngsters' limited life experiences. In the initial intake with parents, the interviewers assessed the likelihood of parental influence, such as encouraging or briefing the children on the *correct* statements, to eliminate the possibility of fraud. Stevenson did report that he had rejected some cases when interviewers discovered that parents had briefed the child.[115]

In a study by Nicholas Spanos et al. of 110 students recruited for a past-life study, 35 had a past-life experience. The information reported was of historical periods and cultural contexts that were of interest to the participants at the time. One student, an art major interested in Florentine art, had a past-life experience as the daughter of a nobleman in Florence, Italy. Others had past-life experiences in places their families had vacationed recently. Many, however, gave the current names for locations instead of their ancient names and used the term *BC* when referring to early, pre-Christian era dates. Spanos concluded that the findings supported the researchers' hypothesis that past-life reports are fantasies the participants construct on the basis of their limited and inaccurate historical information.[116]

It is possible that an interest in specific cultures or time periods could be an indication of previous experiences in that place and time. Another interpretation could be that historical information is processed by the student's current mind using current language to communicate, much like a default setting on a computer.

In case studies and empirical experiments, psychologist W. P. Hull came to the conclusion that:

> If the patient has not had an experience, he/she cannot have a feeling. No amount of suggestion can cause feeling. We come into this world with the ability to feel, but we do not feel until or unless something happens. There is a big difference between feeling and imagination. We can imagine almost anything, but you cannot feel anything unless you have had an experience to cause it.[117]

In the case study of Alan Lee, the client speaks in verifiable ancient languages and, when translated, the transcript has the appropriate date references. Lee was a client of Irvin Mordes, a psychiatrist at the Maryland Psychiatric Research Center in 1974. Lee was a thirty-two year old who had no schooling beyond the tenth grade and was fluent only in English. He had no known or evident psychological problems. The sessions were audiotaped. Lee received an induction to the unconscious level and reported sixteen lifetimes during these regression sessions. In several lifetimes Lee demonstrated the ability to write with the appropriate handwriting and in the appropriate languages according to the reported place and time, often changing hand dominance. Experts in ancient languages confirmed the handwriting and linguistics.

During one session, Lee started talking in a heavily accented voice. He described living in Italy until migrating to the United States, where he romanced women and became an actor. While in hypnosis, he was asked to write a letter. He signed it "Rudolph Valentino," and dated it "5 Margo 1926."[118] Subsequently, it was sent to handwriting experts for comparison with an actual signature of the silent picture star. The signature was authenticated. Again in trance, the subject was asked to write a letter to Pola Negi, a silent film star then in her eighties and known to have been Valentino's lover. Accompanying the letter was an explanatory note asking for verification of the information contained in the sealed letter. No reply came from Pola Negi. Finally, her secretary contacted the hypnotist and told him of Negi's reaction to the contents of the envelope. Negi replied that she was too old for the young man and that contacting him would only prevent him from living his current life fully. The contents of that letter remain unknown.[119]

These regressions ruled out possession and cryptoamnesia, because the information produced was not easily available in this country. The possibility of Lee's accessing the collective unconscious was remote, and since the subject expressed emotional involvement in several of the lifetimes recorded on tape, it was *very* remote. There were no unsuccessful research findings reported in the Alan Lee case.

One of the best methods of verification is comparing information about a particular event with others who also witnessed the same event. One can expect individual differences in the details, but one might also expect a consensus as to the core event. An outsider, researcher, or jury would reasonably be able to tell that they were the same event.

In past-life cases, comparing information on the same event has been rare, because therapists are careful about confidentiality in discussing cases. Occasionally, two or more clients recount the same event from their separate viewpoints. In one published case, *Mission to Millboro*,[120] the therapist Marge Rieder had eighteen clients who reported lives from Millboro, Virginia, during the Civil War. In another published case, the regressionist Janet Cunningham encountered in her office almost an entire Ogallala tribe in the Dakotas, of which she was also a member at the time of their massacre. This is recounted in *A Tribe Returned*.[121]

Research on each case ascertained that the events had occurred, although the events were not of major historical importance. When Rieder's group visited twentieth-century Millboro, members correctly identified buildings and pictures. Several members independently identified West Point photographs of one of the characters. Rieder noted that not everyone who thought he or she was connected to the Millboro group reported a life during that time or place when regressed. If Cunningham had the same experience, it was not reported. However, Cunningham did report that some tribe members were reluctant to talk about their experiences.

When we analyze and compare the two case studies, it seems that only the verifiable information was given in both instants. There were no data on erroneous information reported. None of the clients regressed or the locations reported were of historical importance. Both initial groups started with standard regressions.

With the eighteen inhabitants from Millboro and the thirty tribal members agreeing on the basic events, cryptoamnesia would have to be ruled out, as well as any type of possession or attachment. This leaves the collective unconscious or reincarnation as possible explanations. To have eighteen or thirty people all tap into the same unconscious memory within the same time span, each manifesting different personalities, would be highly unusual. There is the remote possibility of a group psychically tuning in to the same historical event. This takes expertise and experience in psychic awareness. According to Cunningham's report, perhaps four of the thirty might have had the ability. These cases would appear to be good examples of actual memories of past lives. However, very few (about five of the forty-eight, fewer than 10 percent) reported any therapeutic effect from the regressions. Most did report a change in their lives, such as increased tolerance and improved personal relationships, which could have been the result of group dynamics and the general support of other group members.

The basic regression techniques used at that time were primarily to elicit past-life information. Any therapeutic changes were an uncommon side effect.

# Retrieval Process

The retrieval of memories depends on the amount of information supplied by the retrieval cue and on the similarity of expectations and beliefs about the event as to what was encoded.[122] Human memory is influenced by expectations of the individual about what should have occurred as well as by what really did occur. The fabrication of false memories that match the expectations of the pattern of recall by the therapist may occur.[123]

In a review of the empirical literature on retrieving memories with regression techniques, Nash found no evidence for literal memories of childhood events. There were eighty empirical studies included, with publishing dates spanning from 1926 to 1985. It was found that there might be ability to access emotional material, but this does not imply an accurate reliving of a specific event.[124] Loftus, Nelson, and Usher and Neisser published articles describing their research in 1993, wherein they stated they could not find empirical evidence that adults could recall concrete episodic memories after birth.[125] I found this interesting, because many of my clients, in recalling a prenatal or early childhood event, will have the event acknowledged by a family member. But then, I didn't start working with prenatal events until 1990.

The core element of the retrieval process in a therapeutic situation is some type of altered state of consciousness brought about by one or a combination of hypnotic factors, such as induction, visualization, or bridges. *Bridges* are the use of physical sensations, such as coughing, itching, forced breathing, or touch, as in massage. Edith Fiore, Bruce Goldberg, Ian Stevenson, Helen Wambach, and Brian Weiss mainly used hypnotic inductions as a means to access past lives.[126] Visualization was the means of choice for accessing past lives by Marcia Moore,[127] for example. Bridges were the method of choice for Morris Netherton, Tad James, and Roger Woolger among others.[128] Stanislav Grof, psychiatric researcher, used accelerated breathing as a bridge into memories for healing.[129] An altered state of consciousness is considered to be any state other than normal waking consciousness. The altered state is also reached when consciousness is focused on a different timespace other than ordinary awareness of the present timespace. One example would be when you are looking for your car keys. You go to the place you normally leave them. Then you mentally retrace your steps. As you are mentally retracing your steps, you recall what you were carrying, what you were wearing, and what happened when the phone rang. In doing so, you access an altered state. Another example would be when you are looking at photographs of your childhood or visiting former neighborhoods and you start a daydream, a reverie, however slight, that shifts attention, although briefly, from the here and now to the past, so memories can surface.[130] The actual techniques are identical to those used in age regression, but moderate adaptations include directions to give permission to access other memories not limited to the current life experience or to go into another life. An example of the regressionist's direction might be, "Go to the original event that caused the current situation."

Another consideration is the validity of information obtained under or with the use of various techniques. After over 1,500 case studies, Helen Wambach claimed her hypnotically regressed subjects consistently gave historically accurate information.[131] Others such as Cunningham, Rieder, Wambach, Snow, and Stevenson, also have had many clients recall lifetimes with sufficient details to verify historical facts.[132]

The majority of Wambach's case studies were performed in group sessions, with the participants completing standardized forms immediately after their regression experience. The main criticism of Wambach's case studies was the preselected time periods. Because the time periods remained constant, the participants could easily know ahead of time about the time frame of the story they were to recall. The time periods—AD 100, AD 1750, AD 1900, and AD 3000—allowed them to draw on readily available information. Wambach used the same verbiage to lead participants forward as well as backward through time. This was compensated for, in part, by Wambach asking about details of daily living, such as the evening meal, the utensils used by the people at the meal, the taste and texture of the meal, and the description of the place where supplies were purchased or obtained, as well as the method of payment or exchange. The consistency of the details was the amazing part of the experiment.[133]

## Summary

The regression I did with Pam (chapter 1) started out with a past life and then went through genetic memory to the source of her problem. Because her past (other) lives, her mother's life, and her father's life are all recorded in each cell, we might have been able to shorten the process *if* she had not been concerned with the story. But it was the story she wanted.

Memory, it seems, is the storage of experiences auditorily (by ear), kinesthetically (by emotion or feeling), olfactorily (by smell), or visually (by seeing) perceived. Regression is the recalling of those stored memories. Regression therapy is the refiling, reframing, and/or reprocessing of those memories. The history and progression of the various regression techniques follows in the next chapter.

The stories that a client tells a regressionist depend on the regressionist's beliefs, stated and unstated, as well as the vocal directions the regressionist gives to the client. The history of a person's regression work up until the current time also affects one's experience during a regression.

# Chapter 4

# History of Regression

This chapter continues the discussion of regression techniques, which started with the hypnosis work of Breuer and Freud in chapter 2. The emphasis is on the use of regression to access past events and past lives. Therapeutic changes are often an unintended result, although some regressionists use events recalled during a session as the basis for therapy. The chapter also reviews historic information from the context of regression as a means of recovering memory. In chapter 3, we saw that the issue of memory is at the crux of regression work.

## Josef Breuer and Sigmund Freud

After working with Bertha Pappenheim in 1880, Breuer continued using regression to access catharsis-producing events. Breuer and Freud agreed on the desirability and necessity of abreaction for the client's improvement. Charles Darwin disagreed with Freud and believed it was not necessary to reexperience the traumatic event.[134]

After Freud stopped using hypnosis, he encouraged free association from his patients. The following is a transcript from one of his cases:

F (Freud): Have you seen anything or had any recollection?

P (Patient): Neither the one nor the other, but a word has suddenly occurred to me.

F: A single word?

P: Yes, but it sounds too silly.

F: Say it all the same.

P: Concierge.

F: Nothing else?

P: No.

F: I pressed a second time [I assume this was the pressure of Freud's hand on both sides of his patient's head], and once more an isolated word shot through her mind.

P: Night-gown.

[He continued this line of questioning]

P: Concierge . . . night-gown . . . bed . . . town . . . farm cart.

F: (After asking her to put it all together, she then told the story.)

P: When I was ten years old and my next elder sister was twelve, she went raving mad one night and had to be tied down and taken into the town on a farm cart. I remember perfectly that it was the concierge who overpowered her and afterward went with her to the asylum, as well.

(After continuing this method of investigation [with Freud], the patient produced another series of words that led to the final story.)

P: They slept in one room, and on a particular night they had both been subjected to sexual assaults by a certain man. [It is not uncommon for clients to change from first person that is experiencing the event to third person that is observing during a traumatic event.]

The mention of this sexual trauma in the patient's childhood revealed not only the origin of her first obsessions but also the trauma which subsequently produced the pathogenic effects.[135]

Freud used the term *regression* to describe the process by which he led the patient's attention to the traumatic scene—which resulted in producing the symptom in order to find the mental conflict involved in it and to release the suppressed emotion, usually through catharsis.[136]

Carl Jung (1875-1961) learned the regression methodology from Freud and continued to pass it along to his students. In his work, the need for catharsis was gradually deemphasized. Jung encouraged patients to use their imagination as a transformation technique.

Another one of Freud's colleagues was Otto Rank (1884-1937), an Austrian psychoanalyst, writer, teacher, and therapist born in Vienna as Otto Rosenfeld. Rank split from Freud when he suggested that birth trauma was the main cause of neurosis.[137]

## Alberto de Rochas

Hans TenDam, in *Exploring Reincarnation: The Classic Guide to the Evidence for Pastlife Experiences* (2003), traced the modern concept of past-life regression to the first mention of regression by Eduardo Colavida, a psychic researcher and spiritualist in 1887. Albert de Rochas experimented with magnetism and hypnosis in Paris and had patients recall past lives in 1893. In 1911, he wrote *Les Vies Successives*, the first book about past lives. It is still available in French. De Rochas found that when he led people back to their childhoods, then further back to birth, then even further back to the first concrete experiences they could perceive, they would go back to a time before they were born, prior to being in the womb.[138]

De Rochas used mesmerism. His method was to have his client sit in a chair,

> [W]ith his right hand on the subject's forehead and passes were made along the length of the body with his left hand. The more passes, the further back the subject regressed. When he wanted to bring the subject back to the present, he made horizontal movement with both hands in front of the subject, starting from the body's vertical middle line. If he continued these passes, the subject went past the present and into the future.[139]

Some of de Rochas's clients went back ten lifetimes.

## Stanislav Grof

In the 1950s, Stanislav Grof, research psychologist, pioneered the concept of rebirthing—at first using LSD. Later, in collaboration with his wife, Christina, he found that a process of deep breathing and relaxation, now called *holotropic breathwork*, could produce results similar to the effects of psychedelic drugs. By the 1960s, there were two psychological systems: Freudian and behavioral. Freudian theories have already been discussed. Behavioral theory stems from the idea that humans are animals. As such, all our behaviors are learned and can be unlearned the same way as animal behaviors. In 1967, Abraham Maslow, Anthony Sutich, James Fadiman, Miles Vick, Sonya Margulies, and Stanislav Grof met to form a new approach to psychology that would cover "the entire spectrum of human experience: the various non-ordinary states of consciousness."[140] They named it *transpersonal psychology*.

During this time, information on work with past lives was scarce and usually limited to the work of psychics and deep hypnosis. In 1927, Paul Brunton described a technique that would allow individuals to discover their own past lives through a daily practice of reviewing the day backward, event by event, hour by hour. It takes years of work and dedication to go back to birth and then to earlier lives.[141] Winafred Lucas reported successfully experimenting with this method, recalling complete conversations that had occurred over the previous two years.[142]

In the late 1960s, I was introduced to Edgar Cayce and his writings. Cayce was known as the "sleeping prophet" through association with the title of Jess Stern's book by the same name.[143] A major concern on my mind was the topic of reincarnation and past lives, which I wanted to know more about. I consulted two psychics who said they could replicate Cayce's method, but they each told me a different story. Wanting a third opinion, I investigated Scientology in Los Angeles. L. Ron Hubbard had started this movement in the 1950s; it was then called Dianetics. His method promised enlightenment and healing after only five weeks. *Auditing* was the name of this process, whereby the client would remember a troubling situation and the resulting symptom would then disappear.[144]

I went into their office for an introductory "audit." Sitting in a cubicle, I held in each hand what looked like a tin can connected to wires, the other end of which went into a boxlike machine. An auditor (conductor) asked me to talk about my concern, and then he directed me to go back before and before each point in time I had previously recounted. I went back to my childhood. When I asked him to clarify the instructions, he said that the conductor was considered part of the machine and thus not permitted to give me information or assistance. After talking about an incident in my childhood, I felt no changes in perception, feelings, or emotions. The auditor explained that I needed more sessions, but when I learned the cost of the series, I left the office.

By the early 1970s, the use of hypnosis to move clients backward chronologically was generally accepted. Denys Kelsey, after fifty years of specializing in psychiatry, began using hypnosis successfully with his patients. He introduced the process to modern psychiatry, in which it was eventually called hypnoanalysis. Kelsey believed that the origin of patients' ongoing problems might be not only from their current past but also from former lifetimes. He further believed that these origins might be accessible to therapy and that patients might perceive and process experiences concurrently.[145]

From the 1960s on, the barriers that prevented recall of birth, prenatal, and past-life experiences started thinning. Was it possible that Sheldrake's (see chapter 3 on Memory) morphic resonance theory was working here? Grof and others were using breathing and imaging to trigger birth memories. The most frequent barrier that regressionists faced when leading clients on time travel, however, was the regressionists' own disbelief in their clients' abilities.

My own first attempt to review one of my own past lives was a dismal failure. My boss, Dick, had been a hypnotist for the military during the Korean War (the movie *Manchurian Candidate* was an overdramatization of the military's use of hypnosis). He offered to help anyone in the office to stop smoking or lose weight. I suggested he help me see a past life. He was positive that it couldn't be done. I was more stubborn, claiming that it was possible. He tried at least four times without success.

Other barriers might be that the client isn't ready to see the real cause or that the regressionist's instructions are confusing to the client. A few clients seem to unconsciously enjoy confusing the process. Sometimes it might not be the right time for a past-life regression. If the client has some problems in the current life that need attention, then recalling the past might hinder the solution to the present challenges. Or perhaps there is an attachment preventing the client's progress (see chapter 4 section on Attachments). Special induction techniques have been developed to bypass many of these barriers and to solve difficulties that may arise during regression.

## The Christos Technique

In the early 1970s, Gilbert Glaskin, a novelist and playwright in Australia, worked with the Christos Technique. He followed directions from an article by novelist Jacqueline Parkhurst, in *Open Mind Publications*, in Western Australia. Using imaging and massage, primarily on the feet and forehead, this process intends to induce in the client lucid dreams that would allow recall of a previous incarnation. A guide directs the person to go out of body and land in another time, usually a former lifetime.[146]

In the induction, a helper massages the feet and ankles of the client, who is lying on her back, as the guide massages her forehead. The massaging lasts from three to five minutes. In the second stage, the client is given mental exercises, such as visualizing various parts of the body growing two inches longer, then shrinking back to normal size and, finally, extending outward in all directions, like a balloon expanding. The third stage is used to stimulate details of visualization that encourage a client's use of imagination. Visualization is indicated by the client's rapid eye movements (REM) with the eyelids shut. For example, a person is asked to imagine standing outside his front door, then floating up to one thousand feet above the house. The REM would indicate whether the client is experiencing a controlled lucid dream. In the fourth and final stage, the client is told to forget all preconceived notions and move down into what may be a totally alien environment. Once the client lands, he is asked to describe his body from the feet up. The entire process takes just over twenty minutes.

This technique does not always move the person into another lifetime. In a lucid dream, as in nocturnal dreams, one may relate symbolic stories that can be interpreted as a dream might. Glaskin found that when he discussed theories about past lives with the client before the session, the probability of recalling a past life increased.[147]

## Hypersentience

Another innovator in the regression field in the mid-1970s was Marcia Moore, astrologer and altered-state researcher. In 1976, Moore published *Hypersentience,* which spelled out visualization inductions that anyone could do. The process starts with progressive relaxation and then counting down. The second stage is going to a childhood memory, encouraged by the use of imagination to assist the memory. The facilitator asks a question, such as, "What do you want—really want?" In the third stage, a person is directed to visualization exercises. At the end of the third stage, the client is asked to walk down a flight of stairs into an underground cavern and then to go to a higher place (through the count of one to twenty), where the person meets a spiritual guide. After talking to the guide, the client uses a bridge to enter another lifetime. After the lifetime is recalled, the client is counted back[148] (see Appendix C). This is the induction method I used from 1977 to 1988. I achieved success and had many return clients using the hypersentience method.

A couple of years later, in 1978, psychologist Helen Wambach conducted large workshops (often hundreds of participants) leading people into past lives and gathering information on customs, clothing, and artifacts. Her book *Life Before Life* (1979) and an earlier book, *The Wambach Method and Manual for Pastlife Recall* (1978), coauthored with L. Lee, are based on research concerning past lives and prenatal memories. She used relaxation and a standard hypnotic induction before bridging with questions to lead participants into another lifetime.[149] She completed three research projects: One was with 1,088 participants over ten years and asked questions about specific time periods, clothing, footwear, money, housing, and so on. With the exception of eleven responses, all descriptions were consistent with historical records. A second research project took 750 participants into the time between their past and current lives. In her last effort, Wambach took over 2,500 participants through future-life progressions, although not many were able to travel into the future. Of the 2,500 people in the study, 6 percent reported being alive in the AD 2100 period, and 13 percent in the AD 2300 period. Wambach was working with Chet Snow on *Mass Dreams of the Future* (1992), which Snow published after her death.[150]

Also in the 1970s, Edith Fiore, a clinical psychologist and trained hypnotist, asked clients to recall past lives during age-regression sessions and published *You Have Been Here Before* (1978). Later, while working with a client, she found she was talking to another voice, an angry voice. She developed techniques to release spirits—souls that had died and attached to another living being instead of finishing their dying process. The subsequent book, *The Unquiet Dead* (1987), opened the way to spirit releasement therapy. Fiore later teamed with William Baldwin to write the foreword to *Spirit Releasement Therapy: A Technical Manual* in 1995. Her clients led her to working with those who had experienced UFO abductions, which was the topic of her book *Encounters* in 1997.

Dick Sutphen, a hypnotist, started giving public workshops during the 1970s and assisted hundreds into past lives. What he began as an all-day or three-hour workshop gradually condensed to a session lasting just an hour. Similarly, Henry Bolduc, who was studying hypnosis, started to explore the readings of Edgar Cayce during this period. He began leading people into their past lives using hypnosis and eventually gave workshops on past-life regression. The barrier between the current life and other lifetimes was diminishing.

Past-life recall workshops lasting one to three hours have become a standard during many hypnosis conferences. Most hypnotherapists can lead their clients into some type of past-life recall, using a preferred hypnotic induction. The International Association of Regression and Research Therapy (IARRT) has trainings during its annual conferences and at other times throughout the United States and other countries (www.iarrt.com). The National Guild of Hypnotists (NGH) conferences also usually have one or two past-life workshops (www.ngh.net).

## Hans TenDam

Hans TenDam, president of the European Association of Regression Therapy (EARTh),[151] described the five levels of memory recall used to relive and identify with a past life, in his book *Exploring Reincarnation* (2003). The first level, *memory*, occurs when clients are aware of current circumstances and surroundings, while at the same time they recall past details, such as where they left the car keys. The second level, *recollection*, happens when clients recall some of the images and sensations, such as what was happening when they put down the car keys. *Reliving,* the third level, starts when recollection is complete; clients feel what it was like to eat the ice cream at four years of age, and yet they remain as they are now. *Regression* starts when clients experience their lives at age four and also forget everything in between now and then. During the hypnotherapy session, they may hear themselves answer, but their conscious mind is unable to intervene. For example, a client might be regressed to the late 1800s in England, where she is living as a daughter of a blacksmith. As that girl, she might not know the name of the queen. Her conscious mind might be yelling, "Victoria!" but the client is unable to vocalize it. The fifth level is *identification,* a state in which any awareness of the current present vanishes. Clients may question the regressionist about why questions are being asked about things everybody knows.[152]

Because the initial regression needs to be deep, the regressionist might choose a more formal hypnotic induction. This is followed by physical and mental relaxation. The client is directed to focus on bodily sensations, taking his attention away from the immediate environment. Next, the hypnotist stimulates the imagination by asking the client to perceive a garden. The regressionist then asks him about details in the garden, the creek or river, and his sensations, such as odors, colors, and any breeze or wind. Then the client is directed to follow a path, cross a bridge, or go through a mist, as in the Christos Technique. This will lead to a past life or a psychodrama or waking dream.[153]

Often, the unconscious mind will take the opportunity to present for processing current emotional situations that have been ignored. TenDam suggests that in discerning a psychodrama from a past life, the regressionist needs to ask for emotions and bodily sensations.[154]

Past-life recall sessions have developed beyond evoking a previous life and processing the death experience, to continuing the recall through the between-life state. This proceeds to the decision to enter the current lifetime. The information gathered during the decision time is related to the subject's purpose in the current lifetime. The information is not always readily accessible, probably due to its potential to affect the client. If the client's unconscious mind deems she would be unable to process the information to her benefit, it will block the information.

## Summary

It seems that Sheldrake's theory of morphic resonance has been displayed in current times. In the 1950s and 1960s, past-life recall was an anomaly. Delving into a past life was considered only an Eastern religious practice or thought. When people such as Helen Wambach and Dick Sutphen gave regression workshops to hundreds of people, the process started becoming easier. It also became easier to access past lives in an hour using standard hypnotic inductions. Going forward in time was not contemplated seriously until Wambach did her studies. Her meager results in leading people into the future were to be expected, however, based on morphic resonance. As regression therapy was becoming more of a possibility, it also became more of a probability.

Currently, past-life recall is primarily a nontherapeutic process. The purpose is simply to recall many details of a previous life. The same techniques are often used to move clients forward in time in a process of progression. In my practice, I have found that moving clients forward a hundred or a thousand years into the future is possible. Although moving them ten years into the future is quite possible, a progression of three to four years is not likely. I rationalize that the near future is already in the making: knowing the outcome, if it were positive, could cause an event not to happen; if it were negative, it might cause undue anxiety. Once information is known, the future changes, or has the possibility of changing, because the present has changed.

When I am moving clients into the future in the current lifetime, the information is often difficult to translate. Clients tend to try to make logical sense out of the information. For example, one client and girlfriend, Doris, wanted to explore her future to see what was happening five years from the present date. What she saw was that she was sitting under a tree, alone. When asked about her family, she said her son was gone and her husband didn't care where she was. It left her depressed. She did enjoy sitting under the tree, however. I saw her frequently thereafter, as a friend. One day, she said the session was correct and made perfect sense. She had gone to the beach to meditate and was sitting under a tree. Her husband was working and had said she could do what she wanted; he would be home when she got back. Her son was away at college and had a serious girlfriend.

While flying across the United States in coach class, I conducted a brief session with a businessman who owned various companies. He was stressing about organizing his advertising budget, so I suggested a progression into the possible future to see probable results. He thought about one project and the money he had currently allocated to it. We took it forward, and he saw the investment making a favorable profit. In the second project, he reduced the investment. The forward result was okay, but not what he had expected. We came back to the present. I asked what else he could do. He stated that he could double his investment in advertising. Then he stated this intention as a positive: "I am doubling my investment in advertising." Going back to the same time in the future, he found the project was a huge success and had won awards. Unfortunately, it was not a publicly-traded company.

## Comments

Past-life recall began as an inquiry into the current past history of a client. It evolved into research into a client's past, in not only the current life but also previous lives. Spiritual questers have been looking for answers and found some of the answers in their past lives. Many regressionists use the information found in past-life stories as the basis for ongoing psychological therapy. In the next chapter, regressionists will use the opportunity to change behaviors at the time-space of the original event.

# Chapter 5

# Regression as Therapy

Up until the late 1970s, regressionists used their methods primarily to uncover information. They considered as only incidental any changes a client might experience. The information they gathered became the basis for both traditional psychoanalytic or behavior therapy and the new transpersonal therapy. When the clients recalled an original event, however, they would often notice a profound change in themselves. If you were to learn or remember that you have been a success in school and not the class dummy, for example, wouldn't it be natural to hold a different outlook on life? Wouldn't your future likely change as well?

When more psychologists and psychiatrists started using hypnosis, the regression field took on new meaning. After these regressionists began doing work with their clients in the original time frame, the desired changes were more consistent and reliable. Regression thus became an effective therapeutic modality.

By the end of the 1970s, there was enough interest in past-life work for Ronald Jue, a clinical psychologist, to arrange a conference for psychiatrists and psychologists at the University of California, Irvine. Professional medical journals carried a notice of the event, and those with proper credentials attended. At the next conference, the attendees chose the name Association for Regression Research and Therapies (ARRT). Ongoing conferences allowed regressionists to share findings and discuss advances in the field, while the public gained a reliable source of referrals. In 1996, the organization became the International Association of Regression Research and Therapies (IARRT) in order to include practitioners from outside of the United States.

## Morris Netherton

During the 1960s and 1970s, Morris Netherton was director for the crisis intervention program in California. In three county juvenile detention centers, he participated in the design of short-term therapy procedures for children from troubled homes. He developed a past-life therapy technique that bypassed the need for formal inductions by using a bridge into a past life. Netherton considered past life to be anything before the present moment. Yesterday is a past life. The bridge could be a word or phrase, a physical feeling, or an emotion. Netherton built on the tradition Freud had started, leading clients to the hypnotic states that result from prior traumatic experiences and remain unresolved in their current problems. The Netherton technique revolves around the memories right before birth, including time in the womb, the mother's moods and experiences during pregnancy, and birth trauma. It is during these situations that a client has the potential to create his positive and negative survival patterns for the coming life. [155]

After eliciting a detailed history, the regressionist directs the client to the moments just before entering the birth canal, where the person will relive his thoughts and feelings up to the first moments with his mother and father. Then the client follows the emphasized emotion, feeling, word, or thought back to its beginning, its origin in this life, then back even before experience in the womb and further back to origins in another life—until it is obvious to both client and regressionist that it is the beginning event. During this time travel, the regressionist encourages the client to experience catharsis (release of negative emotions) as a signal that the emotions connected with that event have been neutralized. The regressionist assists the client to reframe the event, or see it from the perspective of others (such as perpetrators or victims), or perhaps both. Once the original event has been processed (emotions relived, released, and understood), the client can embrace a change.

In this method, Netherton used a physical feeling and emotion, which is similar to the way psychologist Fritz Perls used gestalt techniques. Perls talked to a body part to gather information, such as its purpose and how best to resolve the problem.[156] Netherton addressed the sensation in the body part and then followed it back to the origin of discomfort and the resolution. After studying this method for three years (until 1989), I have had success with many clients.

The technique is also a way to process dreams. Bob came into my office concerned about a recurring dream. Bob was not sure about the validity of past-life theory, but his marriage was at stake. He had wakened his wife with his thrashing, yelling, and crying during the night. I explained to Bob that I needed to know his background to be able to help him identify metaphors from his life. I could thus help him understand his dream language. I began eliciting a detailed history, but when I asked Bob to describe his dream, his face started tensing. His eyes were squinting, almost tearing. I noticed this abreaction because there was nothing in my office that would normally cause tearing.

The following is a transcript of the session. My thoughts and comments are included in brackets:

Pomar: Pay attention to your body. Describe what is happening as it is happening.

Client: It seems as if I see a dashboard with lights on and with the control panel flickering. It is filling up with water. Could be a cockpit of a plane or a car. The instruments are round. The flickering could be due to water or my eyes or the electrical connections shorting out.

[At this point, I follow his first observation that it is a plane and the flickering is due to water. His conscious mind is still present and trying to make sense of the scene. Bob is a successful businessman and accustomed to making sense out of odd situations.]

Pomar: Be there. What are you wearing?

Client: A brown military jacket. Why don't I have a flight suit on?

[I decide not to answer the question. I make a note to guide him to a situation where he can answer the question himself.]

Pomar: Look at your name tag. What does it say?

Client: It is on the left side. It should be on the right, but it is on the left. It is fuzzy. I can't read it.

Pomar: What military are you in?

Client: Air Force? I think German.

[By fixing the incident at a specific point in timespace, Bob is able to leave the event where it originally occurred.]

Pomar: What year is it?

Client: 1939.

Pomar: How old are you?

Client: Twenty-six.

Pomar: Go back before you were in the cockpit.

Client: I am in a room of people. I am in a brown uniform. I shouldn't be here. I don't want to go. I don't have a flight suit on like the others.

Pomar: Where are you going?

Client: I don't know. All I know is that I don't want to go.

Pomar: Go further back to before you were in that uniform.

Client: I am on a farm. My family isn't exactly poor. We don't have much. I don't want to farm. I am going to be a pilot. I like to fly. It is in Germany.

Pomar: Then what happens.

Client: I am in school. We are learning to fly for Germany.

Pomar: Go to the first time you soloed.

[I am looking for a time of happiness. As soon as I ask this question, a smile comes over his face.]

Client: It feels great. The sky is clear. There are fields and mountains in the distance.

Pomar: Where are you flying over?

Client: Belgium? Belgium. I really like to fly.

Pomar: Go to the next significant event.

Client: My plane is not ready.

Pomar: Why isn't it ready?

Client: Something is wrong.

Pomar: What is wrong?

Client: The fuel line is not right.

Pomar: What about the fuel line is not right?

[My questions include Bob's exact wording.]

Client: Water is in the fuel line.

Pomar: Then what happens?

Client: We go into the flight room.

[Now, maybe we can answer his first question: Why isn't he wearing a flight suit in the airplane?]

Pomar: What are you wearing?

Client: A brown uniform.

Pomar: Are you in your flight suit?

Client: No. My plane isn't ready. I can't fly.

Pomar: Who are you flying for?

Client: Germany! [He says this proudly, with a slight smile.]

Pomar: What is the next thing that happens?

Client: I am in a plane. My plane was ready.

Pomar: Go before you are in the plane. Go to the words telling you, you can fly the plane.

Client: I am being told to fly. My plane is ready.

Pomar: What is the next thing that happens?

Client: I am flying over water. I am going down fast. [pause] I hit the water hard. Oh, my. I am not ready to die. My girl. I wanted to have children with her. The cockpit is filling fast. But not as fast as I thought.

[Tears come out of his eyes. It appears that Bob is trying to hold back tears.]

Pomar: Let the tears come.

[Bob has been holding back emotion. This seems like a good time to encourage abreaction, appropriate abreaction for that event. Perhaps then he won't need to act out the scene at night in the dream state.]

Client: [His body begins shaking, and tears flow from both eyes.]

Pomar: How soon until the body dies?

Client: Not as soon as I thought.

Pomar: What words are going through your mind?

Client: I don't want to die. Too young. I wanted to have children.

Pomar: Continue through the dying process. (silence)

[I leave the definition of the dying process to the client. His concept of the dying process might be different from mine.]

Pomar: Any promises made to you or to anyone else?

Client: No.

Pomar: What did you leave undone?

Client: I left my *frauline* [girlfriend]. Didn't get married. Didn't have children.

Pomar: What would you like to say to your parents, your mother and father, that you didn't get to say before you left that body?

Client: Nothing.

Pomar: To your girlfriend?

Client: [tears] I want to marry you and have children with you.

Pomar: Look into her eyes. Do you recognize them?

Client: Yes. I think she has remarried this time.

Pomar: As long as you are both alive, there is a chance this time. If not, perhaps in another lifetime.

[I am careful in this wording. He is currently married to a woman who he considers is someone with whom he had a past-life connection. In this state, clients are most suggestible. My first thought is that he might take this as a sign that he could look for her at this time, or at the next time of marital strife. I noticed he used the phrase "as-as," so when it was appropriate, I use the same phrasing. Using the same wording keeps the client focused in the event and not needing to translate my usual terminology into his own.]

Pomar: Continue through the dying process. Is there someone else there?

[In most times, during the dying process, there is someone or something assisting the soul onward and upward. I am trying to get Bob focused on going forward.]

Client: Someone is taking my left hand. I am right-handed. I can't see who it is. They feel familiar.

Pomar: Continue on.

Pomar: Go to the place you can look over that last life as a pilot for Germany.

Client: I was born on a farm. Mother and father loved me and wanted me to continue with farming. I didn't want to be on the farm. I joined the air force to fly. I was going to marry my girlfriend. Then I died. [tears]

[Since the tears are gentle tears of regret and loss, I do not pursue an attempt at catharsis, which is coming naturally.]

Pomar: Continue on. Go to just before you entered the current life.

Client: I am being told it is time. There is a whoosh. I am in water.

Pomar: Are you inside or outside?

Client: Inside.

Pomar: Where?

Client: Mother?

[I learned that he frequently answered my question as a question.]

Pomar: Go to your birth.

Client: Pressure. I am being wrapped. It is too tight. I feel Mother. She loves me. The man is not my father.

[I feel the time is almost up, and Bob has experienced enough emotions already. Much more material remains for a future session. The question unasked is, "Who is the man?" It could be a doctor or an attendant or someone else.]

Pomar: Come forward to the present time. When you are here in the room, take a deep breath and open your eyes.

Client: I feel there is someone here.

Pomar: May I talk to them?

Client: Yes.

Pomar: How old are you?

Client: Two to three years old.

Pomar: How long have you been with Bob?

Client: A long time

Pomar: How long?

Client: He was little.

Pomar: What is your name? What can I call you?

Client: Helmet.

[I transcribe names phonetically. Sometimes, I ask the client to spell it out. This time I didn't.]

Pomar: Where were you before you were with Bob?

Client: In a plane drowning.

[Bob repeats the story. It seems that Helmet and Bob are the same at one point. But there is a difference in the way each speaks about the other.]

Client: There was a health problem when I was two to three years old.

[It seems as if Helmet died in the plane in 1939. Bob was born in 1941. However, sometime early in the womb, Helmet left and someone else took over. A couple years later, Helmet returned to Bob's body. Did the original owner leave? This could be the earliest, youngest instance of a walk-in[157] in my experience. Questions will have to wait until another session]

I talked to Bob on the telephone a couple months later. He said he had been sleeping the best he had in a long time. The depressions he had before the session had not returned.

## Comments

Because of Bob's immediate abreaction in the regression session, I started taking everything he said at face value. The emotional content of his memory precluded any memory falsification. He didn't need any formal inductions, because he was already hypnotized by the action, the trauma. The dream was a natural trance state. Because he was already in the event, I had not checked for attachments before starting. Afterward, when it was almost obvious that there might be two beings in the same body, I considered sorting. However, Bob had had enough traumas for one day. As in regressions with previous clients, once the death of the suspected attachment had been completed, I saw no further evidence of his presence. A few months later, I talked to Bob. He reported that he had experienced no more nightmares and the thrashing and crying at night had not reoccurred.

# Roger Woolger

Roger Woolger, a practicing Jungian analyst, became interested in the past-life experiences of others and joined a group of psychologists who researched past-life regressions. Jung took the position

[T]hat [the idea of] reincarnation was in principle improvable but was nevertheless one of the most widespread of all religious beliefs and must in itself be accorded the status of an archetype, a universal psychic structure.[158]

Woolger relived a past life in southern France where the Catholic Church was engaged in a crusade to eliminate the Cathars, also known as the Albigensians, a heretical group, according to the Church. He found himself a "crude, peasant-turned-mercenary soldier . . . in the thick of the most hideous massacres."[159] These memories related to some of his personal history and explained his pacificism—yet simultaneously explained his urge to kill during an elementary school scuffle. This experience resulted in further exploration with a fellow analyst, because Jung had "insisted all would-be analysts undergo analysis themselves, so that they would not project their unacceptable qualities onto future patients."[160]

In explaining the past-life phenomena, Woolger suggested that every other life is a piece of a part of us, in the way Jung considered that each part of a dream symbolized a part of the dreamer. Woolger emphasized that it is not necessary for either the analyst or the patient to believe in reincarnation or past lives. However, one should consider the memory as real while the event is being recalled and thus, at the least, a hypothetical event used to facilitate the session.

There are two ways past lives can influence present behavior. The first is that the character in the recalled episode is often recognized as similar to the current personality and is an *other self.* The second is that the character's story is being reenacted in the current life because it is still unfinished.[161] This does not always mean the karma, the law of cause and effect, is not finished. It can simply mean that the actions and reactions of a situation have become a habit.

Woolger's method of leading patients into a past life can be distilled into five steps:

1. The therapist leads the client through relaxation exercises and gives directions to focus on the chosen central issue.

2. The therapist says to the client when necessary, "It doesn't matter whether you believe in reincarnation or not; simply follow the story as if it were real for the duration of the session."[162] The regressionist treats whatever the client says as the truth, "which is real for the patient."[163] The therapist encourages a client to relive, in its fullness, the major event and turning point of that other life, assuming the most catharsis will come from the crucial points of conflict. The client is taken completely through the event to its conclusion.

3. The therapist directs the client through the death of that recalled past-life personality. The client experiences that life fully in that body, releasing the blocked energy of the old traumas. During the death process, the therapist encourages the client to let go of the shocks and traumas to that body. At this point, the death brings a sense of detachment and completion of that life and its experiences. The client is able to leave those memories and experiences.

4. The therapist encourages the client to continue relating his or her experiences through the after-death period. This is an opportunity to compare that life with the unresolved issues of the current life.

5. At the end, the therapist guides the client back to reentry into the current time-place. Events of the previous life and their relation to the current life are discussed, to provide continuity and an opportunity to reflect on the lessons they offer.[164]

# Comments

Woolger's method is similar to Netherton's with the exception of the technique of accessing the past life. Netherton uses a verbal, emotional, or physical bridge into a past-life experience. Woolger uses relaxation exercises first, then the bridge of focusing on the central issue at hand. He uses traditional psychological techniques to process the events, including the catharsis. In his book *Other Lives, Other Selves* (1987), Woolger warns that "guiding regressions and research into past lives should be undertaken by those fully trained in psychotherapy."[165] Regression, especially past-life regression, is not a parlor game, even in light of the historic episode of Bernstein and Bridey Murphy.

In my experience, psychotherapy training and experience are probably not necessary to recall a past life. If you want to use regression and past lives as a therapeutic modality, however, some training in psychotherapeutic techniques is recommended, for the well-being of the client and confidence of the regressionist. Most past-life trainings include beneficial psychological techniques, and colleges and online universities typically have courses to assist regressionists in their practice.

# Hans TenDam

Hans TenDam, an international management consultant and president of the European Association of Regression Therapists, states in his book *Deep Healing* (1996) that "regression therapy is simple."[166] He considers that many problems "result from traumatic experiences that occurred in the past . . . that never having been assimilated become repressed."[167] This results in repressed reactions to the client's problems that are reinforced by weaker, but similar, experiences. These accumulated reactions to similar experiences occur naturally, even though the various reactions are not appropriate to the specific events they accompany.[168]

TenDam, like Freud, Breuer, and Netherton, believes that catharsis is necessary for any successful treatment and is, therefore, the goal of each session. He defines catharsis as cleaning, liberating, and purifying the emotions and providing a physical release and psychological growth in understanding the issues. This understanding is the insight that the psychotherapist seeks in order to produce lasting results.[169] In contrast, psychologist Michael Newton believes that the client has suffered enough during the original event and that desensitization (or neutralizing) the emotions is all that is needed for healing to take place.[170]

In a way similar to Netherton, TenDam doesn't use formal hypnotic inductions. In TenDam's view, the process of remembering itself produces a hypnotic trance state. He notes that when clients are absorbed in telling their story, their perception of time diminishes. The person also does not hear outside noises and enters a "spontaneous and self-induced hypnotic trance."[171]

As clients go through life, many experiences are integrated into the fabric of their personalities. Some sort of therapeutic intervention is needed when a part of the past that has not been integrated is activated and creates problems or discomfort. Regressionists allow clients to revisit the troublesome event and release emotions through catharsis. This emotional release produces emotional peace. Likewise, when one understands an event in present time, purification occurs, to produce intellectual peace. The client begins to accept the past as past, which leads to congruency within the client's own self in the here and now.

TenDam considers that we are always in the "continuous present"[172] and that the words used to direct clients into the past are merely figures of speech. Any actual movement in time, in his view, can be only toward the future.[173]

# Hypnoanalysis

Medical hypnoanalysis is an evolution of psychoanalysis and psychotherapy that uses hypnosis to locate the root cause of a problem or symptom through regression techniques. According to the Hypnotic World website, which provides information in a question-and-answer format, the difference between hypnoanalysis and psychoanalysis is that the latter requires years of reviewing the patient's life (a broad view); conversely, hypnoanalysis requires only the hours needed to deal with the patient's reaction to a particular situation (a specific point in time and space).[174]

On the American Academy of Medical Hypnoanalysis (AAMH) website, hypnotic inductions are used along with free associations during the sessions to follow the trail of memories to the originating event that caused the negative emotion. If the memories might be painful, the therapist is able to help the patient remember without experiencing the associated negative emotion, therefore avoiding catharsis. The therapy is complete when one of the following occurs: (1) the patient does not return, (2) the therapist decides the therapy is not working, or (3) the client gains understanding about the root cause—the originating event—and the precipitating behavior lessens.

## Comments

Hypnoanalysis seems like a bridge between psychoanalysis and hypnotherapy regression. The hypnosis used in hypnoanalysis invokes a light state, because the conscious mind needs to be aware of the root cause and to understand the problem. Further research could consider how many hypnoanalysts have patients who spontaneously access a past life in response to suggestions to go to the previous memory.

## Spirit Releasement

During the late 1970s and 1980s, when regression therapy was starting to include past-life work, anomalies began to arise. In my work, I noticed something strange was happening. I found that clients were recalling past lives that had no relevancy to themselves or their past situations. They commented that the regression did not make sense. To remedy this, I started cautioning clients that they could be picking up on someone else's vibrations. If the first regression was not relevant, we would do another. In the second regression, the past life recalled was usually appropriate, and the client was satisfied.

Then, one time in the mid-1980s, I had a client named Kathy who said she was very psychic. During the induction, her face scrunched up, and she reported the presence of other beings in the room who were not angels. I searched my brain for any information I might have received in any of my conferences or trainings on what to do next. I was entering a new phase. Being familiar with what I call *house cleaning*—the removal of spirits from haunted places—I asked if the other beings belonged to the house. She said they were inside, pointing to her chest. The three of us talked, and I asked them to leave, with Kathy's permission.

After bringing Kathy to full awareness, I asked her opinion of what had just happened. She told me of mischievous spirits around her and of her battle with them. She also told me of her psychiatrist, the prescriptions he had given her, and how she had refused to take the medications. What I learned from this experience was to ask about medications and doctors before working with a client. I was doing past-life recall and hadn't previously considered the implications of medical treatments. I warned Kathy about the necessity of daily meditation and prayer and use of the White Light before doing any—*any!*—altered-state work or time travel. Later in my official training, I learned the importance also of getting a detailed history, which I now take from the client before starting any process.

The thought came to my mind that perhaps the lifetime my client recalled could be the lifetime of someone else (perhaps a past life of an attached spirit)—it was obviously not one my client's past lives. For the next few years, I would assume that if a lifetime presented itself that was not my client's, it was that of a spirit without a body. Also, because I felt an ethical conflict, I did not address these uncalled lives. When I learned the Netherton technique and followed the client through the death of the recalled lifetime, however, subsequent reexperienced lifetimes would become relevant.

I talked to Bob on the telephone a few months after his session. He said he had been sleeping the best he had in a long time. The depressions he had experienced before the session had not returned. He sent me an e-mail giving permission to use his story. Right before *Confessions of a Regressionist* went to press, Bob called for another session. He was having problems. We started where we had left off. After a hypnotic induction, I asked if there was anyone else there. The following is an excerpt from my notes:

Bob: Not me in mirror.

Pomar: May I talk to the person in the mirror?

Bob: [Nods yes.]

Pomar: I am Barbara. What is your name? What may I call you?

Bob: Helmet. [German accent]

Pomar: We have talked before, I believe.

Bob: [Nods yes.]

Pomar: Are you happy?

Bob: [yes]

Pomar: Do you miss your fiancée—your frauline?

Bob: [silence]

Pomar: Do you miss your family?

Bob: [Silence—he seems to be thinking.]

Pomar: Wouldn't you like to see your frauline again?

Bob: [Tears are forming.]

Pomar: You can. She has been waiting for you. Your parents are waiting. Would you like to see them again?

Bob: Yes.

Pomar: Look for a warm, bright light. Go over to it. They are up, on the other end. The light is the way to get to them, where they are waiting. You may reach into the light and feel the cool warmth and how comfortable it is. [Bob's hand moves forward.] When you are ready, go into it. Feel yourself float up, as if you are flying. [He was a pilot]. Look up; you are starting to see someone. Is it your frauline? Can you see others?

Bob: [He nods yes.]

Pomar: Would you like to stay?

Bob: [Nods yes and starts to sniffle and snuff the tears.]

Pomar: You can stay. They will take you and show you around. Bob, can you say good-bye to Helmet and thank him for his help and company?

Bob: Good-bye, and thanks.

Pomar: Look over and see the light starting to encompass you. Feel the light, love, peace, and joy filling you—filling the empty spaces that Helmet left. [pause] Look into the mirror. What do you see?

Bob: Me, smiling.

[Because Bob saw himself in the mirror, I could assume that Helmet had left, and I could talk to this unconscious mind. By talking directly to the unconscious mind, I could determine any blocks or problems that could interfere with his life. Then I could ask directions on how to proceed.]

Pomar: May I talk to your unconscious mind?

Bob: Yes.

Pomar: Unconscious mind of Bob, are there any blocks that prevent Bob from doing what he is here, in the current life, to do?

Bob: He has—.

Pomar: May we go to the source of the—and neutralize them?

Bob: Yes.

Pomar: Good. Thank you for your help. Let's come back to consciousness and discuss what has happened before proceeding.

When Bob was back to full consciousness, we discussed Helmet leaving and possible sadness and grief. We had time. I asked him if he wanted to proceed. Bob reported feeling lighter and wanting to get along with his life. I felt he had done a great service for Helmet and that we could proceed with the session.

Edith Fiore's book *The Unquiet Dead* (1987) answered several questions. Her work explained that attachments were generally spirits of people who had died but had not completed the dying process. Instead, they had chosen another living body to continue their lives. This explanation reminded me of the depossession rituals of the Roman Catholic Church and the movie *Rosemary's Baby*. At the time, I had not yet encountered evil spirits.

In 1992, regressionist William Baldwin had completed *Regression Therapy, Spirit Releasement Therapy: A Technique Manual.* Irene Hickman, an osteopathic physician, had used hypnosis and developed reliable regression techniques that are illustrated in her book *Mind Probe-Hypnosis* (1984). She also devised a method of remote depossession work in *Spirit Depossession* (1994), in which the therapist hypnotizes a proxy for the client who is suspected of having an attachment. She directs the proxy to "go to the client" and "look for the attachment." She also asks the proxy to relay all responses of the attachment. During dialogue, the therapist then coaxes the attachment to leave. It usually does.[175]

After my experience with Kathy, the psychic client, I would begin regression sessions by leading clients to a deeper hypnotic level and having them talk with their unconscious mind. Meanwhile, I asked if anyone other than my client was there. I got answers, sometimes positive.

Soon I developed a method (see Appendix B) whereby, at the beginning of a session, after I took the history of a client, I would ask if I could talk directly to her unconscious mind. I would get permission to help the client and get the client's unconscious to help find out if there were any blocks to the change desired. When the blocks were resolved, I would lead the client through an induction and deepening and then take her downstairs to a hall with a mirror. If the client saw in the mirror an image of herself and what she was wearing in the chair, I would ask permission to assist the client with the changes requested. Permission was usually granted, sometimes enthusiastically!

If the client described someone who wore something other than what she was wearing or someone of a different age, different sex, or something else—perhaps even just a blur or a mass of energy—I would ask the client if I might talk with the person or the energy in the mirror. The response was usually yes. I would then ask if the client would relay the response from the person or the energy. We would talk, and eventually I would ask the someone or the something else—the one attached—to finish the dying process by going up into the light. We repeat the process for each attachment.

When there was more than one attachment, I would ask the first one identified to take the others with her into the light. I would repeat this procedure until the mirror showed the client herself dressed in the same clothes she was wearing in the chair in my office.[176]

When a client said he could not get anything, or there seemed to be something blocking him, I would ask the client to describe the block. After I identified the block, I would ascertain its purpose for the client. Another way of dealing with the purpose was to ask, "How else can the purpose be resolved?" If all else failed, we would remove the block, the barrier, with a sledgehammer—an imaginary hammer, of course—or whatever was appropriate in the physical sense.

## Comments

Spirit releasement has become an integral part of regression work. Regressionists have found that it is much easier and quicker to work with a client without unnecessary attachments. Often symptoms and problems presented are those of the attachment. Early discovery and release allows the rest of the session to progress productively.

As mentioned, attachments are usually spirits of people who have died and not finished the dying process. Spirits have given me various reasons for their attachment. The host may have requested help while still a child and the spirit of someone else may have come too close and attached. The host may have been passing the scene of an accident, and the spirit of one of the victims, not wanting to die, attached to the nearest body. Some are afraid of dying, because of the unknown or because of fear of retaliation (hell) for something they had done while alive. Some attachments have been deceased family members who did not want to leave, or did not leave because the client was not ready for the family member to depart.

Rarely, an attached spirit states that its purpose is to hinder its host. Once questioned, the attachment indicates that it is not happy but afraid of the consequences from its *boss*. While the questioning continues, the *boss* is usually identified as Lucifer, Devil, Bad Spirit, or such, who gives assignments to the spirit. When I ask if one of the assignments is to remain hidden, attachments usually say yes. Then I comment, "Since I know about you, you aren't hidden anymore, are you?" The attachment answers no and is in a bind. So, I present a way out: "Go to the Light, and finish the dying process. There is an angel who will protect you and guide you to a place where you can rest and be healed. Later, if you desire, you can have another body of your own." Most of the time, the being is ready to leave. Sometimes it needs to be talked to, gently but forcefully. The goal is to encourage the attachment to leave, go into the Light, and continue its death process uninterrupted.

Rarely, but it does happen, a client will have an attachment that was sent to harm or discourage the client. This can be discovered when talking to the image in the mirror. When I ask its purpose, the image will eventually say that it was sent to hinder the client. At this time, the hypnotherapist's imagination becomes necessary. Neale Donald Walsch, philosopher and writer, has said that there is no evil but beings do evil on Earth. The purpose of some beings, it seems, is to teach humans that goodness does exist by showing the opposite.[177]

Occasionally, release of the attachment is all that is necessary to make the presenting symptoms disappear. When the client has let go of a major influence, I caution him about possible feelings of loss, accompanied by tears and grieving, such as the feelings he might have when a close neighbor or friend moves away. We spend the rest of the session integrating the experience. Often I suggest that we schedule another session for the following week. During the follow-up, the client often remarks that the presenting symptoms or problems have dissipated.

## Spiritualism and Family Constellation

Marcia Rodriguez Daian, a psychologist practicing in Brazil, gave another version of spirit work at the 2007 World Regression

Congress held in Rio de Janeiro. Daian's work is based on family constellation therapy, whereby family members—or, in this case, volunteers representing family members—have a group-therapy session to contact spirits of the deceased. Spiritualism is a major religious belief in Brazil that was brought over from Africa by slaves during the Portuguese colonization period. The people believe that spirits can enter into someone, usually a minister, and communicate with still-living family and friends. In this instance, since the family members of a client were not at the conference, other participants represented them. In the chosen case study, the client showed concern for her son, who was demonstrating behaviors and speech patterns that had also been present in her deceased brother before he had committed suicide. Another brother had been showing the same behaviors before his unsuccessful suicide attempt.

The regressionist said prayers and asked the spirits of family members to take their places inside each respective volunteer at the conference. The volunteers were designated in the role of a certain living family member—such as mother, father, siblings, uncles, aunts, and children—of the concerned client. After a short period of time, each representative would tell his or her version of the story. When it was time for the child volunteer to contribute, everyone assumed that the spirit/soul talking through him was the client's son who had committed suicide. It was a surprise to all that it was instead the spirit of another child who had been aborted a couple of generations before and later entered three persons—the brother (the successful suicide), his brother (the unsuccessful suicide), and the current child. The attachment was jealous of the life, the love, and the attention the brothers and the child were receiving from their host families. It wanted to cause a sense of loss to the mother to compensate for the loss of that spirit's own life by abortion.

The regressionist allowed the child's spirit to express emotions and offered explanations so the spirit would understand what damage it had done and possible reasons why it had not been permitted to enter life at that time. Daian asked the child's spirit what it needed. The spirit wanted acknowledgment and love. The surrogate mother and other family members each vocally gave love

85

and acknowledgment. The child's spirit said it would return through normal channels (birth) at another time. At the end, everyone offered prayers of thanks and asked the spirits to return to the places from which they had come.

Afterward, I interviewed one of the surrogate family members. She didn't believe in Spiritualism (in which spirits without bodies communicate through humans). However, she said something had entered her and begun speaking. She hadn't had control over what was said. In addition, the utterances were not made with her phraseology. When I asked about the current status of the spirit, she said that it had left. A conference attendee asked Daian if the incoming spirits ever stayed in the surrogates. Her response was no.

## Comments

Daian's spirit work is similar to Hickman's remote depossession. Hickman would have someone in her office travel mentally to the target person and look inside to find the hitchhiker. In Spiritualism, family constellation work, the spirit of another is asked to enter into the person and speak. I don't know whether this method is frequently used in the United States.

## Tad James

In 1988, Tad James, clinical hypnotherapist, published *Timeline Therapy*. His method does not use a formal induction and specializes in eliminating negative emotions and limiting decisions. Negative emotions are primarily anger, fear, and sadness, which may result from the effects of traumas and phobias. *Limiting decisions* are based on beliefs that limit and control reactions while attracting circumstances to enforce a particular belief. James considers all events to exist on a plane that he has trademarked *the timeline*, which stretches from the very far past to the very far future. The therapist traces the root cause of a worrisome effect by leading the client back above his timeline to the original event. The theory is that each event has a purpose and all behavior is learned (as in behavioral psychology). When the client discovers the lesson of the event, the event no longer has any emotions connected to it. The more emotions an event has, the more persistent the memory. After the attached emotions are removed, the event fades into a distant, forgettable memory. By going farther back to a point in time before the root cause has occurred, the unconscious and the conscious mind can feel what it was like prior to the troublesome event. The unconscious can relearn, remember its original programming, and bring it forward along the timeline. The timeline is the imaginary line that is used to organize concepts of time. It can be individual with each client. [178] Once the original programming has been reestablished, the negative impact is neutralized with the new perception. The upcoming example of my client, Bud, is a good example.

Another good example is when I became the client in my own therapy session with Linda. I felt I was being taken advantage of by my husband, friends, and family and was not able to speak up about it. Linda had been trained in timeline therapy and was visiting locally. After questions and a discussion about the session, we decided the limiting decision I needed to address was that I didn't feel good enough about myself to speak up for myself. I went above the timeline toward my past and stopped at an event located in my father's genetic line—back two generations. I went to this place to learn what I needed to do in preparation for actually doing it. I got the impression that I was a male child being berated by his father for not doing something the way the father wanted it done. But the father had not told the child what to do or how to do it. I then went to a time before and relearned and reprogrammed my self-confidence. Next, I returned to the event and found that the emotions were no longer there. Thus, I had gone back and picked up his (my) original confidence and brought it forward to each event in his timeline in which he wasn't able to address himself. At the end, I came back along my own timeline to the present.

# Comments

In this regression, the content of the past-life experience was not important to the regressionist or me. None of my previous regressions had touched on the problem that surfaced. The timeline therapy was a quick and effective solution. The result was that when my husband asked me to do something I didn't have time to do; I realized that he did not really expect me to do it. I just chuckled and said I would do it the next day. He either did it himself or waited until I did it later. Before the session, I would have worried and stressed over trying to do the requested task. Sometime later, I experienced my improved self-confidence when a girlfriend who was a successful businessperson asked for a free session. I said that my therapy work involved valuable time and was a business for me. She paid for her session, and we are still friends.

When the cause of a problem is genetic, an inherited response rather than from one's own experience along the timeline, past-life therapy can take one to the original event in the genetic memory. Lipton (see previous chapter) learned that memories of both father and mother are present in every cell in a person's body. In the Netherton method, the regressionist makes no differentiation as to the lineage of the source, giving only the directions, "Go to the original event." In timeline therapy, the client receives more specific instructions: "Is it along mother's timeline? Is it along father's timeline?" TLT supposes that by going to the source and changing one's perception (and thus the impact) of the event, one changes the DNA programming. As a result, all future holders of that DNA will experience change.

The following case of my session with Bud offers an example of using timeline therapy to reduce a physical symptom. Bud's complaint was the urge to regurgitate after a hearty meal, accompanied by tightness in his upper esophagus near his heart. He had visited the Mayo Clinic, which advised that the problem was not with his heart. Then the Mayo doctors performed a procedure to eliminate the problem. Bud did not experience difficulty in swallowing for a year, but the trouble returned. The difficulty started after he ate bits of something dry. Because Bud's complaint involved a specific problem and the doctors had done what they could, I decided to introduce timeline therapy. Bud understood that I didn't need the story but that he was welcome to share when he desired. When he did, I would ask questions to get the entire story.

During the initial session, and with Bud's permission, I used a formal hypnotic induction to talk directly to Bud's unconscious mind. I asked the reason he was having a difficult time swallowing. His unconscious mind said that Bud needed to meditate. I then asked what was blocking Bud from meditating, and he said, "Past experiences in this lifetime." We went along his timeline to the cause: his first meditation class. The class was taught by a yoga teacher and the meditation students were hippies whom Bud, a surfer, did not like (surfers and hippies did not get along in the 1970s). He agreed with his unconscious to meditate regularly.

During the next part of the session, I explained TLT and led him above his timeline to the first time he had difficulty swallowing. He told about a time when he was seventeen years old. He was dining in a restaurant when he began choking on a lobster. He thought that he must be allergic to lobster. The lesson he learned from the TLT was that he was to relax and meditate and that the difficulty in swallowing would go away.

Something told me there was more involved, so we scheduled another session. The following is the transcription from that session:

Pomar: Go back further, above your timeline to birth. Look down Mother's timeline.

Client: Nothing there.

Pomar: Anything while you were inside Mother?

Client: No.

Pomar: Look down Father's timeline.

Client: It is Father's father. He has gray hair, and he's with Grandmother on a houseboat. Paddle boat on river. He is inside.

Pomar: Talk as your father's father. Be there. Be him.

Client: I am inside. A lot of people are playing poker.

Pomar: Describe what you are wearing.

Client: A fancy outfit. I am not a player. I run the gambling thing. It is a great job. I am the Head Dog. Got shot.

Pomar: What is your name?

Client: Steve McCormick.

Pomar: Go before you got shot. Go to the event that led up to you getting shot.

Client: I am talking to a pretty girl in a plumed hat. I see guys verbally sparring across a gaming table. I excuse myself and walk over. I pull out my gun from my left side; the handle is tilted to the front, with my right hand. I get shot.

Pomar: Where do you get shot?

Client: Lower ribs. I don't believe it; it goes through me.

Pomar: Go above your timeline. What is or are the lesson or lessons learned?

Client: I didn't need to butt in to others' arguments. If I didn't pull my gun, I would not have died.

Pomar: Go to the moment, the second the bullet entered your body. Follow the bullet as it enters your body.

Client: Enters lower ribs, bottom of heart, top of lungs, out my back.

[I am looking for any possible residual pains from this event.]

Pomar: What are the words going through your mind?

Client: Hope she doesn't get hit. It's about my time. I am not distressed. I don't believe it. That guy shot me. I had a lot of hair, long hair.

[I notice Bud has a shaved head.]

Pomar: Was there anything you would like to say to the girl you didn't get a chance to say?

Client: I'll be back.

Pomar: Follow the bullet. Where did it go?

Client: Into the wall next to the girl.

Pomar: Did she get hit?

Client: No. It passed her.

[This past-life experience seems to be the potential origin of the heart problem, but it doesn't relate to the esophagus or to the difficulty in swallowing. We need to go back farther or along another line. Next, I give the nonspecific direction to go to the initial event without specifying the lineage.]

Pomar: Go to the event, the initial event that resulted in the esophagus problems.

Client: I am a blacksmith in a shed. It has a straw roof and sides.

Pomar: What happens?

Client: I am in the shop, pumping bellows. Nothing is good, don't feel healthy. I am dirty, not happy.

Pomar: What is the next thing that happens?

Client: I break the shaft. The red-hot end pops off and starts a fire.

Pomar: What is the next thing that happens?

Client: I have fallen down.

Pomar: Go before the end pops off.

Client: I strike the shaft and slip to avoid the red hot-tip and fall. Everything is blurry. I fall . . . Am choking. [pause] Breaking lower back. Gasp! [pause] Got to get out. Damn God. Damn dog. I fell over dog.

Pomar: Is there anything you left incomplete in that lifetime?

Client: I could have joined the army, but instead I stayed here. [Tears start coming out of his eyes.]

Pomar: What is in the tears?

Client: I was miserable most of that life.

Pomar: What are the lessons you learned?

Client: Life does get better. I helped a lot of people. Died completed. I just performed. I stayed with peers, learned to keep mouth shut, stayed by myself.

[At this point, I think briefly about asking a follow-up question: "Died completed?" From his tone of voice and expression, however, I believe Bud knows what has been finished. I do not need to know. I continue by placing this incident in a specific time-place.]

Pomar: What is your name?

Client: Vlatimore Brosky.

Pomar: How old are you?

Client: Twenty-three.

Pomar: What year is it?

Client: 1647.

Pomar: Where are you?

Client: Suffolk, England.

[We go back to a time before the fire, when he was happy and healthy, so the body and the unconscious can remember what it is like.]

Pomar: Go to earlier in that life, before you were a blacksmith, healthy and happy.

Client: I am a kid outside playing, sitting on grass.

Pomar: How old are you?

Client: Three. The grass is itchy on my bare legs.

[We go forward to get the family and basic family dynamics. This is not a part of timeline therapy, however. When Bud expresses a desire to know more about his past and I have a feeling that there is something more, we continue forward.]

Pomar: Go forward to when you were with your family.

Client: See two things. They have blond hair, blue eyes, in Sweden; and they have dark hair, dark eyes, dirty and poor.

Pomar: Let's go to the life in Sweden.

Client: We are happy; things are light. Have two siblings. Dad makes butter and has milk cows.

Pomar: Go to the most significant event in that lifetime.

Client: Marry a cute blonde girl. We have sons.

[This sounds like wishful thinking and a nice life to balance what could be a difficult life in the other direction. In the current life, his grandfather had a dairy farm that specialized in butter, so there might be a connection, after all. I skip ahead. When reliving an experience in another lifetime, by going through the death process, the client is better able to leave negative feelings and emotions in that body, in that life, and not bring them forward.]

Pomar: Go to the end of that life.

Client: My son has grandson that takes over farm. I am 83. Die of old age.

Pomar: What year is it?

Client: 1722.

Pomar: What are the lessons learned?

Client: I was very happy, wanted to travel but decided to stay with family.

[The lifetime as a farmer is not the same as a blacksmith. This seems to be an example of parallel lives or perhaps wishful imagination of what he wanted to happen. When presented with two options, I take both. The first is more pleasant, to give the client confidence in the process. The second is usually a more difficult life but has more probabilities for growth and change.]

Pomar: Go to the dark-hair, dark-eyes family.

Client: We are dark, dirty, and poor in the Balkans. Family is disgusting, dirty, with much yelling. There are lots of mouths to care for. Father is a blacksmith, a cheat, and a sneak.

Pomar: Go to next significant event.

Client: Father doesn't come home one day. I am going to England with my uncle.

Pomar: Go to the words telling the reason he is taking you away.

[By asking for what words were spoken, I make sure that the conscious mind of the small boy, the client, will not need to interpret their meaning. Sometimes what is spoken is not what is heard or interpreted.]

Client: Mother is pushing me to go with Uncle, to go to England. We have to leave. The village is going to be overrun by [unclear transcript].

Pomar: What is the next thing that happens?

Client: We travel by boat.

Pomar: What is the next thing that happens?

Client: We arrive. People are different.

Pomar: How are people different?

Client: They have light hair.

Pomar: What is the next thing that happens?

Client: I am apprenticed to a blacksmith shop. I like Uncle. It is better here. I am an outcast.

Pomar: Why are you an outcast?

Client: My language and looks. I work to do a good job, keep to myself. I have my own shop.

[The comment about Uncle does not fit in here. I make a note to follow up on it, but the opportunity does not easily present itself. It might be an interesting side trip for later, but is not the focus of the session.]

Pomar: Go to the end of that life.

Client: I am working in the shop, forming a shaft. The tip is red hot and falls off. I jump to get out of the way and fall over my dog. My lower back is broken; I have no feeling in my back or legs. I can't move. The tip starts a fire. I start choking; my throat closes. My sphincter muscles in the esophagus close to prevent smoke from getting down my throat. Have pain in my chest and lungs. Heart is beating, hurting. I die in the fire. It is a long time before anyone finds me.

Pomar: Is this the cause of the current esophagus problems?

Client: Yes.

Pomar: Can you leave it back there? The unconscious was trying to save your life, because as long as you felt the pains you were alive. Do you need to feel those pains anymore?

Client: No.

Pomar: As you go through the dying process, leave all the pains in your back, throat, heart, lungs, and esophagus in that body. Can you do that?

Client: Yes.

[I summarize, stating fact that the pain is not needed for survival anymore.]

Pomar: Anything left incomplete in that life?

Client: Did not join the army.

Pomar: Who would you like to say something to that you didn't get to talk to before you died?

Client: No one.

Pomar: Did you have a wife?

Client: No.

[I do not ask about a girlfriend or if he has any children. This is not a part of timeline therapy. However, because he has identified with the blacksmith and spent time in his body, he needs to leave those aches, pains, and experiences in that life and not have them follow him to the present.]

Pomar: Go back to the time you are outside playing in grass.

Client: [He nods.]

Pomar: Feel the comfort in your throat, esophagus, lungs, and body.

Client: [He nods.]

Pomar: Let the unconscious mind remember how the body is to feel after a meal. Bring that feeling forward. Bring it above the timeline to each time you had problems with your throat, esophagus, and sphincter muscles. Go down into the event, get what you have learned, save them in the place you keep what you learn. Then go to before that time, picking up the feeling of happiness and comfort, and go on to the next time.

Pomar: Go to age seventeen when you were eating at the restaurant.

Client: Hmm. It is not allergy. There are shell pieces in the lobster I have eaten. I am trying to cough them out.

Pomar: Continue forward to each event where the sphincter muscles are getting tense. Pick up what you have learned and come forward to now. Now, go forward to a time when in the past the sphincter muscles would act up.

Client: It is October 10. We are eating dinner, laughing, and talking about the fish we have caught.

Pomar: Are there any thoughts about your throat or esophagus?

Client: None.

After the session, when I was typing the notes, I realized that there was a split during the childhood. This was the first time I had encountered the origin of a split in another lifetime. Because it is not uncommon for a personality to split during the current life as a response to a traumatic incident, I wondered what the incident was that had prompted a split. There is much, still, for me to learn.

I talked to Bud the following year. He had gone on the fishing trip that October. He said he neither had thoughts of the throat problems on the trip nor had he had any problems with choking since.

The major benefit of TLT is that the content of a client's past-life recall does not need to be shared with the regressionist. Once the therapist has explained the process, the client just follows the directions. The clients can nod their heads to indicate when a part of the process has been completed. Because the major portion of time in a typical regression involves eliciting the story behind the problem, the time per session for TLT is thus reduced.

The problem event can also be genetic (see previous chapter on memory). When I followed the source of my problem with self-confidence back by following the gene memory, first along my timeline and then my father's timeline, self-confidence was restored. Because the originating event happened to another person, a relative, any between-life information was not relevant to me. The same was true for Bud when he traced his great-great-grandfather's genetic memory back to the source of his chest pain. Then Bud returned to his own timeline and went into his past life as the blacksmith. After the end of the blacksmith life, he could have continued to the between-life (along his own timeline), but we left this for a subsequent session. When the cause is genetic memory, which is along either the father's or mother's timeline, continuing to the between-life is not an option. At that point, the relative (not the client) is being regressed. The information is thus from another's life and not applicable, or probably not even accessible, to anyone else.

*Barbara H. Pomar*

# Comments

The purpose of past-life recall is to gather information. In past-life therapy, the purpose is to help the client change something. Many, not all, regression techniques may be combined for the benefit of the client and the most expeditious solution of one's problem. With timeline therapy, content may or may not be shared with the therapist, so the full story of the lifetime is not necessarily accessed or processed. Only the relevant event and time before—way before—is accessed, along with any necessary lessons that the event can provide.

With Bud, there was a seeming conflict with time periods, a possibility of having lives in two separate places at the same time. With Pam (chapter 1), the cause occurred centuries ago, yet in both cases the healing took place almost immediately. What was happening? How can it be explained? This is further discussed, along with other questions regarding the nature of time itself, in the next chapter.

In the development of past-life work, there seem to be the two different means of conducting a therapeutic regression. In one, the regression follows a pattern of thought or words or feelings. The client is encouraged to demonstrate or release pent-up emotions by talking about the event. In the second, the regression follows a timeline or a bridge. The client observes but does not need to discuss impressions. Both methods produce therapeutic changes in the client. Within both regressions, the client is directed to look at the trauma from a different angle or point of view. It seems that the reframing of the event is the main therapeutic technique.

## Summary

Past-life regression had a following by the 1600s, when the first book was written about it in France. Breuer found that when he returned his patients to the origin of their symptoms, the symptoms would disappear automatically. Freud started using regression techniques to obtain histories from his clients. Although both Freud and Breuer stopped using hypnotic regression in their practices, past-life regression continued like parlor entertainment. It was this popular version that enticed Tighe to recall a past life that resulted in the book *The Search for Bridey Murphy*, by Michael Bernstein.[179] This popular 1950s publication resulted in others, and it caused both medical and psychology professionals and amateurs to become interested in past-life regression work.

In the late 1960s to 1970s, psychologists and psychiatrists started using regression as a therapeutic modality. Some clients spontaneously recalled a past life. Then, in the late 1970s, medical professionals held the first past-life conference. From that point on, there have been annual past-life conferences, and workshops in giving past-life sessions have become a part of hypnosis conferences. The fields of past-life recall and past-life therapy started to become part of the mainstream. They haven't quite reached that status yet, but past-life work is being considered and talked about more and more, especially via television and radio talk shows.

There is, however, still the problem of the belief that there is no such thing as past lives. When asked why they disbelieve, many people say that a minister or pastor has told them there is no such thing or that it is written thus in a holy book. Beliefs are not easily changed by logic. It is my belief, nevertheless, that a logical premise or reason underlies every belief. In chapter 7, I discuss various beliefs in time and the scientific evidence of quantum theories regarding the nature of time. Perhaps readers can find an answer to this puzzle there.

# Chapter 6

# Between Death and Life

In ages past, knowledge of the after-death time was the realm of religions and philosophers. People consulted priests, psychics, and mediums to inquire about life after death. Before passing from his body in 1926, the magician Houdini left a code that was to be kept in secret and revealed only after he had later contacted someone from the other side. This would be proof of survival after death. Arthur Ford said that Houdini had revealed the code to him, although this possibility was clouded by controversy.[180] By the 1970s, more people were reporting their near-death experiences (NDE). Keith Williams has an extensive website dedicated to the research and stories of near-death experiences of those who were officially declared dead (www.near-death.com). After they revived, these individuals told incredible stories, changing our ideas about existence between death in one lifetime and another birth. Until recent times, the ability to access such experiences intentionally was not considered possible or even thinkable.

In 1975, Raymond Moody, psychologist and medical doctor, published his research about near-death experiences in *Life After Life*.[181] The NDE travelers had many things in common in their stories:

1. They were declared dead by a doctor or others.
2. They had feelings of peace and quiet.

3. The tranquility they experienced was frequently followed by an annoying noise: a ringing, buzzing, or whirling.
4. They felt they were being pulled through a dark tunnel.
5. They felt they were out of their bodies and looking down at what was happening.
6. They met others. Sometimes the others were known; other times a spiritual (nonphysical) being told them it wasn't their time.
7. They met a nonphysical being, sometimes described as an angel, which communicated by thought.
8. They reviewed their current life with a nonphysical being.
9. They came to a barrier, such as a field, park, river, stream, mist, and so forth. They were not allowed across just yet.
10. They came back, but sometimes it was not by their choice. They were told there was more for them to do; they were not finished with their current lives. Sometimes—rarely—they were they told what they still had to do.

These experiences are not completely new to all cultures. For example, *The Tibetan Book of the Dead* (*TBD*) has been in existence for many centuries, and many English translations are currently available. This book is customarily read during the dying process and then repeated over the deceased, guiding the dying person through the dying process and thereafter by describing what to do and how to approach and handle each step.

The steps that the deceased will take according to the *TBD* are as follows:

1. Leaving the physical body.
2. Raising up and leaving Earth.
3. Orienting to the nonphysical state.
4. Meeting with a being or beings, or no one.
5. Reviewing one's current status and former life.
6. Meeting with a series of deities (guides).
7. Choosing rebirth.[182]

In Tibet, one is to read the *Book of the Dead* periodically and commit it to memory as a way to live on Earth and as preparation for death. It comforts us to know what will happen after the physical body is gone, the choice we will face, and how to make the choice. In the Western world, religious leaders teach that the afterlife reflects the actions of a person's current life, without possibility of change once we are there. This doctrine is to be taken on faith, without question. When we began recording more NDEs in the West, more people started wondering what really does happen after death.

## After Death from Arthur Ford

Ruth Montgomery, a Washington, DC, reporter and former president of the National Press Club, knew Arthur Ford, the well-known psychic involved with Houdini's passing.[183] After Ford's death, Montgomery started communicating with him through inspired writing. During this process, he eventually described his death and what had happened after his final heart seizure. After reporting that he "gloriously moved about . . . without as much as a railroad ticket or a walking step," [184] Ford then described meeting people he had known in his last life. Montgomery wrote about his experiences after death, which in 1971 became the book *A World Beyond*.

Ford related what happens after death through the stories of various souls, which have the following in common:

1. The new arrivals find themselves wherever they decide they should be, or in a situation that exaggerates their previous life.
2. They are met by those who are willing to help, once they decide they would like to go someplace else.
3. They meet with friends and loved ones and are introduced to others and made acquainted "with the laws that govern transportation and conversation with others."[185]

4. They go to a place of healing if they had disabilities or a traumatic death.
5. They go to classrooms or study areas.
6. They go to a place where they choose their next life.[186]

Although not all souls had the same experiences, most had some similar ones. Those with expectations from their religious backgrounds experienced such expectations first. Most had someone to meet them and guide and teach about life without physical bodies. Their experiences reflected their immediate past lives. Those who wanted to keep learning went to learning centers.

Montgomery asked Ford about immortality. His response was, "Time has no meaning here. We are ageless, having existed since the beginning, and we are without end. Thus we are *here*, and that is all there is to time."[187]

## The Dying Process

Morris Netherton's therapy followed the client's past-life experience through death. The directions were "Then what happens?" or "What happens next?" Netherton's clients' experiences were similar to those of Moody's NDEs. He and others started to direct the client to a place of review of the previous life. The regressionist assisted in a discussion between the newly deceased (the client between lives) and the loved and unloved ones from that past life. The goal of the client was forgiveness of both himself and others that he knew in that lifetime, as well as acceptance of the event as a learning experience. An example with a former client follows:

[Irma has finished reliving a life in the early twentieth century. As Tony, she has pulled her friend Andy away from a fight, where Andy is threatening to kill somebody.]

Pomar: What happens next?

Client: I get him into my car, and we drive away.

Pomar: Then what happens?

[As Tony, she is not talkative. I mentally send words of encouragement to her. From previous clients, I have learned that because the conscious mind is present and reacts to vocalizations, the unconscious mind is aware of thoughts as well as vocal words.]

Client: A deer jumps in front of the car. I swerve to miss him and hit a tree. We die in a flash of light.

Pomar: What do you want to say to Andy?

Client: I am sorry. Don't leave me. I am sorry for hurting you. I'll make it up. I will be punished for hurting you.

Pomar: What does Andy want to say?

Client: The accident was just life. I'll see you again. We are friends forever—one of my husband's favorite sayings: "I'll see you in another life."

[Both had relatively short lifetimes. I ask what is undone and receive no response.]

Pomar: Go to the time before the current life. How do you know it is time to return to Earth?

Client: My father has a hand on my neck, the nape and back, pushing me. I don't want to go. I am afraid of dying, pain; living will be a struggle.

[I am surprised at her father or anyone else having to push her. I don't follow up on who father is. I also don't ask the question "Why are you afraid of dying?" It would have added to the story. However, Irma knows what she is saying, even if I don't.]

Pomar: What are the words you perceive?

Client: No matter what happens, I can't be hurt. We are eternal. Not to be afraid. Do what my heart tells me—no matter what. Light is all around me, inside me.

Irma had another regression to the eighteenth century in Virginia, as a popular, wealthy male surgeon. He died in his sleep at age eighty-two. He was aware he had met his goals in that lifetime. When directed, "Go to the time before the current life," Irma reported angels, Ariel and Michael, were helping with the decision. Her assignment was to continue healing and to experience joy and to enjoy life. I asked if they had anything to tell Irma. She said they replied, "Helping others and teaching people to be joyful and to experience spirituality . . . Money is not imperative . . . The value is in love . . . When you give, you get back . . . Money is there when you need it."

Irma had been trying, unsuccessfully, to start an alternative healing center. Her second love was in art, which gave her the most joy. A few months after the last session, she reported giving up the idea of a center and concentrating on producing art for an art show. I heard joy in her voice.

Netherton considered past lives of the client's parents as just another past life of the client, because one can reach beyond the womb through genetic memory. In his writings, Netherton did not consider soul memories as separate from the genetic memories that follow a being into the next womb. During the 1980s, he continued to follow clients' other past lives, past their deaths and into the review period, until the clients went through the tunnel or the light and were met by someone. At that juncture, the regressionist would bring clients either forward to current time or into another lifetime.

# Afterdeath—To the Womb, Birth, or What?

De Rochas wrote in 1911 about his subjects' afterlife experiments. Then, in 1944, Michael Newton, psychologist and hypnotherapist, published his research in afterlife experiences in *Journey of Souls*. Newton described cases of clients who reported their adventures after a death in a past life, until their entry into their current mothers' wombs. This was the first time many became aware of the possibility of intentionally accessing the afterdeath state as a goal of regression. Newton came to call this work *spiritual regression*.[188]

In my experience, it is possible to access this period from the back door, from this life, regressing back through the womb. However, as Newton commented, that does not permit individuals to be aware of the experience of leaving the body, and they may be confused or incomplete about the experience during a regression or when they take on a new life. The confusion could arise from gaining surprising information from the between life, of which the client previously has had no knowledge, and which may reflect upon the immediate previous life. Instead, Newton takes his clients through the following steps to warm up for the new experiences with a quick review of a past life. Then he leads clients to reexperience a previous death, to review the in-between life, to preview the next life with choices, and to end in the womb.

Part I. The regressionist briefly directs the client through an immediate past life. This allows the client to naturally reexperience the events following physical death. Also, it "allows for memory warm-up," so the client can become "familiar with the process and become more responsive to questions."[189]

Step 1. Newton's process begins with a hypnotic induction to a fairly deep level, which is practiced with the client before the actual regression session begins.

Step 2. The regressionist leads the client down a staircase, where one step represents each year of the client's life, beginning with the present and recalling only happy events.[190]

Step 3. The regressionist questions the client about activities in the womb before this lifetime and then leads the person through a time tunnel to another time and place in another body. The client recognizes the body. If the client is hesitant, the regressionist asks, "What does your heart say? Let your heart choose the body."

Step 4. The client describes the body, location, and another event in that life. Next, Newton directs the client, "Move to the last day of your life on the count of three . . . Describe what is happening."[191]

Part II. Taking the client through death and beyond.

Step 5. Newton directs the client, saying, "As you move out of your body . . . You can float away when you are ready."[192]

Step 6. The regressionist asks the client questions about what is going on around the body. For example, "Who is near and what is their relationship to you?" or "What are you feeling?"

Step 7. After the client has answered the questions and completed the death experience, the regressionist encourages the client to move on "in perfect comfort . . . releasing all negative energy from your life"[193]

Part III. The stages comprising the path after death are not always sequential. Newton refers to this as *Now* time.[194] ("Nows" are explained further in chapter 8, on Time.) The simple explanation is that everything happens simultaneously but is perceived by the traveler as being present in different Nows. A fraction of a second may be experienced the same as a span of centuries. This reminds me of what Peter wrote in the New Testament: "A day is as a thousand years" (II Peter 3:8). Clients will usually report the following steps in varying sequences once they have left the body in death and have decided to leave the Earth.

Step 1. The newly deceased follow a light or experience a pulling upward.

Step 2. They meet a light being. Newton directs the client to watch the light turn into a being. Some of my clients meet a loved one from the previous past life. (One of my clients reexperienced a life as a cowboy who spent most of his life on horseback, and he met his favorite horse.) They eventually meet a being to guide them in this dimension.

Step 3. They go to a place of healing if the death was traumatic or they had health problems.

Step 4. They go to an orientation room, where they review their previous past life in the context of the goals that were set for or by them for that lifetime.

Step 5. They meet their cluster group, souls that tend to incarnate together. Some remain in the spirit world to assist and direct actions. Others are in body to do the work. These have been called soul groups.

Step 6. They meet with their council, a group with two or more members, including a speaker or director of the meeting. The council gives guidance, advice, and comments on various lives and progress through the clients' lifetimes. The new arrivals are given encouragement and constructive criticism. The clients' guide might be there as an advocate (similar to an attorney). Clients may report being before the council more than once.

Step 7. They select their next life, body, and time of return. The selection may be included in the last meeting with the council or may occur in a different area and time. Often the client has a choice of bodies to best accomplish the goals or assignments of the next life. Sometimes videos are shown of crucial events in the life to assist in the selection. The timing of entry is often coordinated with other group members and the future parents.

Newton's process continues and ends with entry into the fetus in the mother's womb. Netherton's process continues through the birth process to being held by the mother. A good example of a client following this process is Brenda, who was interested in the spiritual part of past lives. Brenda had finished reliving a life as a priest in the mid-1400s. A cart had overturned on top of her, resulting in a quick death.

Pomar: Go, before the cart overturned, to the event that led up to the cart overturning.

[We had relived her previous life, and we went to the end of that life as an entry into the between world.]

Brenda: I am loading the cart with wood with other people helping. The horses are nervous, and the cart moves. The horses shy and the cart falls on its side, with me underneath. I die quickly. I see people lifting the cart off of me. It is too late. They are very sorry.

[Brenda has been given instructions to report the story in first person, using the present tense. This gets the client into feeling the story, instead of just reporting it.]

Pomar: Go above the life and tell the story of that life.

[Normally, I would have waited until after processing the death scene. However, because Brenda has reported her death without emotion, only a hint of surprise on her face, I decide to get the full story. Not all deaths are traumatic. An interesting note is that my clients experience deaths at early ages and in historically early time frames without emotional content. That is, the death is accepted as a normal event. Could it be that children, who have recently experienced *before* life, are not afraid of afterlife, and that those who have had no experience of a painful period before death are not afraid of it either?]

Brenda: I grew up in a small village with my mom. Didn't know my dad. We had to work and help for food. It was a poor village. A castle is in the distance, behind the meadow. I like to go help them in the castle. At seventeen [when he was seventeen, not the priest], the priest invites me to join them. There is a lot of laughter. The master priest dies and a lot of good workers died when the new one came who pushed us a lot. Didn't this Frederick know what was happening? I leave and go into the woods. Come to a meadow and see a house, a very small house. I go to the door, and the man is there. I ask to work for room and board. He lets me work for him cutting wood. We are stacking wood to take to market. Lots of people are helping. Dogs are running around. The horse is not accustomed to being with a lot of people and is skittish. He shies and rears up. The cart overturns on me.

[I don't ask about Frederick. By the time the story is over, I do not want to review. In hindsight, it might have added to her story.]

Pomar: Where are you? What is the nearest town, village, or city?

[The question should have been: "Where are you taking the wood?"]

Brenda: Inner France.

Pomar: What are the lessons you learned in that lifetime?

Brenda: I did no harm. I was good and helped others.

Pomar: What did you gain spiritually?

Brenda: People were poor. Lots of them were thieves. I was not. Never harmed anyone or anything.

[Brenda has asked about spiritual matters during the initial interview. So I inquire about her spiritual journey. During the initial interviews, I ask about my clients' religious preferences and practices, including meditation. Unless a person indicates a spiritual interest, I do not inquire.]

[I again return to the scene of death.]

Pomar: Go to after the wagon overturns. What happens?

Brenda: I am looking down and see myself. It isn't me. I am free. Light.

[There is a huge grin on her face. I know the journey will be easy for her. So I go directly to the end of the afterlife to find her purpose for the current life.]

Pomar: Go to the decision being made before birth in the mid-twentieth century.

Brenda: I just came back home to relax. It was a hard life. Not going back just yet; guides are older and bigger. They know more and are more advanced.

[Brenda has other things she wants to tell me. I have learned that the client actually controls the session. The regressionist has to be aware and follow the leads, fleshing out the details.]

Pomar: Listen to the thoughts, words said. What is being communicated?

[Without physical senses, one has to use mental or telepathic communication. Some people are not used to receiving communication mentally. This is to give them confidence in relating what they at first might think is their imagination.]

Brenda: I just want to go back. I am being told, "Not yet. Why do you want to go now?" I reply, "I can do so much. It is boring up here." They say, "You have just come up." They talk together. The three of them talk.

Pomar: What is being said next?

Brenda: They tell me, "Okay, you can go. If that is what you want. You can go back down. You will need a lot of patience. The time will come when they will need you. You are going back too soon."

Pomar: May we ask questions?

[Since there is no time in the between life, I assume that we can ask for clarification using the present tense. It is usually successful. This is usually one of the most interesting parts of the regression for the client. I use the word *we* because I am asking for the client.]

Brenda: [Client nods her head, indicating affirmative.]

Pomar: What will people need help with?

Brenda: Help with disasters. People will need help. Have to be strong. One of the pillars. Have to be a beacon of light. Help where you can. Show the way home.

Pomar: How can she be prepared?

[I am putting myself in the client's place, trying to ask clarifying questions that might be useful to her.]

Brenda: Just wait. She is ready. She will know when. Time will come when all will be awake. It is your time, too. Patience helps. *Patience* [emphasized] helps. Don't worry too much. Time will come, and it will come whether you worry or not. You also can't speed it along. It is all in a timetable. Just be good and help prepare you. Stay focused. Watch for signs.

Pomar: What signs?

Brenda: You'll smell it in the air.

Pomar: What smell?

Brenda: Chemical, burning; chaos. The day will be just beautiful. Then suddenly, everything breaks loose. People are dying very fast. No water.

Pomar: What happened?

Brenda: A storm, like a big eruption, earthquake, rocks falling, mountains trembling, flames. There is a stench everywhere. People are crying; everybody needs help. I am fine.

Pomar: What about her husband?

Brenda: He is home.

Pomar: Where is Brenda?

Brenda: Outside, everything is happening. People are crawling out from rubble. Everybody is shocked. There are lots of dead people.

Pomar: What happens?

Brenda: I help everybody I see. Give what I have. Find things to help. Just be with them. Talk to them. Tell them they are not alone. We have to work together. We have to all come together, all of us, all of humanity. Not here to work for ourselves alone. We as a group have to improve.

Pomar: Anything else you would like to tell us?

Client: [Shakes her head no.]

[As Brenda has already reviewed the decision phase, it is time to come forward to present and integrate the experience.]

Pomar: Continue on through birth. [pause] Continue forward to the present time. [pause] Continue forward to my office in the chair. When you are ready, take a deep breath; stretch and open your eyes.

## Comments

During the initial interview, Brenda told of a pleasant, unstressed life during her previous sixty years. She had a feeling there was something else she was to do this lifetime and thought perhaps that by knowing about a past life she might get an idea. This story was the second past life she reviewed. When she remembered, the telling of the details and descriptions improved. By the end of the session, she was leading herself. I was the transcriber, adding questions to get more details. I found it interesting that she started talking in the first person, present tense when I questioned her guides. In reviewing the session, I wish I had asked about the "timetable." Frequently, I have been able to get to the purpose of the client's life during the before life decision time. It has only been since 2005 that some of my clients have been told that the reason for the current incarnation is to help with coming disasters.

## Summary

Netherton and Newton have found that the journey of the client after death is very similar to the journey described in *The Tibetan Book of the Dead* and read to the deceased after death. The primary benefit of afterlife review is to give clients a dress rehearsal of death and what can be expected. This relieves most of the fear of death and can give the client confidence in the future. Another purpose is to give the client a context for the current problem or symptom. The council can give suggestions on the current situations of the client for favorable (to their total growth) outcomes. Often the client can view the effects of a successful transaction that is not beneficial in the long term and then can see the probable effects of a seemingly-less-than-successful event that has greater benefits later on. It is up to the client to put the principles learned to work.

## Comments

I was amazed when I compared what is described in *The Tibetan Book of the Dead* with near-death experiences reported by Ford—in both his stories from those already on the other side and his clients' recall after a death and before reentry to Earth. They all seemed to agree on the various steps and, except for the *TBD*, they all said the order was not exact and could vary. It seems that it is very possible to access the afterlife and better prepare clients for what they most likely will experience.

Most of Newton's experiences with clients have been duplicated by other regressionists. It is my experience that the trance automatically deepens as the client navigates time, while relating details, reliving the experience, and becoming more engrossed in that other timeframe. It also is possible to negotiate with the council on behalf of the client to have a specific or general situation modified (such as a physical ailment or having to pick a difficult job). This needs to be done in a spirit of loving cooperation and concern for your client.

Clients may not remember the scenes that come up for review. Nor do I have records to verify how accurately they are viewing the happenings in these scenes. Newton does not address this question. Viewing the probable future does not negate free will. The future results from every decision we make, and each new decision changes the future. Clients have free will in how they perform their chosen or designated part in the scene. They also are able to choose many details in each life, such as their parents, their tasks, or something they want to do. How they navigate through this life, however, is up to each individual. Visiting the in-between life often acquaints clients with helpers on the other side and aids in identifying those on this side who are there to help.

Newton believes that to successfully navigate the between life with the client, the regressionist needs to have a solid spiritual life and a regular practice of meditation or prayer, according to the regressionist's personal beliefs. The client will experience that which the regressionist allows to be. Any doubts the regressionist might have need to be suspended. The client will react and often take on the doubt, thus preventing the between session. Not all clients are able to access this state. Those who are able might not experience all stages or report all stages.[195] Most clients are met by someone. Many continue to the healing room, if needed. They might appear before the council with life choices, and then go on to birth. Occasionally someone, such as Bob the pilot, will go from death (in the water) to the womb (in the water) directly. When I took Bob back into the previous body and went through the death again, while asking questions during the dying process, he received more information. Due to time constraints, we didn't explore the between region.

Currently, candidates for board certification by the International Board of Regression Therapy are required to demonstrate competence that includes between-life regressions.

## The Case for Belief in Past Life—A Synopsis

People have believed in past lives for thousands of years. In the Orient—in India, for example—it has been part of the spiritual heritage for at least three thousand years. In 1969, a Gallup poll showed 20 percent of the population in the United States believed in reincarnation, that is, the rebirth of the soul in a new body after death. In another poll taken in 1982, 67 percent of the population believed in life after death, and 23 percent believed in reincarnation. In 2001, the percentage slightly changed to 25 percent when the Gallup organization took another survey about belief in reincarnation. Gallop polls taken in 2004 and 2005 indicated that 81 percent of Americans believed in heaven and an afterlife, and 20 percent in reincarnation; another 20 percent were not sure of their belief in reincarnation.[196]

Ian Stevenson devoted much of his professional life to interviewing children about memories of previous lives. For a child to come to Stevenson's attention, the child must have already demonstrated spontaneous memory of a past life. Of the over three thousand cases that were brought to Stevenson, two thousand were eventually published. Carol Bowman, a social work counselor specializing in children, wrote two books about children who remembered a past life: *Children's Past Lives: How Pastlife Memories Affect Your Child* (1997) and *Return From Heaven: Beloved Relatives Reincarnated Within Your Family* (2003)[197]. Many people, including my husband, have recalled a past life either on their own or with guidance. Déjà vu experiences could be recalls of other lives. Wambach and Sutphen (see chapter 4) took thousands of people in groups to previous lifetimes, and Wambach conducted a research project leading people forward in time (progression).

In chapters 2, 4 and 5, I show many ways of accessing past-life information. Much depends on the motive and the intent of the regressionist and client. If only the story is desired, then one technique is used. If therapeutic change is desired, then the instructions are different.

What is it that people are recalling in past-life sessions? This question is the focus of chapter 3. Some can make up or fabricate stories to please the regressionist (false memories) or interpret information from outside sources as being part of a past life (cryptoamnesia). The source of these memories can be identified with direct questioning, perhaps using ideomotor responses. Some stories can belong to the past lives of attachments. The attachments can be identified and released early in the session. Some past lives may have genetic origins. As Lipton found in his research, we have memories of both parents in every cell in our genes, and a specific past-life memory could be found in the genetic memory. Jung identified the collective unconscious as being a depository of all of human experience. Jung's collective unconscious is similar to Sheldrake's concept of formative causation. When requested to review a situation, clients could be accessing the collective unconscious or the morphic field to obtain experiences that might explain a question to the regressionist—or they could actually be recalling their own past lives. If the change is accomplished as the client desires, what is the difference?

There are times when clients spontaneously recall past lives, such as those psychiatrist Brian Weiss recounts in his book *Many Lives, Many Masters: The True Story of a Prominent Psychiatrist, His Young Patient, and the Past-Life Therapy that Changed Both Their Lives* (1988). At that writing, Weiss had not considered the possibility of past lives. He was neither a believer nor disbeliever. However, when a client desires to recall a past life, it is important that regressionists believe they can lead the client into the past. The intent of both the regressionist and the client needs to be clear as to the purpose of the session: it is to recall a past life of the client while observing any emotional attachment to the events that come up. Sometimes the client is not emotionally inclined. This can be ascertained by observation while asking for a happy memory and watching for smiles and so on. The inability to express appropriate emotions could be an issue to be explored. If, at the end of the session, the client professes that the recalled memory has no relevance to his or her current life, then an attachment might be involved. Once the attachment is released, a successful recalling of a past-life memory usually occurs.

When clients who desire a specific therapeutic change are asked to recall an original event that has resulted in a current situation, the recalled life might be theirs or a genetic memory. Either way, the therapeutic change can be made at the original event. To ascertain if the recalled memory is genetic or the client's own, one may ask questions early in the session. I have found that more specific directions at the beginning of the session will produce more specific information in the recalled memory. When I take the history of the client, we agree on the purpose or goal of the session. While using the Netherton method, I simply direct the client: "Go to the original event that precipitated the current condition." The unconscious mind will do just that. The original event might involve an incident in the mother's life, in the client's own current life, or in one of his or her past lives. When TenDam reviewed the results of a questionnaire he sent to clients three months after their last appointment, he found "results increased when present-life regression work was used in addition to pastlife regression work."[198]

As Edgar Cayce (1877-1945) was one of my first sources when I started understanding the concept of past lives, I researched his readings on time and space. Cayce went into a self-hypnotic trance and would answer questions posed by those present or who had written letters. The readings from letters asked for information on a variety of subjects, mostly medical conditions. Cayce was also known for his past-life readings (61 of the over 14,300 readings that he gave). When I was researching the readings, there were seventy-six mentions of time and space within seventy-three readings. The earlier readings talked about time and space being part of the third-dimensional world, the material world. Time and space do not exist in the infinite; they exist only in the material world.[199] Could this mean that past, future, and other lifetimes exist only in the now, the present? And would this also mean that in nonmaterial existences there is no time, no separation between events, no separation between cause and effect? Let us explore what time is, in the next two chapters.

# Chapter 7

# Time: Absolute to Relative

Our review of regression up to the twenty-first century shows that clients seem to remember something and that the remembering effects changes in their current lives. However, some people still question the reality and existence of past lives. Perhaps the history of time and quantum theories might provide another part of the answer. Sean Carroll, theoretical physicist at California Technical College in Pasadena, California, began his book *From Eternity to Here* in this way: "According to researchers at the Oxford English Dictionary, time is the most used noun in the English language."[200] St. Augustine, theologian in the fifth century, best noted for developing the doctrine of original sin, wrote, "What is time? If no one asks me, I know. If I wish to explain it to one that asketh, I know not."[201]

My research identified three kinds of time: personal, relative, and scientific. *Personal time* is a concept with which everyone is familiar. The ancients geared their life on sunrise to sunset or sunset to sunrise, that being what we call a day. Later inventions were created that divided the day into equal segments. When it was more important for people to be on time, for example, at the beginning of the Industrial Age, time became an absolute. Lives were adjusted for time. Yet, even in the twenty-first century, there are cultures in which being on time is dependent on the situation and/or the culture. In many Latin and mid-Eastern countries, being fifteen minutes or even an hour late is still considered being on time. In

Germanic and English countries, by contrast, five minutes late is five minutes late. We consider things we have done or experienced as past, and things and events we have not experienced but hope to as future. We currently live in the present. Memories are current recollections of past events.

*Relative time* is the time relative to an event. For example, time moves slowly when we are children waiting for our birthdays or Christmas. When we get older, birthdays appear to come closer together. *Scientific time* is absolute. Clocks move at the same speed wherever they are.

Einstein wrote about the relativity of time. He noted that the perception of time depends on the relative motion of observers. Previous measures were replaced by new conceptions of scientific time, as time went from the absolute of Newton to the nonexistent of quantum theories as discussed in the next chapter. The problem could be that if time does not exist, then the past and future do not exist. Therefore, we must ask, where does that leave our impressions of past lives and past-life memories?

## Absolute Time

In the days of classical philosophy, according to Aristotle and Ptolemy, the basic concept was that one could work out all the laws of the universe by pure thought using logic. There was no need to check by what we would call scientific experimental observation. However, Aristotle observed that the natural state of a body is to remain at rest unless acted upon by some force or impulse. In most cultures, people observed that the sun rose and set, therefore the sun revolved around the Earth in a periodic fashion, called a day. This was absolute. This conception of time was absolute.

However, in the eastern Oriental world before the second century BC, the Sautrantic Buddhist school[202] argued against the concept of time as being absolute—by demonstrating that past, present, and future are interdependent and that any notions of an independent past, present, or future are not real. Apart from the temporal phenomena upon which we construct the ideas of time, there is no real time that is an absolute, having an existence of its own.[203]

In the early 400s, St. Augustine asked, "How can the past and the future be, when the past no longer is and the future is not yet? If it always were the present and never moved on, it would not be time but eternity."[204] In current language, we would say, "Time is not possible because the past is a memory and the future a dream."

Later, Galileo Galilei (1564-1642) expanded on Aristotle's work by demonstrating how the real effect of a force is always to change the velocity of a body. Velocity is a combination of speed and direction. Acceleration is the rate of change of velocity with respect to time. Velocity is the rate of change of direction with respect to time. Theoretically, a body would keep on moving at the same speed in a straight line,"[205] and the "concept of motion makes sense only as it relates to other objects."[206] Unless we have an absolute standard of rest, which is one of the major problems for physics, "we cannot determine whether two events that took place at different times occurred in the same position in space."[207]

Isaac Newton (1642-1727) experimented on his own but had a watchful eye on what had happened between Galileo and the Church. In 1615, Galileo took a stand that the Earth revolved around the sun (heliocentricism). Through the Inquisition, the Catholic Church (the Church) disagreed. Galileo recanted in exchange for a reduced sentence that confined him to house arrest indefinitely. In 1992, John Paul II made a formal apology for Galileo's treatment by the Church, and the heliocentric system became an acceptable belief for Catholics. Newton (and the Church) worried about the lack of absolute position or absolute space, because this concept conflicted with the idea of an absolute God. Both Newton and Aristotle believed in absolute time. Newton wrote, "One could unambiguously measure the interval of time between two events and this time would be the same regardless of who measured it, providing the person used a good clock."[208]

In the middle 1600s, Galileo and Newton, along with Wilhelm Leibniz, a German mathematician and philosopher, were working separately on laws of the universe. With Kepler and Copernicus, Galileo learned that the Earth moves, even though it appears to be stationary amid the revolution of the stars, sun, and moon. Newton was aware of Galileo's troubles and tried to couch his discoveries in ambiguous, more acceptable, terms. In his *Philosophiae Naturalis Principia Mathematica* (1687), Newton expounded by saying that absolute time flows equitably, equally for all observers, and uniformly without relation to anything external. He described this natural process as running in only one direction and said that time is like an arrow. Later, mathematics proved time could flow in both directions. [209]

According to Newton, the entire world's history can be determined from two snapshots taken in quick succession. If the motions of a body are known at some instant, the known physical laws, along with the initial conditions of the event, or of the body, determine all future movements. Newton believed that the initial conditions were originally set in place by God when he created the universe.[210] Time, in Newton's science, was absolute. One second in England was one second anywhere in the universe. Time was absolute.

Wilhelm Leibniz (1646-1716), who also claimed to have first discovered calculus, said time is made up of different instants of time, an infinite number of them. He argued that time is an entity that fuses space and time into a single notion for a possible arrangement or configurations of the unity. He argued that space and time do not exist separately.[211]

Time was calculated on the rotation of the Earth. Soon discrepancies were found in measurements of the Earth's rotations, which were attributed to the tidal effects of the moon. Astronomers looked for a more accurate natural clock and found the solar system. They assumed that Newton's laws governed the solar system. Time defined in this manner was called Newtonian time. It is now called *ephemeris time*, termed for the publication that gives the position of celestial objects at any given moment. For more than a decade it was the official time standard for civil and astronomical purposes. A clock is any mechanical device constructed so that it marches in step with ephemeris time, the unique simplifier.[212] Currently, atomic time, which relies on quantum effects, is used as the standard. Atomic time is measured by atomic clocks and is calculated from the microwave signals from electrons, because electrons are emitted from super-cooled atoms at a predictable rate.

## Relevancy to Regression Work

Past lives have been acknowledged, although in a minor manner, in most of the Western theologies. However, they were considered to be isolated in a linear timeframe and not readily accessible to the everyday human.

## Relativity Theories

In 1865, James Clerk Maxwell (1831-1879), a British physicist, combined the partial theories that were being used to describe electricity and magnetism, and

> [F]ound that a single field carried both electricity and magnetism . . . . [Maxwell] called that force the electromagnetic force and the field that carries it the electromagnetic field . . . The wave-like disturbances in that field would travel at a fixed speed like ripples on a pond. When he calculated the differences between the waves and the peaks, they exactly matched the speed of light, 186,000 miles per second.[213]

In 1905, Albert Einstein (1879-1955) formulated the theory of relativity, which says that "the laws of science should be the same for all freely moving objects no matter what their speed."[214] Observers must have their own measurement of time, and identical clocks carried by different observers need not agree. He established the need for three special coordinates (east-west, north-south, and up-down) plus one time coordinate to locate any particular event, termed space-time. The concern of physicists has been with the mathematically calculable nature of reality and how everything can be explained by mathematics. By showing that the appearance of physical reality may vary from one frame of reference to another, the unchanging, invariant, aspects of physical reality may be explained. Space and time are not two different things but are one space-time continuum, confirming what Leibniz had said two centuries earlier.[215]

Einstein later revised the theory of relativity and called the revision *special relativity*. This said that the speed of light was the same to all observers, and it explained what happens when things move at speeds close to the speed of light. Two events that happen at the same time in one frame of reference may occur at different times when seen from another frame of reference.

Einstein's special theory of relativity "has verified that travel into the future is as possible as is going backwards."[216] If an astronaut were to travel near the speed of light, it might take him, say, one minute to reach the nearest stars. Four years would have passed on Earth, but for him only one minute would have passed, because time would have slowed down inside the rocket ship. Hence, he would have travelled four years into the future, as experienced here on Earth. Brian Greene (1963-), professor of mathematics and physics at Columbia University in New York, wrote:

> Special relativity declares a law for all motion: the combined speed of any object's motion through space and its motion through time is always precisely equal to the speed of light . . . Light travels at the speed of light . . . Time stops when traveling at the speed of light through space . . . [217] (Light doesn't age).

Greene explained that since the timeframe is dependent on the observer, someone in a distant galaxy can see events in their present as happening at what we, on Earth, would call our distant past. And, if they could speed up, they could see what was happening in our future. All "[E]vents, regardless of when they happen from any particular perspective, just *are*. They all exist. They occupy their particular point in spacetime."[218]

Greene's findings were inconsistent with Newton's theory of gravity, which says that at any given time objects are attracted to each other with a force, the size of which depends on the distance between them at that time. This means that if you moved one object, the force on the other object would change its position instantaneously.

In 1908, Herrman Minkowski (1864-1909), Einstein's mathematics teacher, announced that space by itself and time by itself are doomed to fade away and that only a kind of union of the two will preserve an independent reality. Minkowski created a simple diagram of space-time, showing the mathematical relationship of the past, present, and the future. For each individual they met and forever met at one point—now. Now is specifically located and will never be found at any other place than here. Now is wherever is the position of the observer.[219]

Einstein worked to find a theory of gravity that was consistent with special relativity. In 1915, he proposed the general theory of relativity, which describes space-time as not flat, but curved or warped by the distributions of mass and energy in it. Time has a beginning and runs differently for observers at different heights in a gravitational field. Time moves more slowly closer to the Earth's surface.

Werner Heisenberg (1901-1976), a German theoretical physicist, developed the uncertainty principle that expresses the limits nature imposes on our ability to predict the future using scientific law. To predict the future position and velocity of a particle, one needs to measure the present (position and velocity) accurately. In order to measure the position, one needs to put light on it. The more light on the particle, the more accurate is the measurement of its position. However, even the smallest bit of additional light will disturb and change its velocity. "The more accurately you try to measure the position of a particle, the less accurately you can measure its speed, and vice versa."[220]

Einstein postulated that space-time is curved because it is bent by a gravitational force. He proved mathematically that time travel is possible; it is a matter of engineering. According to quantum theory, "it is possible for space-time to be finite in extent and to have no singularities that form a boundary or edge . . . The surface of the Earth is finite but has no boundary or edge."[221]

The theories of time can be compared as follows:

1. Newton's absolute time is one dimensional. In absolute time, events develop with age, the passing of time. Past develops into present, which develops into the future. It can be described as a line drawn with a series of finite points infinitely close together.

2. Einstein's general relativity of time has two dimensions, as the wall with length and width, where all points on the wall are in contact with other points on the wall. He then adds a third dimension, space. For example, a pilot flying reports his direction (north-south and east-west) and altitude. Einstein's special theory of relativity adds a fourth dimension—time. To keep appointments, we need the address (or intersection) of north-south and east-west, up-down, and time.

3. Later, the concept of the *spacetime continuum*, where all events exist, was developed. It says everything already exists completely in the now. We can see all—past, present, and future—at the same time, with one glance.[222]

In the nineteenth century, the second law of thermodynamics, covering the concept of entropy, stated that all processes observed in the universe have directionality. It was observed to be in conflict with the fact that Newton's laws should work well in either direction. In 1906, the Austrian physicist Ludwig Boltzmann (1844-1906) "introduced a theoretical definition of entropy as the probability of a state" (using statistical arguments to describe how atoms behave).[223]

# Relevancy to Regression Work

Before the 1980s, lifetimes were generally assumed to be linear and sequential. Two opposing thoughts existed: (1) There is no such thing as a past life, and (2) there are past lives. Both were strong beliefs, creating a schism that is the basis for this work.

# Chapter 8

# Quantum Theories of Time

In 1925, Werner Heisenberg, Erwin Schrodinger, and their colleagues found that "electrons acted like waves and could make quantum leaps in their seemingly chaotic motions within the atom."[224] The explanation of these observations was originally called quantum mechanics because of the mechanical qualities found in a multiple of discrete units called *quanta*. Quantum mechanics—a subject that covers the small, micro world—is currently called quantum theory. Today, the terms *quantum mechanics* and *quantum theory* are used interchangeably.

In 1906, an English physicist named J. J. Thomson was awarded the Nobel Peace Prize in Physics for the discovery that electrons are particles. However, in 1937, his son, G. P. Thomson, also an English physicist, was awarded the Nobel Peace Prize in Physics for his discovery that electrons are waves. The quantum theory is based on the idea that particles, such as electrons, could be described not only as pointlike particles but also as waves having properties of both. Schrodinger's celebrated wave equation—a key to physics and chemistry—states that "the wave represents the probability of finding the particle at that point."[225]

In the classical double-slit experiment, protons are shot one at a time through slits to a wall, where a pattern is observed. If they were particles, the protons would produce a certain pattern reflecting the slit on the wall. If the protons were waves, they would produce a wave pattern, a semicircle, on the wall. In this setup, what determines whether a particle or a wave reaches the wall? The outcome stems from the objective of the observer, who is viewing the protons going through a slit to form a specific pattern. The event thus becomes reality, and any other options cease to be real or to exist. There have been three interpretations of this experiment:

**Copenhagen:** In 1920, Danish physicist Niels Bohr and German physicist Werner Heisenberg wrote that nothing happens until it is observed. Einstein didn't agree, saying, "I like to think the moon is there, even if I am not looking at it."[226]

**Many-Worlds:** In 1957, Hugh Everett found that every possible outcome exists. Each outcome exists as a part of the original observer, and each observer is unaware of the other outcomes.

**Two Places at the Same Time:** In the beginning of the twenty-first century, Roger Penrose, Oxford mathematics professor, was researching the possibility of protons being in two places at once. In the theory of quantum mechanics, extremely tiny objects "exist in a state of constant flux, allowing them to occupy not just two locations but an infinite number of them simultaneously."[227] Penrose designed an experiment that, if a success, would show that when an object splits, one part is able to turn a mirror. The gravitational pull will force all parts back together quickly, but before this happens, a camera will have captured the particle as it splits and rejoins.

Students at the University of Santa Barbara, California, built the equipment, which was assembled at the University of Leiden in the Netherlands. The experiment was completed in 2011, with a finding that the particle traveled faster than the speed of light.[228] New experiments are being designed to duplicate the findings or refute them.

The classical "Schrodinger's Cat" experiment proposes that a cat be put into a box along with a time-release capsule of poisonous gas. The radioactive decay of an atom (a random event) would determine when the capsule releases the gas, killing the cat. In another version, the decay of an atom would affect the trigger of a loaded gun. The gun would shoot the cat. There could be several outcomes, according to various theories:

**Classical Physics:** The cat is either dead or alive when the box is opened.

**Quantum Theory:** The cat is dead or alive depending on the decision of the observer who views the opened box.

**Many-Worlds:** The cat is both dead and alive. Mathematically, it is represented as the sum of a dead cat and a live cat. When the box is open, the world—as well as the consciousness of the observer—splits into two different outcomes. One consciousness goes with the reality that the cat is alive. The other goes with the reality that the cat is dead.[229]

**Penrose:** Ask these questions: "Who counts as an observer? The cat? If not the cat, then why do we count as observers?"[230]

**Einstein:** He was not fond of quantum theory. In a letter to Max Born, he wrote: "Quantum theory is very impressive, but I am convinced that God does not play dice."[231]

The Copenhagen interpretation of quantum theory reflects the dominant influence of Niels Bohr and his school of thought. This perspective says it does not matter what quantum theory is all about. The important thing is that the theory works in all possible experimental situations. Further, what we call physical reality is actually our perception of it. For example, once you open the box and establish whether the cat is dead or alive, the "wave function will have collapsed . . . leaving only particles, and the cat will have entered a definite state" [232] (either dead or alive).

John Wheeler (1911-2008), a theoretical physicist, posed the concept of the quantum foam. This consists of the ultramicroscopic examination of the chaos of space (and time) and includes areas of left and right, back and forth, up and down, before and after. The ultramicroscopic scales (particles) that make up the foam, the central feature of quantum theory, and Heisenberg's uncertainty principle, which states you can know the velocity or the position of a particle but not both at the same time, are in direct conflict with the central feature of general relativity, which is the curved geometrical model of space (and spacetime). When the calculations of quantum theory and Heisenberg's uncertainty principle merge, the result is infinity. "An infinite answer, which is not an acceptable answer to a mathematician or physicist, can be nature's way of telling us we are doing something wrong."[233] In other words, it is back to the drawing board.

In essence, quantum theory

1. is a logically consistent system that is self-consistent and consistent also with all known experiments;

2. has experimental evidence that is incompatible with our ordinary ideas about reality;

3. is believed by most physicists, as well as most Hindus and Buddhists; and

4. has as its greatest problem one of measurement.[234]

Stephen Hawking (1942-), Lucasian Professor of Mathematics at the University of Cambridge and a theoretical physicist and cosmologist, listed twentieth-century findings in quantum science as follows: (1) the length of time between events depends on the observer, (2) time is not completely separate from and independent of space, and (3) insights into the properties of light work well with apples, planets, or things that travel slowly but not for things moving at or near the speed of light.[235]

No wall separates microscopic and macroscopic worlds: there is instead a continuum from one size to the other or from one world to the other. According to Kaku, Nobel laureate Richard Feynman was fond of saying that "no one really understands the quantum theory."[236]

## Relevance to Regression Work

Quantum theory is usually used as a rationale for arguing that there is no such thing as a past life. True, if all time is now, then there is no past, no future, and then no past life or future life. Penrose's proposed experiment, if successful, will open up other possibilities. If—a big *if*—people could be split, the client in 2009 could travel back to 1700 to change the emotional charge of an event whose effect was bothersome in 2009. This change could result in a different 2009. The change would facilitate the collapse of the split, reuniting the two personalities. A split personality has been known to occur after a traumatic event, whereby a part of the person splits to avoid unpleasant memories. Another part sticks around, stuck in the time-space of the original event. The psychologist, psychiatrist, and shaman each use varying techniques to bring all pieces of a person together. Hypnotherapists are not trained to regress split personalities, and in some places, such as California, are prevented from doing so by law.

## String Theory

As it matured, quantum theory produced two relevant, but conflicting, theories: first, Einstein's theory of general relativity, which encompasses large-scale phenomena; and second, quantum theory, which governs the smallest scale. Then a third evolved:

superstring theory, which combines the general relativity theory and the quantum theory into one master equation.[237]

In physics, conflicts between theories seem to resolve themselves into development of another theory. For example, in 1800, Isaac Newton claimed that if one were to run fast enough, one could catch up to the speed of light. But in 1968, James Clerk Maxwell's theory of electromagnetism proposed that one cannot go faster than the speed of light.

Albert Einstein resolved the conflict with the theory of special relativity in 1905, which says that space and time are malleable, dependent on one's state of motion, and that no object can travel faster than the speed of light. By 1915, his theory had evolved into the general theory of relativity, stating that space and time can warp and curve in reaction to pressure of matter and energy. Space and time are not inert or static but active players in our universe (because the universe is a gently curving form of space). However, quantum theory describes the universe as a frantic microorganism. The conflict between theoretical descriptions of space was eventually resolved in the mid-1980s by string theory, which says spacetime has many "dimensions tightly curled into a folded fabric of the cosmos."[238] Hawking, in a *Briefer History of Time,* wrote the following about string theory:

> Basic objects [or particles] are described as things that have length but no other dimension, as an indefinitely thin piece of string. These strings may have ends (so-called open strings) or . . . take the form of closed loops (closed strings). A particle occupies one point of space at each moment of time. A string . . . occupies a line in space at each moment of time. Two pieces of string can join together to form one string; in the case of open strings they simply join at the ends, while in the case of closed strings such as the two legs joining on a pair of trousers. Similarly, a single piece of string can divide into two strings.[239]

In the 1960s, scientists found that "the strong forces between particles would correspond to pieces of string that went between other bits of string, as in a spider web."[240] (See Hawking's description of strong forces in M-theory.) The observed value of the force between particles meant that the strings had to be similar to rubber bands with a pull of about ten tons.[241]

String theory suggests that "the microscopic landscape is suffused with tiny strings whose vibrational patterns orchestrate the evolution of the cosmos."[242] Elementary particles of the universe are not point particles. Greene, a professor of physics and mathematics at Cornell University, describes the tiny strings as

[O]ne-dimensional filaments, somewhat like infinitely thin rubber bands, vibrating to and fro . . . They are the ultramicroscopic ingredients making up the particles out of which atoms are made . . . They are so small that on the average they are about as long as a Planck length.[243]

Greene describes a Planck length as "a millionth of a billionth of a billionth of a billionth of a centimeter, so that the particles appear pointlike when examined by our most powerful equipment." For example "if we were to magnify an atom to the size of the known universe, the Planck length would barely expand to the height of an average tree."[244]

In a later book, *The Fabric of the Cosmos,* Greene describes the length of a string. As the string gets energy, it starts vibrating faster, and the length starts increasing; "there is no limit to how long it can grow . . . It could "grow to macroscopic size."[245] The energy from the big bang could have produced long strings that "could very well stretch clear across the sky."[246] The two, three, and p-branes might be larger than a Planck length. (Branes are discussed under Edward Witten's M-theory.)

Height, width, and depth are three dimensions. Time is the fourth dimension. And the fifth dimension is space, as presented by Theodor Kaluza in 1919. If the fifth dimension of space were reduced and reduced, it would split into two equations: Einstein's standard theory of relativity and Maxwell's theory of light.[247] After Einstein read Kaluza's paper, he took two years to evaluate and respond. Eventually, he wrote, "The idea of achieving (a unified theory) by means of a five-dimensional cylinder would never dawn on me . . . At first glance, I like your idea enormously . . . The formal unity of your theory is startling."[248] Later, superstring theory came about.

## Relevance to Regression Work

If events could be considered as a group of point particles, and a lifetime is considered a string of events, then the emotional connections between events could be the strong forces, or pieces of string, that connect lifetimes. If string theory is thought about in this way, then regression work could disconnect unwanted connections between the lifetimes. It is at this point that many regressionists, as well as many physicists, discount string theory.

## Superstring Theory

Michio Kaku (1947-), a theoretical physicist, said superstring theory poses that the electron and other subatomic particles are nothing more than different vibrations on a string acting like a tiny rubber band. Depending on how an individual strikes the rubber band, the rubber band vibrates in different modes, with each note corresponding to a different subatomic particle. In this way, superstring theory explains the hundreds of subatomic particles that have been discovered so far in our particle accelerators. Einstein's theory emerges as just one of the lowest vibrations of the string.[249]

The unique feature of the superstring theory is that strings can vibrate in ten dimensions. The theory breaks down, mathematically, if one tries to create a string theory in other dimensions. Since our universe is four-dimensional, the other six dimensions must be collapsed or curled up, like physicist Theodor Kaluza's fifth dimension.[250]

In 1964, string theory was being discussed. It was similar to the standard model of the universe in that it was incomplete without a mention of gravity.[251] By 1974, Joel Scherk of the Ecole Normale Superieure, and John Schwarz of the California Institute of Technology added gravitons, the "smallest bundles"[252] of the gravitation force, which placed gravity in the quantum theory. They showed that string theory could describe the nature of the gravitational force, but only if the tension in the string was "a thousand million million million million million million tons (1 with 39 zeros after it), the so-called *Planck tension.*"[253] The predictions of quantum theory would be just the same as those of general relativity on normal length scales, but they would be different at a very small distance, a Planck length.[254]

John Schwarz with Mike Green, of Queen Mary College, posed that

> [S]tring theory might be able to explain the existence of particles that built in left-handedness, such as some particles we observed . . . String theories lead to infinities, but it is thought in the right version, they will all cancel out (this is not known for certain). String theories . . . seem to be consistent only if space-time has either ten or twenty-six dimensions instead of the usual four.[255]

With spacetime, string theorists say on a very small scale it is ten dimensional and highly curved. But on bigger scales, the curvature or the extra dimensions are not seen.[256]

Between 1984 and 1986, scientists wrote "more than a thousand research papers on string theory . . . ."[257] Five string theories were developed, but researchers found the mathematics difficult to solve. Even determining the equations proved to be difficult, and only approximate versions of them have ever been deduced. So, the string theorists have been left to finding approximate solutions to approximate equations.

# Relevance to Regression Work

Superstring theories seemed interesting to me but not really applicable to regression work. The concepts didn't yet seem complete. There had to be further developments.

# M-Theory

In 1994, Edward Witten (1951-) of Princeton's Institute of Advanced Study and Paul Townsend of Cambridge University speculated that all five string theories were in fact the same theory, but only if we add an eleventh dimension.[258] By reexamining the origin of each of the five theories, Witten found that the translation of the theories combined into a cohesive single theory—M-theory.[259] Michio Kaku surmised, "Perhaps the universe itself was a membrane, floating in an eleven dimensional space-time. Perhaps our universe exists in a multiverse of other universes."[260]

Witten's M-theory (*M* has not officially been defined, although many people assume it means membrane)[261] brings the various string theories together and asserts that strings are really 1-dimensional slices of a 2-dimensional membrane vibrating in 11-dimensional space. These one-dimensional slices are called membranes. "The higher dimensional cousins are named two-branes, and objects with three special dimensions called three-branes and objects with p-dimensions where *p* can be any whole number less than 10."[262] Branes are "'more massive than strings" and have "minimal impact on a wide range of theoretical calculations . . . here are a variety of circumstances, still hypothetical, . . . . in which case the brane *does* have a significant impact on the resulting physics."[263] "The possibility that we are living in a three-brane—the so-called *braneworldscenario* [universe]—is the latest twist in M-theory."[264]

Hawking asked the question,

Why did one time and three space dimensions flatten out and the others remain tightly curled up? One possible answer is the anthropic principle, which is paraphrased as, "We see the universe the way it is because we exist." There are two versions of the anthropic principle, the *weak anthropic principle* and the *strong anthropic principle*. The weak anthropic principle states that in a universe that is large and infinite in space and/or time, the conditions necessary for the development of intelligent life will be met only in certain regions that are limited in space and time. Intelligent beings . . . observe that their locality in the universe satisfies the conditions that are necessary for their existence.[265]

Hawking described the strong version as follows:

There are many different universes or many different regions of a single universe, each with its own initial configuration and its own set of laws of science . . . Only in the few universes that are like ours would intelligent beings develop. As for the question, "Why is the universe the way we see it?" if it had been different, we would not be here."[266]

Or would we just be different?

## Relevance to Regression Work

When first reading about string theory, it seemed to be the ideal explanation for regression work, as each string could be considered a lifetime. The relevant past lives were close, almost adjacent, to the current problem situation. With a bridge from one string to the adjacent string, the emotional attachment could be neutralized, causing the event to be a nonevent, similar to any unimportant event, such as an everyday breakfast or putting on clothes in the morning, in the person's current memory. It needs to be an actual event that does not, however, leave an emotional imprint. The purpose is to detach the strings, so the client can live a life unencumbered by past emotional attachments.

Theoretically this explanation worked. By following a string from the physical ailment or emotional state back to its origin in a specific event, then dissolving the attachment or string, the client may experience immediate relief. An example is Bob (Helmet) in chapter 5. We followed his emotional state (his tears) back to the airplane crash. Once the tears and emotions were completely expressed and left in that specific timespace, he no longer had the disturbing nightmares.

I found that string theory does not fully explain lifetimes that are not sequential. Therefore, there has to be another explanation.

## Many-Worlds Theory

In orthodox quantum theory, as the observer sees the proton go through a slit, that event becomes reality and any other options cease to be real, to exist. This observation started Hugh Everett (a student of John Wheeler at Princeton), Neill Graham (a physics doctoral student), and others thinking.

Physicist Hugh Everett (1930-1982) wrote in 1957 that the universe can and must be divided into at least two parts, an observing part and an observed part.[267] In quantum theory, the problem is to determine when the multiple possible outcomes collapse into one observable outcome. In many-worlds theory, the collapse does not occur; the multiple possibilities continue to coexist. "Each incarnation of the observer sees one of the possible outcomes."[268] Greene in *The Fabric of the Cosmos* (2004) surmises, "These individual processes take place independently of each other. Each incarnation of the observer is unaware of the other's existence."[269]

Later that year, Hugh Everett, John Wheeler, and Neill Graham posed the Everett-Wheeler-Graham theory, which states that at the moment the wave function collapses, the universe splits into two worlds, two separate branches of reality. Each is doing something different. Each is unaware of the other. Each is creating its own separate branch of its own reality. This theory is also called the many-worlds interpretation of quantum mechanics. If a consciousness or a sentient being observes the split, the consciousness also splits, creating two different editions. Each consciousness is unaware of the other's existence.[270]

John Bell, British physicist from Belfast, claimed

[T]hat the really novel element in Everett's theory had not been identified. The novel element was a repudiation of the concept of the *past* . . . He looked for the quantum property that enabled Everett to make his many-worlds idea plausible and pointed out that the accumulation of mutually consistent records is a vital part of it . . . Bell showed that "record formation" is a characteristic quantum property. At least under cloud-chamber conditions, the wave function concentrates itself at configuration points that can be called records.[271]

Barbour would call them "time capsules" (explained in Timelessness Theory). [272]

Classical physics considers the past as a continuous path through the configuration of space. History is highlighted as a path. Bell claimed that we have no access to the past. We have only our memories and records. These memories and records are, in fact, present phenomena. With them, the actual existence of the past is immaterial.[273]

At any instant, just one event is actualized at random in accordance with its relative probability. The higher the probability, the greater is the chance of actualization. According to Barbour,

Sentient beings within them will possess memories and records within them that convince them they are the product of history. This will be an illusion. In reality, the points realized at successive instants of time are chosen randomly and jump around in a wildly unpredictable manner in the configuration space.[274]

A question that Kaku posed is that if there are parallel universes, why aren't we aware of them? The *decoherence theory* states "that all these parallel universes are possibilities, but our wave function has decohered from them."[275] We no longer vibrate in unison with time and no longer interact with them. That means that in your living room you coexist simultaneously with the wave function of dinosaurs, aliens, pirates, ex-mates, and so on. "All of them believe firmly that their universe is the real one, but we are no longer in time with them."[276]

Barbour wrote, "Mechanical laws of motion allow for immensely large numbers of possible situations. Interesting structure and order arise only in a fraction of them."[277] This leaves statistical arguments, which give dull situations or the so-called *anthropic principle*, which states that if the world were not in a highly structured but extremely unlikely state, we should not exist and be here to observe it.[278]

In the movie *Back to the Future*, Doc Brown goes to the chalkboard and explains his time travel. He draws a horizontal line representing the timeline of our universe. Then he draws a second line, which branches off the first. It opens up when you make a decision that changes the past. Likewise, whenever you travel back into the past and come forward, the past forks into two, and one timeline becomes two, or what quantum theorists call *many-worlds*.[279]

## Relevance to Regression Work

The many-worlds interpretation of quantum mechanics is currently the regressionists' favored explanation for regression and past lives work, as well as for the existence of other lives. Many regressions take a client to the original event. At that point, the event is reframed. The client sees it from hindsight in reference to current life and in a cosmic or spiritual framework. This perspective changes the client's mind-set in order to realize the lesson the event was to illustrate. With this understanding, the client starts on a different timeline.

Another way to work with the decision point is to take the client back to that point to see what other decisions could have been made. The client could also travel each decision to see what the outcome of the alternative decision would have been. Sometimes the original event might be the best of several possible difficult or unhappy choices.

The big problem with this theory, as I see it, is the immense number of potential lifetimes that could stem from the decisions of just one lifetime.

## Timelessness Theory

Since the second century BC, Buddhists and Hindus have written about the past and future as nonexistent. The present is reality, according to this view. In Western cultures, many philosophers, religious teachers, and theologians have stated that there is only the Now, the present. Newton wrote about the possibility of time going backward and forward. Minkowski proved mathematically that there is no such thing as time. But what do these views tell us about our sense of personal history and our experience of shared history?

Waking up one morning with a headache, Julian Barbour (1937-), a theoretical physicist, took two aspirin and went back to bed, thinking. The night before, he had been discussing Paul Dirac's doubt regarding the fusions of space and time into spacetime and the unification of Einstein's general theory of relativity with quantum theory. Later, while walking through a garden, Barbour thought, "time is nothing but change."[280] Upon further reflection, he expanded those thoughts into his statement, "Change is the measurement of time, not time the measurement of change."[281]

The best way to describe it without going into the particulars of physics and mathematics is that each instant, what Barbour calls a Now, is concrete and distinct. He considered Einstein's and Newton's space and time as "redundant as a role on a stage," a nothing.[282] The world does not *contain* things. It *is* things. The Nows exist in nothing.[283]

Barbour considers these Nows to be similar to three-dimensional snapshots. The three-dimensional snapshot can be explained as many people taking regular two-dimensional snapshots and comparing the information to build a three-dimensional picture of the world:

> These three-dimensional snapshots are jumbled up in a heap. A different person, given the heap, could relatively easily, by examining the details, arrange them in the order they were experienced. . . . This imaginary exercise brings out the most important property of experienced time: its instants can all be laid out in a row. These instants are laid out in a row. . . . in a linear sequence. But it [change] is created not by invisible time but by concrete things.[284]

In Barbour's timeless theory, all conceivable Nows, some in multiple copies, exist. However, there are too many to arrange in a continuous sequence. All conceivable states can be present simultaneously.

Sometimes simple Nows can overlap, creating complex Nows—what Barbour calls time capsules. These time capsules contain past and future as well as all sensory feelings and emotions. The past is actually contained in present records. The greater the consistency of the records, the more real the past becomes. The past is nothing more than what we can infer from our present records. According to Barbour, there are two facts consistent with the notion of time: First, the abundance of evidence, for time is literally written in records, such as fossils, newspapers, and minutes of meetings. If the secret of time is in reducing time and motion into the time-capsule structures located in our brains, and if our short-term memory storage and retrieval are the functions of the structures, then any impressions of motion and perceptions of time will have been condensed into a common center of specific structures situated in individual Nows. Second, the creativity of nature speaks insistently and consistently of time; the appearance of time is a deep reality. Time capsules can offer a more radical explanation of the properties of time. The timeline may be redundant. Barbour concludes, "The instant is not in time—time is in the instant."[285]

Each point, each Now, does not have a unique starting point. Each Now, representing a different possible configuration of the universe, is present as potentialities, at least in different quantities. Barbour describes a mist consisting of a distribution of various Nows. Where the Nows are the densest, creating the mist, there is a greater probability of experience. Barbour goes on to state,

> If there is only one Now, all your memories are then illusions in the sense that you never experienced them. If lots of Nows are chosen, then you believe that you did experience them all. It is possible that all Nows are available. It is consistent with the many-worlds hypothesis . . . It truly is impossible to say how many of your memories are real. All we know is that the present is "real." The view that all instants exist together and at once in eternity is commonplace thinking among Christian theologians and some philosophers claiming time does not exist.[286]

Motion is implied, and interpreted by our brain, from the rapid sequence of Nows. Consider this example: Are Buster the dog that starts after the stick, and the Buster that catches the stick, and the Buster that brings it back all the same? The gross physical structure appears to be the same. However, the number of atoms in the tiniest of things is huge and in a constant state of flux at the subatomic level. An immense number of cells are being generated, dying, and sloughing off constantly. There are billions of Busters; only the stability of his gross features (color, size, and so on, which don't change) enables us to call him one dog. If we cannot and do not look closely, we think he is one package. Because we abstract and detach Buster from one of his Nows, we think that a dog ran. Dogs don't run. They just are.

Zeno of Elea, a fifth-century pre-Socratic philosopher belonging to the same school as Parmenides, came to the conclusion that motion is impossible. He explained that when an arrow shot at a target travels halfway to the target, it still has half the distance to go. However, when it has gone half again the distance, it still has half of that way to go.

So, theoretically, it never gets to the target. As Barbour's timelessness theory explains, the arrow that left the bow is not the arrow that reaches the target.[287] Time does not exist. "Since time is the result of change or motion, motion does not exist either."[288]

Recently, Neale Donald Walsch, in *Conversations With God, Book 2*, wrote of time:

> "Time" is not a continuum. It is an element of relativity that exists vertically, not horizontally.
>
> Don't think of it as a "left to right" thing—a so-called timeline that runs from birth to death for [an] earthly individual, and from some finite point to some finite point for the universe.
>
> "Time" is an "up and down" thing! Think of it as a spindle, representing the Eternal Movement of Now.
>
> Now picture leafs of paper on the spindle, one atop of the other. These are the elements of time. Each element separate and distinct. Yet each existing *simultaneously with the other*. All the paper on the spindle at once! As much as there will ever be—as much as there ever was . . .
>
> There is only One Moment—*this* moment—the Eternal Moment of Now.
>
> It is *right now* that everything is happening . . . There is no Beginning to this, and there is no End. It—the All of Everything—just IS.
>
> *Within the Isness* is where you[r] experience—and your greatest secret—lies. You can move in consciousness within the Isness to any "time" or "place" you choose.[289]

Another way of explaining Barbour's view is as frames in a movie. Each frame is a fraction of an instant. When the movie is run, the frames alternate so quickly that our brain interprets the change in scenery as motion. We are culturally conditioned to perceive change and its subsequent inferences of time. When I look in the mirror, for example, I see changes to indicate that the face I see, my face, has been around for longer than I care to remember.

It seems that Barbour's extension of string theory and many-worlds theory through mathematical formulas best explains no-time. Max Tegmark (1967-), cosmologist at Massachusetts Institute of Technology, also comes to the same conclusion, that all events, all lifetimes, are enclosed in a mathematical structure. Tegmark used the metaphor of a DVD movie in which movement is illusionary to demonstrate that all time exists in each moment.[290]

As I was thinking and rethinking Barbour's explanation, I was looking for another physicist who would agree with him or offer another view. I came across Terence Witt's book that equates time and distance. Witt's views are examined next.

## Relevance to Regression Work

Timelessness theory could also explain regression and other-life work, because each Now contains all previous experience of the Now, including past and future lives. Each Now is a frame in a film or video of the life and existence of a client; it is infinitely thin and infinitely long. Each frame is a link to other decisions, other lives, other dimensions. Each client has the ability to rerun the filmstrip of the chain of Nows. By rerunning the strip and going deeper into the frame of a particular instant, a person can access the original Now of the situation or frame. Because the Now can be accessed and changed by reframing or redeciding, it could be possible to change subsequent events of Now, resulting in immediate change in Now. Though I had learned the language of time as well as the basic theories by this point, my firmness in the belief of actual past lives was weakening.

## Null Physics Theory

I thought I had completed a review of the current theories of time when I came across an advertisement in *Discover Magazine*. Terence Witt had written a book about null physics, which discusses time as distance. This approach makes sense to me, for as a former Southern Californian, I was accustomed to measuring driving distances in time. I used time and mileage interchangeably. Witt's book was advertised as available only through the mail. The author uses plain English, with equations to explain his positions. Because of this, I have used more quotations than usual.

Null physics attempts to describe the origins and the purpose of the universe as we know it. Witt dismisses Big Bang and other theories as inconsistent with the known laws of physics and incomplete in their explanations. His theory postulates that the universe is infinite and "must be the way it is, and the reason why is that the universe is permanent . . . The universe exists because there is no other alternative."[291] Witt explains, "Matter is built from spatial curvature, space is built of geometric points, and points are nothingness incarnate. This means that matter is composed of points."[292] Witt seems to conclude that everything is nothing. However, Witt's points seem similar to Barbour's Nows.

In explanation of time, Witt writes, "There is no *now,* just as there was no beginning."[293] I interpret the statement to mean there is no singular present (*now*). Regardless of the apparent redistribution of the universe's material over time, its entire history can be no larger than the size of any given moment. Unlike in Einstein's theories, it is not an independent dimension. Witt goes further to say that if time had degrees of freedom, then there would be many pasts and many futures, such as in the many-worlds theories. But it doesn't. It is an infinitely thin string having length.[294] Witt's description is reminiscent of string theory.

Time is a fourth-dimensional interconnection among energy forms. Trillions of years may pass before two distant quanta eventually interact. If this occurs in the future, the certainty of this future occurrence existed throughout the infinite past. As Witt says, "Every event is preordained."[295] Witt freely transposes *time* and *change.* "Change is not possible, because it violates temporal equivalence . . . The universe, when viewed in its entirely, remains precisely the same from one moment to the next . . . All moments in time are equivalent because they are one in the same."[296] He concludes, "The universe had no origin; there was no special moment when everything began. Nor will it ever end . . . The universe at one moment is exactly the same as at any other moment. It is governed by the utter immutability of nothingness."[297] Witt acknowledges "that this *ultrastasis* is at first spectacularly counterintuitive . . . A static universe means every moment in the universe's history, and therefore Earth's history, is located somewhere in space at this very instant."[298]

There is no change. Because the change would be evidence that the prior event was incomplete . . . There is one past and one future, because they are exactly the same, the ultimate expression of nothingness as well as causality. "All moments in Earth's history are permanently distributed throughout infinite space."[299]

Earth's history is made up of an infinite number of total instants (brief moments in time, which Barbour says are composed of many Nows). The longer an object's life span, the more instants it has scattered across the universe. The minimum lifespan any object can have is 1 squared divided by infinity. An object's instants have an associated spatial volume, or instance volume. Therefore, the moments of phenomenological time are isolated from each other by infinite distances.[300]

Witt disagreed with Einstein's opinion on the possibility of time travel. He explained, "Time is the difference of space. Reaching the past or the future from our current location would require crossing an infinite distance. Time travel is simply not possible, at least in the physical sense. We might be able to use virtual reality to simulate a bygone era, but we will never be able to actually visit a different moment of history."[301]

Witt does answer the question of an afterlife. He writes,

Everyone is alive and well in the omnipattern. They are separated from us by infinite distance but are indisputably alive. Right now. This instant . . . all of our past images move through their lives precisely the same way they did before their passing . . . Moments are never lost. Every civilization that has existed or will ever exist on any world shares a similar posterity. We are all parts of the indelible community of certainty.[302]

## Relevance to Regression Work

Although Witt states that there is no past, no present, and no future, he does say that every instance exists as it always has. Although physical time travel is not possible, according to Witt, virtual travel might be possible. Infinity encompasses everything and all distance. Therefore, it might be possible to access the past (or future) that is relevant to the current instance. As the past/future is scattered across the infinite universe, past and future lives might be accessible to the individual as current past/future.

Witt states, "Every moment is preordained."[303] Therefore, even if accessing a past life were possible, it would not be possible to change it. And, therefore, any changes in the present life would not be possible. That is, unless it were preordained that the past would be changed in the future so the present could be changed. Hmmm . . .

## Comments

Witt's theory of time is a possible, but not fully probable, explanation of regression work. It does explain the ability to access past and future lives of the client. It also may explain the possibility of forgiveness work with those who have already had past, present, and previous lives. It does not address the possibility of a non-Earthly, nonphysical life.

His theory does offer explanations of moments that are similar to what Barbour calls time capsules. Witt concludes that since there is only the present, there could be no singular moment as the Big Bang. Because all Nows and all moments exist simultaneously, everything is preordained. It always was and always shall be. I have a problem accepting his conclusions about predestination, even though the first part of his theory is similar to other findings. Barbour and Penrose explored only their views of timelessness, however, and did not expand their findings to other areas, as did Witt.

## Folding Time

I came across the concept of folding time a few times in my research when I was examining explanations of past lives. I have looked for more scientific explanations and found that philosophers and theoretical physicists have worked with this idea. Albert Einstein was one of the first, writing about the curvature of gravity and time. Michel Serres, Roger Penrose, and Mark Hadley are the latest to have discussed folding time.

Einstein's special theory of relativity seems to presume that the speed of light cannot be surpassed. In the early part of the twentieth century, the speed of sound was deemed impossible and dangerous for humans. Then, in 1956, Chuck Yaeger broke the sound barrier, and for a time a regularly scheduled supersonic jet flew passengers across the Atlantic in just over three hours. By the end of the twenty-first century, the speed-of-light barrier would be broken as easily and frequently. For example, those who conduct remote viewing are doing this. It could be said that regressionists who lead their clients into another time are changing something, and then they observe the result manifesting in their office during the same session they are doing it. The question is: how do we quantify this outcome?

Einstein and his physics and mathematics associates wrote about curvature of time and space. Research on time travel references the curvature, noting that physical time travel is possible because of the curvature. Traversing time and space using their curvature seemed to bypass the need to exceed the speed of light. It would seem that if a person could physically travel from AD 2010 to AD 1200, mental travel should be as easy. The question is: do we have the ability or feasibility for effecting change? In physical time travel, the question was posed: if a person went back and killed his grandfather before the person was conceived, would the person cease to exist? In mental time travel, regressionists have repeatedly found that a person traveling to another time can change a response or an interpretation of the event and immediately affect the current physical body.

Michel Serres, French philosopher, mathematician, and professor in History of Science at the Sorbonne, compared folding time with "fine pastry dough being rolled back on itself many times to make a sheet of flakey crust."[304] With the concept of time being substituted for the pastry dough, any event is usually located in the same layer (some call it a dimension). After a series of events, the curvature is evident, and time reverses direction back upon itself. Because the layers are infinitely thin, lifetimes can appear to be simultaneous or parallel. Two case studies offer examples: one is of the West Virginia wife and the Virginian horse breeder, Ann (chapter 10), and the other is of Bud, the blacksmith and the farmer (chapter 5).

Roger Penrose described Einstein's spacetime curvature as "closed time-like curves"[305] that make it "possible for signals to be sent from some event into the past of that same event."[306]

Mark J. Hadley, a professor at the Physics Institute at Warwick University in Coventry, United Kingdom, followed Einstein's theory of gravity and took it one step further. One part of the theory says spacetime is similar to gravity curves. Hadley's theory speculates that spacetime is "so intensely warped that it bends back upon itself like a knot" that includes a closed time-like curve.[307]

Consider again Pam's regression (chapter 1), when she changed a decision by making a different decision at the time of the forced mating. Pam and the child survived the childbirth in the tent only to be killed by an animal later. Thus, Pam's history is kept intact, as far as we can tell.

One way of illustrating folding time is to imagine a river meandering back next to itself and at one point going underground, flowing underneath the river that is above the ground (see the cover of this book). Steve Cullidane's finite geometry website (http://finitegeometry.org/sc/gen/dth/DiamondTheory.html)[308] has another illustration. The first picture has a line of adjoining blocks (events). The second picture has these lined up in three rows. If we consider each block to be an event, or one of Barbour's Nows, then we can imagine the timestream folding back upon itself.

## Relevance to Regression Work

As I looked back over cases from my former clients, I saw several reported lifetimes that repeated in similar cultural circumstances. They could have been in the same timeframe and same town. However, I did not always get those details. I just assumed that they were in a different time. Many other regressionists have probably made the same conclusion. Sometimes the directions "Go back to the original cause of—" will result in the client going forward in time. In a conversation I had with M. Rota in September 2005, she told of a regression in which she went back to a previous time, but it was also the same time as a previous regression. She was in the same town and the same time period but in a different body. The purpose of returning to that time period was to correct something she didn't get to do in the other body but that needed to be done. In meditation, she asked, "What happened during the regression?" She was told she needed to finish what she hadn't in that lifetime. Then she was told of folding time.

This was the question I was hoping scientists would be able to at least partially answer. Penrose, Hadley, and others are getting close. Penrose's closed time-like curves seem to explain how regressionists guide their clients to the beginning of the event or the cause of their symptom, to allow for a change in perspective or decision at the original timespace, thereby effectively changing clients' now. As we have discussed, events and lifetimes are layered with the present in the main focus. Having a timestream running though, meandering, and connecting them all together seems plausible. Being able to get above the timestream to access each event or lifetime has been getting easier and easier.

The interpretation of time has undergone a drastic transformation, from being an absolute based on nature's rhythms, to depending on partial observers, to being a fabrication by humans. In the German-British-United States culture, *being on time* is a desired quality to be developed. After I finished writing the chapter on time, I had a strange event happen regarding this concept. My calendar said I had a dental appointment at four o'clock on Monday afternoon. My husband had a dental appointment with the same dentist at two o'clock on the same day. When my husband went in to his appointment, he said I would be coming in soon, but the office went into a panic. When I arrived at four, most everyone was in front, waiting for me. At once, they all tried to tell me that my appointment was not until Wednesday and that they had been trying, unsuccessfully, to call me. I stood there amazed. Just then, someone from the back came out and said that the four o'clock appointment had been cancelled. I smiled, confidently. "I'll take it. It's mine." I was a couple days early, but on time.

Sean Carroll, physicist at the California Institute of Technology, at the end of his article "New Rules of Time Travel" in the March 2010 issue of *Discover Magazine,* described the current understanding of time as being

> [B]ased on the logic and the known laws of physics, but some of it is based purely on convenience and reasonable-sounding assumptions. We think that the ability to uniquely determine the future from knowledge of our present state is important, but the real world might end up having other ideas. If physicists discover that closed time-like curves really can exist, we will have to dramatically rethink the way we understand time; in that case, the universe could not be nicely divided into a series of separate moments of time.[309]

The ultimate answer to the puzzles raised by closed time-like curves is probably that they simply cannot exist. If that is true, though, it is because the laws of physics do not let you warp spacetime enough to create them—not because they let you kill your grandfather before you are born.[310]

## Comments

Folding time is the newest, yet one of the oldest, concepts of time that I have researched. It does offer explanations of regression work. Pam's experience from the Egyption life to the tent to the origin in the mating experience could possibly be explained as a series of Nows along a fold that is so thin that the intenseness of the experience pokes through the fold into the present awareness. Bud's double experience as farmer and blacksmith could also be explained as the time layer being stretched so thin that the being was experiencing both lives at the same time. Both lives had an effect on the present life—one positive (the farmer) and the other (the blacksmith) problematic. This could be similar to the thin layers of phyllo or puff pastry common in French or Greek cuisine, which is used in baklava, for example, where the honey, raisins, or nuts often blend through the layers to result in an enjoyable delicacy. In regression work, the intense experiences combine through the layers of time to influence the present experience. This could also explain the other examples previously reviewed.

## Case for Not Believing in Past Life—Synopsis

For ages, humans relied on consistent time or absolute time, based on the periodicity of the movements of the Earth, moon, and sun. Then Einstein formulated his famous equation and applied it to the relevancy of time. Time depended on the observer and the speed of the observer and the object being observed. Since Minkowski and Einstein questioned the belief in absolute time, time has not been the same. The use of mathematics proved that there is no past, no future, but only the present. This proof supports the philosophers who say that there is only now, the present.

Quantum theory, or quantum mechanics, has gone through changes: The proton is currently seen as both a particle and as a wave. The discovery in physics is astounding: What the observer believes is what happens. Could this be the basis for faith in positive thinking?

New understandings of the nature of time continue to develop. The initial string theory says spacetime has many "dimensions tightly curled into a folded fabric of the cosmos."[311] String theory suggests that the microscopic landscape is suffused with tiny strings whose vibrational patterns orchestrate the evolution of the cosmos. These strings are one-dimensional filaments, somewhat reminiscent of infinitely thin rubber bands, vibrating to and fro. Height, width, and depth are three dimensions. Time is the fourth dimension. Space, as presented in 1919 by Theodor Kaluza (1885-1954), mathematician and physicist, is the fifth dimension. "If the fifth dimension of space were reduced and reduced again, it would split into two equations: Einstein's standard theory of relativity and Maxwell's theory of light."[312] String theory gave scientists many questions, and it was soon transformed into superstring theory.

The superstring theory is based on the string theory, but only ten dimensions are necessary, which resulted in five different theories. Edward Witten once said if an eleventh dimension were added, the five theories could be combined into a single theory.[313]

Going back to the original observations of the particle-wave experiment, Hugh Everett, John Wheeler, and Neill Graham posed the Everett-Wheeler-Graham theory, which states that at the moment the wave or particle function collapses, the universe splits into two worlds, two separate branches of reality. Each branch is doing something different. Each is unaware of the other. Each is creating its own separate branch of its own reality. This conception is also called the many-worlds interpretation of quantum mechanics, or the many-worlds theory. If a consciousness or a sentient being observes the split, the consciousness also splits, creating two different instantiations. Each is unaware of the other's existence.[314] This constant splitting eventually becomes unwieldy when considering past lives. It might mean that each decision produces many different lives. Would each life have its own soul? Theoretically, it would.

The timelessness theory of Julian Barbour states that time is change and "change is the measurement of time, not time the measurement of change."[315] Each instant, what Barbour calls a Now, is concrete and distinct. The Nows exist in nothing. These Nows can be considered as similar to three-dimensional snapshots. "These three-dimensional snapshots are jumbled up in a heap, so any person can organize them in any order they desire to experience such, as in manipulating a movie with many frames."[316] When these Nows are laid out in a row, in a linear sequence, often time is inferred. But the sense of time is created not by an invisible nature of time itself but by concrete things. In Barbour's timeless theory, all conceivable Nows, some in multiple copies, exist. However, there are always too many Nows to arrange in a continuous sequence. All imaginable states or events consisting of multiple Nows can be present at the same time. Because states are created not by invisible time but by concrete things, in Barbour's timeless theory all conceivable Nows—some in multiple copies—exist. However, there are too many to arrange in a continuous sequence. Therefore, all conceivable states can be present concurrently.[317]

Each point, each Now, does not have a unique starting point. Each Now, representing a different possible configuration of the universe, is present as potentialities, at least in different quantities. Barbour goes on to state,

> [I]f there is only one Now, all your memories are then illusions in the sense that you never experienced them. If lots of Nows are chosen, then you believe that you did experience them all. It is possible that all Nows are available. It is consistent with the many-worlds' hypothesis ... It truly is impossible to say how many of your memories are real. All we know is that the present is real.[318]

At the beginning of the twenty-first century, experiments were conducted to demonstrate that time could be controlled. In a Noetic Science Conference in La Quinta, California, in August 2006, Lynne McTaggart and Dean Radin, with the conference attendees as subjects, found that distance between events could be changed beyond statistical chance by focusing a group's consciousness on the desired changes.[319] Time appeared to be an independent factor that is subject to control.

The theories I read about after Barbour's had my mind reeling. It would seem that according to most scientists, there is no past life—only the present moment. What we view as a past life or future life is considered a layer of the present. Also, by consciously changing our view or perception, we can change our present, our past, and our future. If there really is no past life, then what can we deduce about regressionists who are helping all their clients? How does that fit in the general scheme of things? The next chapter puts these quantum theories of time together with the work of regressionists. It tries to answer their questions and explores the purpose of regression work.

# Chapter 9

# Putting the Research Together

The debate between those who believe in the theoretical possibilities of past lives and those who do not shows little progress toward final resolution. Both sides have demonstrated empirical evidence and sound logic. A practical resolution could, however, lie in a synthesis of these seemingly polarized perspectives. Coins have both heads and tails, after all, although we view only one side at a time.

The following is a parallel chronological look at the development of regression therapies and changing theories of time, starting with an explanation of assumed *absolutes* of time and life. These verities are not scientifically proven laws but are, nevertheless, widely accepted as noncontroversial facts of life.

## Ageless Absolutes of Time and Life

For ages prior to the twentieth century, most people considered time an absolute. Time was based on cycles of the moon, stars, and sun and no radical departures were evident. Therefore, people relied on the cycles for daily activities. The beginning of a day was sunset (Jewish tradition) or sunrise (Christian tradition). When eclipses occurred, they were considered *unnatural* and signs from a god. Today, most people, including physicists, rely similarly on the regular rhythms of astral bodies, though most people now accept the scientific explanations behind eclipses.

In the seventeenth century, Leibniz, a rival of Newton, said that all time is made up of "different instants of time,"[320] an infinite number of them. He argued the unpopular theory that time is an entity that fuses space and time into a single notion.[321] Barbour in 1990, Hawking in 2005, and Witt in 2007 discussed and agreed with Einstein's concept of a single space-time continuum that reformulated Leibniz's concept of time to include gravity's effect on the curvature of timespace.

Another absolute has been that a person is born and dies and has memories in between, although there are differences in belief surrounding what happens after death. Many ancient cultures—such as the Egyptians and Hindus, long before Christ—believed that the soul, the invisible part of a human, and the body's memories continue on after the end of the body. Some believed that the soul is immortal, while others denied a nonphysical part of the body and thought death of the body to be the end.

Through history, concepts of the destiny of the soul after death became more varied and, in some cases, more dogmatic. Again, some believed that after the body dies, the soul goes to heaven or hell, while others, such as Pythagoras and certain Hindus, believed souls transmigrate elsewhere, such as into an animal or another human body. Indeed, many books have been written about this subject. Because of the natural curiosity of humans, many people have been interested in how and why they are the way they are and why they exist. The belief in past lives and reincarnation has been discussed in the Hindu and Buddhist traditions for millennia.

## Regression and Quantum Theories

Around the turn of the twentieth century, many philosophical and scientific changes took place. Breuer and Freud started using regression techniques therapeutically. Einstein and Minkowski challenged the common notion of time, proving the relative nature of time and, therefore, suggesting theoretically (mathematically) that there is no past or future—only the present.[322] McDougall and others started testing learning and memory theories using white rats.[323]

After Freud dropped hypnotic regression work, he encouraged patients to consciously recall past events and follow them backward to the origin of their problematic symptom.[324] In the 1920s, scientists experimented to find how learning is transmitted and whether learned behaviors can be transmitted through biological generations. Part of learning transmittal is memory transmittal. Experiments with white rats, such as those conducted by McDougall (as reported in the *British Journal of Psychology* between 1927 and 1938), proved that memories are carried forward from generation to generation. After Watson and Crick's discovery of the double helix of DNA in 1953, scientists found that DNA is the carrier of particular behavior traits and memories.[325] An interesting side note was that sometimes a memory—as evidenced by how fast a specific maze can be run by rats that have learned certain behaviors—might skip a generation in the experiment's rat population and appear in a different family line. This phenomenon was noted at the time but not explained.[326]

Einstein's relativity theories evolved into quantum theories during the middle of the twentieth century. From the perspective of quantum physics, the electron is either a particle or a wave, depending on the expectation of the observer. What we see is dependent on what we expect to see. Experiments were performed that proved the relativity of time. The concept of time evolved because the distance between events became dependent on the location of the observer.[327] Einstein said that space and time curve because of the effects of gravity.[328] Einstein's and Minkowski's concept of no past and no future was being verified. For regressionists, emerging theories of time presented a perturbing challenge: if there is no past, no present, and only now then there can be no past lives or future lives.

Along with changes in psychologists' views of regression therapies and physicists' understanding of theories of relativity, changes in religion also occurred. The new thought that the mind has an effect on the body was popularized by Mary Baker Eddy, who started Christian Science, and by Charles and Myrtle Fillmore, who started what came to be known as the Unity movement early in the last century. The timing of such developments in several mind-body spiritual movements seems to have preceded the theoretical insights that nothing happens until the observer acknowledges the happening and that what happens is what the observer expects to happen.

Concurrently, the precepts of Hinduism and other world wisdom philosophies were introduced to the United States by spiritual leaders—for example, Paramahansa Yogananda (who started Self-Realization Fellowship), Jiddu Krishnamurti (who came from India via the Theosophical Society but later created his own foundation), and Rudolf Steiner (who also broke from the Theosophical Society to found the Anthroposophical Society). These organizations vigorously discussed the topics of meditation, reincarnation, and the survival of the soul after death.

Regression regained popularity with developments in hypnotism in the mid-twentieth century; it became easier for mental adventurers to conduct regression sessions as a form of entertainment. Bernstein made regression sessions popular with his book *The Search for Bridey Murphy* (1965). By the 1970s, however, medical professionals, psychiatrists, and psychologists were finding that past-life memories had therapeutic value and were presenting case studies at the first regression conference at the University of California Irvine campus in 1978.

Along with therapeutic developments in psychology by regression practitioners, there was the emergence of string theory in physics. String theories combined Einstein's relativity theories with quantum theory. A string occupies an extremely small, thin line of such particles in space at each moment of time. The microscopic universe is permeated with tiny strings whose vibrational patterns orchestrate the evolution of the cosmos. They are, as Yoichiro Nambu of the University of Chicago, Holger Nielsen of the Niels Bohr Institute, and Leonard Susskind of Stanford University described: "one-dimensional filaments, somewhat resembling infinitely thin rubber bands, vibrating to and fro."[329]

Space and time are active players in our universe, according to the statement of Einstein's general theory, which describes the universe as a gently curving form of space where "not only are space and time influenced by one's state of motion, but they can warp and curve in response to the presence of matter or energy."[330] Even more dynamically, quantum theory describes the universe as a "frantic microorganism."[331] This apparent conflict between emerging theoretical descriptions of space was eventually resolved by the string theory, which says spacetime has many "dimensions tightly curled into a folded fabric of the cosmos."[332]

When the concept of folded space-time is translated into the language of regression practitioners, one might say it is possible that lives are not necessarily sequential. The events that may be affecting particular undesired behaviors could be happening at the same time in space proximate to the current space occupied by the affected individuals. Because we are accustomed to viewing time as sequential, we habitually order memories of events from early to later. When the phenomenon known as déjà vu occurs, it could simply be that spacetime has warped back upon itself so that one is actually viewing a similar event in another spacetime warp.

When physicists expanded string theories into a postulation of eleven dimensions, it became mathematically unwieldy (and unprovable). Because of the number of purely hypothetical premises occurring in the final theories, many scientists and regressionists eventually discounted string theory altogether.

The many-worlds theory returned to the original slit experiments of Thomas Young, in which one personification of the experimenter sees the electron as a wave and another personification sees the electron as a particle. Each personification exists unaware of the other.[333] In applying the many-worlds interpretation of quantum theory to regression work, one could say that with each decision an individual makes, the other possible decisions and their outcomes are also played out as aspects of the individual's psychic experience. So, by the end of only one lifetime, many other aspects of the individual are in existence and playing out the various results of that particular decision. The sheer number of identical individuals and life paths possibly occupying a single existence is staggering. Several questions demand exploration: What or who determines the major decisions that would result in a split, and what would make a decision major? Would it be a clear, conscious, and intentional decision? How many of each of us are out there? When do the splits happen?

For example, when Pam, the first case in chapter 1, went back to her *decision point* (the time that mating was forced upon her) and made a different decision, her future changed. Then, when she was on the Egyptian slab, she made another decision: not to be afraid of death and to cut the cords on her legs that had stopped the blood flow. Her body changed in current time, with the increase of leg circulation and lessening of pain. If we ask the preceding questions in this case, the many-worlds interpretation proposes many answers. However, the infinite number of lifetimes and situations possible for an individual seems to undermine the theory's validity. In mathematics, when an equation results in an infinite variety of answers, the theorem is viewed as suspect.

One way for regressionists to work is to take the client back to the decision point to see what alternative decisions could have been made. If the client travels each possibility to see what the outcome would have been, the original decision might still offer the best of only difficult choices.

When looking for the quantum property that constituted reality in Everett's many-worlds theory, John Bell found that the accumulation of mutually consistent records is a vital component. Bell showed that *record formation* is a characteristic quantum property, and he called the formulated records *time capsules*. Time capsules contain the past and the future to the same degree as all sensory feelings and emotions that exist in the entire complex of Nows.[334]

History and Newtonian physics consider the past a continuous path through the configuration of space, with history as a highlighted path. Bell claimed that we, as historians, have only our memories and records; therefore, we have no direct contact with the past. These memories and records are, in fact, always present phenomena. According to Barbour, beings that have consciousness will possess memories and records within them that convince them they are the products of history. In reality, the points realized at successive instants of time are chosen randomly and jump around in a wildly unpredictable manner in the configuration of space.[335] Memories exist when we think them into existence. Repetitive contemplation on the same events brings them into reality, into what are referred to as memories or remembered events. Elizabeth Loftus considered memories are not all what they seem to be.[336] If this is so, then past-life regression therapy may provide a procedure to eliminate a destructive memory that doesn't really exist.

## Emerging Concepts of Time and Change

Barbour stated, "Change is the measurement of time, not time the measurement of change."[337] Each instant is a concrete and distinct thing that exists in nothing. Each Now can be compared with a three-dimensional snapshot. Collectively, one's total moments in time are like snapshots jumbled up in a heap. A person could organize them in any preferred order to have any desired experience (as in the editing of a movie with many frames). When these instants are laid out in a row, in a linear sequence, time is often inferred. But this perception is created not by an insubstantial concept but by concrete things. In Barbour's timeless theory, all possible Nows, some in multiple copies, exist. However, because there are too many to arrange in a continuous sequence, all conceivable states can be present simultaneously.[338]

The past is nothing more than what we can infer from our present records. According to Barbour, there are two facts consistent with the notion of time. First, the abundance of evidence for time is literally written in records (fossils, newspapers, and minutes of meetings). Barbour says that if the secret of time is in reducing time and motion into a time-capsule structure in our brains, and if that structure could be made responsible for our short-term memory (the phenomenon of the spacious present), then the actual perception of motion and all appearance of time would be reduced to a common basis of special structures in individual Nows.[339] Second, the creativity of nature speaks insistently and consistently of time. The appearance of time is a deep reality, a reality that is embedded deep within our culture. The concept of time capsules can offer another explanation of the properties of time.

Each point, each now, does not have a unique starting point. Each now, representing a different possible configuration of the universe, is present as potentialities, at least in different quantities. Where the Nows are the densest, creating a mist, there is greater probability of experience. Barbour has stated that

> If there is only one now, all your memories are then illusions in the sense that you never experienced them. If lots of Nows are chosen, then the belief is that you did experience them all.[340]

This view is constant with the experiments done by Loftus regarding memory falsification.[341] A story repeated with emotional intensity is eventually recalled as actually having happened.

Barbour also wrote: "Motion is implied, interpreted by our brain, from the rapid sequence of Nows,"[342] such as illustrated with Tegmark's DVD example (in chapter 8). "Since time is the result of change/motion, motion does not exist either."[343]

Another way of understanding Barbour's view is to consider the rapid change of alternating frames in a movie. Each frame is seen for a fraction of an instant. Our brain interprets the passing scenery as motion. Tegmark said that motion is an illusion and that all time is each Now.[344] We are culturally conditioned to perceive change and inferences of time. If time does not exist and our memories are not real, then regressionists eliminate the emotional connection with unreal events to release the client from attachments to reinforced memories. In an interview with Robert Kuhn, Tegmark describes birth as one end of the spacetime string, death as the other end, and the encompassing existence of forever as reality. He also mentions that it might be possible to visit another spacetime, perhaps through a wormhole.[345]

Timelessness theory could also explain regression or other-life work. Each instant (Now) contains all previous and future experience of the Nows. Each Now is a frame in a film or video of the life or existence of a client. Each client has the ability to rerun the film or video strip of the chain of Nows. By rerunning the strip and going deeper into the frame of a particular instance, the original Now of the situation or frame can be accessed and the future of that specific Now, as well. Because the Now can be accessed and changed by either reframing or making new decisions, it could be possible to change subsequent events of each instant, resulting in immediate change in the present. This approach could be illustrated as each person's life being a string of time, similar to a roll of film that is infinitely thin and infinitely long, and having with each frame a link to other decisions, other lives, or other dimensions.

Terence Witt had a similar view of time, which he called *null physics.* Witt wrote, "Matter is built from spatial curvature, space is built of geometric points, and points are nothingness incarnate. This means that matter [even an event?] is composed of points."[346] These points described by Witt seem very similar to Barbour's Nows in explaining time. Witt wrote, "There is no now just as there was no beginning."[347] According to string theory, time is an infinitely thin string having length. Witt's description is reminiscent of string theory. Witt considers time a fourth-dimensional interconnection among energy forms. If something occurs in the future, the certainty of this future occurrence has existed throughout the infinite past: "Every event is preordained."[348]

Witt used the terms *time* and *change* interchangeably. He considers change is not possible because "it cannot have an origin—temporal equivalence . . . All moments in time are equivalent because they are one in the same."[349] Likewise, he could be saying that all time is now and that all events are equal. Regressionists might agree with Witt that it is our interpretation of events that make them different or difficult when he claims, "All moments in Earth's history are permanently distributed throughout infinite space."[350] Witt's premise suggests that what we see or experience is the way—the exact way—things have always been and will always be. One conclusion that could be drawn is that there is no need for therapeutic interventions, because the future cannot be changed.

Another conclusion could be that therapeutic interventions were already planned.

Barbour and Witt agreed that each instant is a thing, a Now, or a point. Change does not happen. They say that what we perceive as change is only Nows happening at an extremely fast rate. Some people may remember flipping pages of small cartoon books to make the characters appear to move. Movie frames give the same effect—only people of our culture have labeled it *change*.

If all instants occur randomly, if the probability of any one instant occurring depends on the concentration of similar or identical instants, and if what we perceive is what we expect (going back to the slit experiments), then we form our lives each instant, including what we tend to call *past* and *future*. What, then, is happening to produce what we call past-life recall?

According to Barbour and Witt, the past occurs and is available in each instant or Now. Witt says that all time occurs in the present, that all instants occurred at an instant, and that these always were and always will be. So every event has already happened, and what happens is predetermined. The event is somewhere in the present. If every event is in the present, and if what we perceive as now always was and always will be the same, this concept nullifies regressionists' work, since nothing can be changed. What *is* will always be.

A person may not be aware of the precipitating events at all. However, regressionists provide a way, a means, or a bridge to the troublesome initial event that produces a client's bothersome behavior. Once the troublesome event is accessed, a client can change the impact on his or her emotions. Once the impact is diminished, the emotional attachment is lessened, and the event is no longer remembered or accessed as a particularly important event. The event becomes just another point, another Now, and only as important as any other mundane occurrence. Energy released from attachment to the troublesome event could be available for use in the present.

The basic problem with Barbour's theory is that once cream is stirred into coffee, you cannot drink black coffee or separate the cream back out. Intellectually, it makes sense. When philosophical, religious, and physics concepts say that for every action there is an equal but opposite reaction, or karma, the idea that each Now is independent from every other Now is difficult to accept. That is, bad actions or Nows would not be punished, and good actions or Nows would not be rewarded.

Penrose and others have been revisiting Minkowski's and Einstein's concept of folding time-space, sometimes blending with Barbour's Nows. Time and gravity gently fold back in the manner of a meandering stream. The time stream could consist of separate instants, the result being that we live all our life and lives (past, present, and future) in every instant, every Now.

## Summary of Past-Life Theories

Putting all the above considerations together, it seems that the term *past life* is at most a misnomer. The type of experiences the term refers to might more accurately be identified as *otherlife*. It appears that regressionists guide clients over a bridge to another part of their existence, which appears to be in another time-place. This time-place is located within their soul's experience, the nonphysical or pure-energy part of their being. The basic reason clients ask for a regression is to address a recurring problematic behavior. Sometimes, though, clients have no logical reason for a regression, only that it seems to be a good time for one, or they are simply curious. Once questioned, they realize there are questions in the back of their minds that they would enjoy having answered. With a past-life recall session, they are able to reconnect a troublesome feeling with a logical event. The result is that clients become free to live in the present without carrying baggage from some other event. Because they are able to be more focused and present, they achieve their goals with less effort.

# Applying Theories to Case Studies

To see how we might explain clients' regression sessions, let us examine the case studies already discussed. Pam first went to a slab in Egypt, which explained the start of her abnormal blood clotting. Then she went back to a difficult birthing, in which both she and the child died. That problem started with a forced mating in a much earlier time, which had resulted in the genetic mutation that led to the disastrous birthing. When the negative energy was released from each event, the previous event was easier to access. After she had gone to the initial event, the decision point of the forced mating, Pam could finally make the decision she was originally unable to make.

While reexperiencing the terrifying nonhuman invasion, Pam realized she could make a choice, an alternative decision, no matter how difficult the choice might be and how onerous the possible results. She decided to do something that would prevent conception from the forced mating. When she made a decision to mate with someone else, she and the child survived the birth in a later life, though they both died in an accident shortly afterward. Medical doctor Carol Phillips, retired emergency room physician, explained to me (phone conversation on March 28, 2010) that once released, the ovum, or egg, has forty-eight hours to be fertilized for successful conception. In extremely rare cases, two ova are released, and more rarely, each may be fertilized by a different sperm donor. When a pregnancy has progressed more than two weeks, it is almost impossible for another pregnancy to occur.

Next, let's go to the slab in Egypt. She was being killed, part by part, to teach her to be afraid of death. She realized it was her decision to go through that death, and this helped her have no fear of death. Afterward, Pam realized she could always make a decision, even when all choices did not seem good. Her power lay in making the decision. She also realized there were those who did not like success and would do what they could to destroy what they did not like, and that some would call them *evil*.

Pam's session could offer an example of the many-worlds concept of parallel outcomes stemming from a decision point. The session could also be explained by the convenient use of a timeline metaphor to allow the consciousness to jump to another connected event. The release of energy attachments to the event, after the initial decision, would allow energy to be available for subsequent actions, and subsequent decisions would come more easily, possibly collapsing alternative lives. An alternate explanation could be obtained by following the folding time-stream back to the precipitating causal event and changing one's perception of it. Thus, the DNA changed, which also changed the present Now, the current period.

Now, let's look at the session with Bob, which is very different from Pam's. Bob went into an altered state, with abreactions, when merely discussing his dream about the airplane crash. He instantaneously jumped time and space to be in the plane and easily accessed information about that life. Once he realized that the incident was completed, the abreactions stopped, and all difficulties surrounding the crash disappeared. There is a lingering possibility that Helmet was attached at a very early age to Bob, perhaps in the womb. Because of the possibility of an immediate abreaction, I did not look for attachments prior to the session. According to Barbour and Witt, everyone has access to every point, to every Now. Bob was able to access that point, another part of the current complex Now, and he released unneeded attachments that had sapped energy and prevented him from being his total effective self. Again, once the connection had been detached, the problem dissolved.

Considering Bob's dream, the concepts of Barbour's Nows gives *dreaming* new meaning. It could be that in dreaming we access another reality, full of different Nows. Some of the Nows are similar to those of waking experience, but some are not. Another explanation could be that a part of Bob (Helmet) was living in another complex Now and was caught up in the dying process in the airplane; he became, for some reason, unable to move forward. At some point, the part known as Helmet found a part known as Bob and pestered Bob at night—when his conscious mind would not interfere—knowing that Bob would get the assistance needed for Helmet to complete the death process. With this completion, Helmet and Bob would be free. Helmet would be free to continue his existence, and Bob would be free to enjoy a full night's sleep. Another explanation might be that Bob entered a different state of consciousness; some might call it dreaming, remembering, or entering a different dimension. He slid along a fold in time into a simultaneous event in another timespace. By placing his conscious awareness fully into that place, Bob could fully express and release the negative emotions, thereby releasing him from the negative experience. The experience became just another experience, neither negative nor positive.

With Bud, the session started out to be a normal, standard regression to the original event that caused his physical symptom. Because he was symptom free when he came into my office, I proceeded to talk to his unconscious mind. When we started the process of accessing the original event, we took a detour. As Barbour and Witt explain, all events happen simultaneously with the warping of timespace in time capsules.[351] "Time capsules" are the way Barbour describes what Franz Perls referred to as "gestalts" (see chapter 5). There were more layers to the event than I had originally considered. Part of the personal complex of Nows could lie within the genetic structure of the individual. Lipton found memories of individuals' mothers and fathers in each cell in addition to memories of an individual's own memories or perceived memories.[352] We can access any point in a time capsule. Bud's events—the dinner in the crab restaurant, the death on the steamboat, and the death as a blacksmith from the fire—were all related to Bud's current symptom. The shot on the steamboat that came close to his heart was the trigger to his chest pains. The ultimate decision point was when the smoke from the fire was in his esophagus. He was trying to gasp for breath and decided, unconsciously, that as long as he felt the roughness in his throat (esophagus), he could be found, and he would survive.

Looking at Bud's session from the viewpoint of folding time, which is that all time is now, it looks similar. All of Bud's experiences—the blacksmith, the riverboat gambler, the farmer, and the current life as a retiree—are layers or different dimensions of the same time: Now. By changing conscious awareness, Bud was able to access a different part of Now and change a perception that was affecting the current situation. We see this in children. A child can develop likes and dislikes of certain foods yet change them to match the likes and dislikes of a cherished playmate. The child doesn't change, and the food doesn't change, but the child's perception of the food changes.

Bud's revisiting of the seemingly unrelated events led to his relief. It could be that he had to detach from the various unrelated Nows before he could find release from the current symptom. Each memory, what we could call a metaphor, could be an attachment to a problematic Now that, when released, changes part of the symptomatic pattern.

The use of a bridge to access the point of abreaction—or decision point, or an event that starts a cycle of action or reaction—might be necessary only as a training tool (similar to training wheels on a bicycle) to allow the conscious mind to access unconscious memories or other Nows that have relationship to current symptoms. Perhaps the consideration of the use of metaphors is a more convenient way of saying the Nows that are accessed are not really part of the actual experience of the client.

To make the theories of time personal, in each moment (each Now we experience) we are experiencing simultaneously various events that are randomly spread over spacetime. Where our focus concentrates is what we remember and fully experience. When we get entangled in negative emotions of an event (or a relationship?), we leave some of our energy in that situation. Regressionists assist in retrieving that lost energy by severing the situation's ties and by reframing, assisting, and supporting conscious decision-making. Sometimes a disinterested third party, the regressionist, can offer another angle for looking at the event, as in reframing. It is still the decision of the client, however, to accept the alternate view. It is difficult, but not impossible, to do this by oneself.

The genetic explanation of regression is that we carry all our fathers' and mothers' genetic memories back to the beginning, when or wherever that was. We can access those memories, as did Pam and Bud, and effect changes in current circumstances. But that does not explain Bob's recalled experience. It could be that genetic memory is really a propensity to perform certain actions when a certain stimulus is perceived. The stimulus in his case had a major emotional impact (good or bad), so Bud the blacksmith was attracted to a familiar situation, a complex Now, and repeated the response. Barbour suggested that when there are many Nows, a mist forms, and the probability of the Nows repeating becomes greater. When the regressionist helps the client release the old emotions attached to the original stimulus, it becomes a Now too and separates from the other Nows. It is also a possibility that once the original complex Now has been relieved of its emotional charge, it is released from the memory of the client and eventually ceases to be available.

Another experience of Nows is in the between-death-and-birth period. The experiences reported between one life and the next seem to illustrate how the Now time works. NDE travelers and regression travelers report time as being differently experienced. Regression travelers relive several events in detail, often in the same lifetime, including their deaths in that lifetime. Later, after the experience is complete and they are fully conscious in their current bodies, they ask if there is time for another regression, although more than two hours have passed. Or, they are amazed at the events they have covered in such a short period of time. NDE travelers report detailed experiences that take more time to tell than the time they were supposed to have been dead. Newton's clients report that, without physical bodies, when people exist as souls or spirits, time takes on a different aspect.[353] The clients experience each event separately, yet not always sequentially.

Penrose is currently attempting to not only split a speck of dust into two identical parts but also to photograph the split and the reuniting. He believes a speck of dust is the smallest object that can be easily seen. If a speck of dust can split, then theoretically, larger objects could be split. If larger objects can be split and rejoined, then humans could also. So, if a client were to split physically, with one part remaining in the office in 2011 and the other going to 1021, for example, the one leaving could change an observation or concept, and the other would automatically, instantaneously change as well. When both parts reunited in the office, the change would have happened. This does seem farfetched.

Something similar might happen, however, when the regressionist leads the client into an altered state, no matter how mild or how deep. The client might split, with the unconscious going to the problematic situation and the conscious remaining in the regressionist's office. This type of split seems to happen on a regular basis. When the client's unconscious returns to the present, the changes are brought forward as well. Once the client is back together, the changes either have been implemented or are in the process of being integrated into the whole being.

Still, it seems a stretch to make one theory fit all past-life situations. The theory of folding time seems plausible—once it is confirmed and accepted by science. There is a possibility that the correct theory of time has not yet been confirmed. Another possibility is that I have something yet to consider in my analysis.

# Chapter 10

# Questions Answered

The first chapter started with the question "Is there really such a thing as a past life?" After my research on the various theories of time, including the quantum theories of time, my conclusion is that there really is no such thing as the past or the future. Therefore, the term *past life* is at most a misnomer. The past lives that someone recalls and reexperiences are accessed alternate realities, alternate places in the same time but, perhaps in other dimensions. If, for some reason, the action or event was not completed, it seems to bleed through to another place or dimension—this one—for completion or solution. By changing the perception of the original event, wherever it is, and any decisions that were made based on that perception, whatever they are, the current problematic situation is changed.

## The Big Bang

To situate regression work within a larger theoretical context, let us go back to the beginning, to the very beginning. Most scientists agree with the still unproven theory that the universe itself originated with the Big Bang. They have observed the cosmos expanding from a central point and concluded that something started the expansion—a big explosion, the Big Bang. Other commentators, for example Terence Witt, say that the universe has always been constant. [354]

We need to consider what could have produced such an explosion and what existed prior to the explosion. So far these considerations have occupied the realm of philosophy. Scientists have begun working on the difficult questions but, to date without published results. Sean Carroll (see chapter 7) considers the Big Bang to be a singularity, a special, exceptional moment in time. By reversing the observed expansion of the universe back to a condensed, cooled event, one might consider a hypothetical moment when entropy was at the lowest. In this instant, the Big Bang happened. Carroll noticed that the Big Bang is mentioned as a *special time*, not a special place, in scientific literature.[355] He poses this question: What was happening before the Big Bang? Either there was no time before the Big Bang or maybe the universe was in the process of collapsing, becoming denser until the moment it "bounced"[356] into another phase of growth.

However, Barbour and others seem to concur that if there is no time—*timelessness*—then the beginning is happening as another Now, now. Or, if Jeff Tollaksen and Yakir Aharonov, physicists at Chapman University, and others are correct, then the Big Bang could be the result of an event in the future that hasn't been recognized. If so, what happens to our concept of time?[357]

While I was discussing the start of time with Eileen Rota, a philosopher and spiritual teacher, we traced it back to the beginning and postulated (as have others) that the Big Bang came about when Consciousness and Unconsciousness-subconsciousness[358] split from the One. Some call this the God-Goddess split. This split in consciousness could constitute the beginning of time, the initial change, the beginning of distance. It could also be the moment or point when energy began condensing into matter.

Early humans depended on their intuition, or awareness from the subconscious, for survival. They needed intuitional guidance especially to avoid predators and acquire food. During the time of Greek philosophers (Aristotle and Socrates, for example), the development of conscious subjectivity became more important than subconscious awareness. The philosophers would sit and think, observe the world around them, talk, and come to conclusions that would be taken as absolute law.

## Science and Religion

Scientific experimentation was not a major factor in scientific law until Isaac Newton. Before that, followers of the Catholic Church who sought to understand nature considered the Bible to be a scientific text. Later, the logical, thinking part of the brain, which some call the left-brain function, became increasingly important to cultivate. As a result, science and the church began to separate, with matters of the physical world being relegated to science and concerns of the nonphysical world to religion.

Since the soul was invisible, it was in the domain of religion. The *soul* could be defined as the invisible, immortal part of a sentient being. Transmigration or metempsychosis or reincarnation was considered the process of a soul migrating from the physical body to a newer one when the former had become damaged, worn out, or not needed.[359] Most of the world's religions acknowledged the possibility of soul migration in some form until sometime in the mid-1800s.[360]

In the mid-1800s, metaphysicians and psychic researchers were using hypnotism to effect changes in themselves and others. Jose Silva, who founded the Silva Mind Control Method in the mid-1900s, put together some techniques that had been taught from person to person since the mid-nineteenth century.[361] I found mention of some of Silva's methods in other classes about psychic subjects but no references to the original materials from which he had drawn.

## Early Twentieth-Century Changes

In the early twentieth century, revolutions took place in several areas of thought: politics (Russian revolution), culture (women's emancipation), physics (Einstein and beginnings of quantum theory), psychology (Freud), and religion (New Thought and positive thinking). During this period, for example, Freud was delving into the subconscious as a healing modality, while Einstein wrote about the relativity of time. Freud and Einstein were scientific pioneers who expanded on the revolutions of their day.

Freud also brought regression therapy into psychology. Most regressionists observe that clients in a state of self-hypnosis can go into another timespace relatively easily. To provide continuity from events of the previous regression session, clients are directed to "Go to that timespace, to [date and place] where [summarized event] is happening." Or they are directed to "Go to the specific time and place when and where the root cause of . . ." For regressionists, time and space seem to be different dimensions and need to be coordinated to pinpoint a specific event. It could be that our consciousness is conditioned to respond in that manner. Or, it could be just the way the universe and reality actually are.

Another revolutionary change was the new thinking in religion and philosophy of the period. Positive-thinking-type churches, such as Unity (Charles Fillmore) and Religious Science (Ernest Holmes) congregations, and movements stemming from books, such as *Think and Grow Rich* by Napoleon Hill (1937), became popular and prospered during the mid-twentieth century. Other philosophers and spiritual thinkers—such as Paramahansa Yogananda[362] (in lectures and books, 1920-1952) and Norman Vincent Peale (in *The Power of Positive Thinking*, 1952[363])—stressed the necessity of controlling the mind and residing in the present, the Now. Edgar Cayce (from the 1920s) described the mind as the builder that creates the physical (the body).[364] And most recently, quantum theory postulated that the mind of the observer had controlled the outcome of the slit experiments.

# Mid-Twentieth-Century Changes

Toward the middle of the twentieth century, Freud, Jung, and others wrote about the conscious mind as subject to the subconscious and the importance of bringing to awareness memories stored in the subconscious. One of the ways the unconscious mind communicates is with dreams. Freud's patients provided thousands of dreams in their three-times-a-week sessions over many years. This gave Freud the opportunity to study the mannerisms and conduct of patients through minor details, which revealed their secret thoughts.[365] After comparing the content of their dreams with the patients' case histories, Freud drew several conclusions. He found "a constant connection between some part of every dream and some detail of the dreamers' life during the previous waking state, thereby establishing a relation between sleeping states and waking states."[366] He also wrote that dreams are an unconscious language that can be understood by the trained observer. Jung considered that a major difference between Freud and himself concerned dream interpretation. In *Memories, Dreams, and Reflections* (1989), Jung wrote,

> I was never able to agree with Freud that the dream is a "façade" behind which its meaning lies hidden—a meaning already known but maliciously, so to speak, withheld from consciousness. To me dreams are a part of nature, which harbors no intention to deceive, but expresses something as best it can, just as a plant grows or an animal seeks its food as best as it can.[367]

The physicians of the twentieth century identified the autonomic nervous system as a controlling factor in the human system. After the discovery of DNA by Watson and Crick in 1953, scientists found a wealth of information in genes, including biological memories. Later, Lipton (2007) and others found that memory is stored in every cell in the DNA. Regressionists started using various methods, including hypnosis, to access the memory of clients by the mid-twentieth century. After such access, the emotional impact of the memories would change; the automatic responses of the autonomic nervous system changed as well. Researchers concluded that the DNA, the genetic structure of the body, was also transformed.[368] My case study of Pam provides an example of this emotional and physical change. When she regressed to the original event that she called "forced mating" and changed her perception and her decision, her body was different during recall of a subsequent life wherein she gave birth in the tent.[369]

During the early twentieth century, Einstein changed, some say revolutionized, physics. One of the changes was a series of calculations and observations that time was not absolute (as the Newtonians had proposed) but relative to the location and motion of the experiencers and observers. He also discovered the timespace continuum and postulated the invariance of the speed of light agreeing with James Clark Maxwell that nothing can exceed the speed of light. Scientists have performed many mathematical experiments that proved that light travels at the maximum speed an object can attain, although recent experiments with neutrinos, using advanced technology, suggest otherwise.[370] Later, Einstein's special theory of relativity deduced that time and gravity curved. This curvature allowed for the possibility of physical time travel. At the end of the twentieth century, Roger Penrose carried this theory one step further by describing time as folding back upon itself many times.

In the mid-twentieth century, quantum theory said that the witnessing subject, the conscious, neutral mind of the observer, decides the outcome of events. According to the theory, events that are not observed by the observer—the other possibilities—collapse and do not exist. String theories developed out of the quantum theory. The physicists theorized that *strings*, extremely narrow and miniscule in length, hold events. When I heard about string theory, a light went off in my brain. I had originally envisioned time being a spiral, similar to a well-used Slinky toy. Clients could access events vertically on each loop of the spiral (a particular lifetime) and then follow the spiral back and forth in that lifetime. If each string could be a lifetime, then when events were emotionally charged, they could be considered to exist on a string that was physically closer and more easily accessible using the emotion as a bridge to the other string or lifetime. Netherton, TenDam, and Woolger used *bridges* (similar to *strings*) as connections to past events. The Netherton method was my preferred technique. My client Bob (see chapter 5) provided a good example of how the method works.

Everett's many-worlds theory (see chapter 8 on Quantum Theories) postulated that the unwitnessed events of quantum mechanics do not collapse. In this theory, the unwitnessed events and an aspect of the observer's consciousness split off from the original timeline and continue on a different time track.[371] This split initiates parallel lives. Richard Bach illustrated this splitting of consciousness in his novel *One* (1989).[372] My client Ann in 1984 was the first example in my experience with parallel lifetimes, and my most recent was Bud.

Ann wanted to know about her past lives. She was one of my first clients on the East Coast. Using Marcia Moore's hypersentience method (1976) (see chapter 4), we went back to the late 1800s in West Virginia during a snowstorm. She was alone, sitting in a rocking chair with an infant daughter. Ann was hungry and cold. Her husband had been gone for quite a while to get food and wood for a fire. When I asked what happened next, she told me of a scene on a warm spring day in Virginia on a horse farm. A man was showing his son the land and saying, "This all will be yours someday." After we went back and forth a few times, getting more information about each life, I mentally made the note to check the anomaly of being in two different locations during the same time frame. When Ann came back to present reality, I asked her opinion, but she didn't know what to make of it. However, the process had relieved her questions about her fear of freezing to death and explained her love of horses.

There are three possible explanations. One is that at one point she fantasized so richly about a life so different from the one she was living in West Virginia that her immediate next life gave her the opportunity to live the life she fantasized about. Another explanation is that somewhere in her past she made a decision. That decision resulted in a split in her. One part reincarnated in a female body that was to live a difficult life. The other part reincarnated in a male body to live a life of comfort and ease. The third explanation is that at one point she decided to experience a completely different life during the same time period. This would mean that sometime after the life as the housewife in West Virginia she chose to reexperience the same time period as a wealthy male. It would be interesting to go back in time even further to see what the choices were and follow through in more detail her between-life choices.

It could be that clients regressing to the root causes of their problems, that is, to the original causational events, change their mental interpretations of the events and the emotional reactions to their present memories of the past. Because the event being remembered is actually a present memory of an event recalled in the current time, the present memory changes when the emotional and mental effects are released and the result is changed in the present, the Now.

The original question—If all time is now, how can regressionists lead clients to a past-life time and affect their symptoms and situations in the present?—has at least one answer. If we take the premise that each individual moment is all there is, and that there are layers (strings or Nows) within each moment, and that each layer has infinite sensory potential, we can access the layer that has the root of a situation and change the effect by changing the response to the event (therefore also affecting the DNA). Is it possible that when you change the response, you do, in effect, collapse an alternate timeline? If so, while the client comes forward along another timeline, situations (as well as responses to situations) could be changed. A new question arises: Does the client come forward to the present along a different timeline, resulting in a change in the present situation, or does the client remove the negative reaction that drained positive energy, thereby bringing the additional energy forward to be used in a more practical way in the present? In digesting the two different theories of time, I discovered yet another in the making.

# End of the Twentieth-Century Changes

Jeff Tollaksen, a physicist at Chapman University in Orange, California, has proposed an answer. Tollaksen and Yakir Aharonov, another physicist at Chapman University, are currently researching how events in the future may affect present events. The mathematics work. John Howell, physicist at the University of Rochester, and his team performed experiments that resulted in backward causality. In one experiment, they measured light from a laser, which was then shunted through a beam splitter. According to Merali (2010), Howell described what happened next:

Part of the beam passed right through the mechanism, and part bounced off a mirror that moved ever so lightly, due to a motor to which it was attached. The team used weak measurements to detect the deflection of the reflected laser light and thus to determine how much the motorized mirror had moved.[373] . . .

Searching for backward causality required looking at the impact of the final measurement and adding the time twist. In the Rochester experiment, after the laser beams left the mirrors, they passed through one of two gates, where they could be measured again—or not. If the experimenters chose not to carry out that final measurement, then the deflected angles measured in the intermediate phase were boring[ly] tiny. But if they performed the final, postselection site, the results were dramatically different. When the physicist chose to record the laser light emerging from one of the gates, then the light traversing that route, alone, ended up with deflection angles amplified by a factor of more than one hundred in the intermediate measurement step. Somehow, the later decision appeared to affect the outcome of the weak, intermediate measurements, even though they were made at an earlier time.[374]

187

These experiments in backward causality could imply that the work regressionists do with their clients result in changes in the past that could also affect future events. It could also imply that the original cause of the Big Bang is still what we would call in the future. That the Big Bang is really the result of a future event. So, could all events be happening now? Is it just that we can perceive only a bit at a time?

Hawking and Mlodinow, in the October 2010 issue of *Scientific American*, wrote, "[A]ccording to the quantum physics, the past, like the future, [is] indefinite and exists only as a spectrum of possibilities."[375] This suggests that the past can be changed if it is in *a spectrum of possibilities*. The regressionist takes a client to the original event, changes one's perception, and the present changes as a result.

Part of what regressionists do is sever the negative emotional connections of otherlife events that impact the present lives of a client. When one can live fully in the present, with conscious and unconscious/subconscious mind acting as one, one can fully actualize his or her full potential. It is theorized that once we achieve unity within ourselves, unity with others, perhaps all others, will be achieved. This unity will eventually bring us back to the Big Bang and, ultimately, to the place we were before the Big Bang.

Instead of *past* or *future lifetimes*, these terms should perhaps become *other lifetimes*. The problem with using the terminology *other lifetimes* is that current usage of *past life* is so ingrained in the profession and in the general public. In a discussion with TenDam at the 2008 World Regression Congress in Rio de Janeiro, Brazil, he reminded me of the time that had been spent trying to change the terminology in various regression conferences, for example, the AAPRT and IARRT conferences in the 1990s. So, similar to the situation with words such as *hypnosis* and *gay*, the current usage has evolved into a different understanding than the original, literal definition.

As for the initial questions "Are past lives real?" or "Are there no such things as past lives?" here is another take. "Yes, Virginia, there is a Santa Claus" Francis Church wrote in an editorial in response to

Virginia O'Hanlon's letter in 1897.[376] In reality, Santa Claus—Saint Nicholas—was a real historical character. Now parents assume his role in teaching about generosity and providing happiness to others. Small children believe as the concept is presented to them. In the case of past lives, the concept is a convenient explanation for unexplained memories of *past* events. Science is explaining, however, that there really is no past and no future, but only now. There really are no past lives separate from our present reality. Regressions have indicated that most of humanity has had more than one reasonable life span; our experiences have been layered upon experiences, giving us the impression of multiple lives because our brains have not been wired to understand such levels of experience and time. TenDam alludes to these layers in his books on past-life therapy and reincarnation. And in my own experience, only after three years of concentrated study am I almost able to understand the quantum concepts of time.

## Comments

This brings me back to the Slinky I had as a child. It was a symmetrically-arranged coiled wire that hopped down stairs. When coiled, the Slinky appeared to be a solid tube, similar to one life. When it was extended and well used, the coils would separate, illustrating the various lifetimes that make up a single life. Often the coils would become irregular, illustrating that certain lifetimes might possibly be shorter than others. Sometimes the coils overlapped, which could allude to the possibility of overlapping lifetimes.

After I started reading physics explanations for time, I continued using the Slinky explanation of how lifetimes work in my sessions with clients by supposing Barbour's Nows were located on the Slinky wire, one now leading to another.[377] Could it be that when a person is faced with an emotional or difficult decision, a part of that person might split off after the decision has been made and thereafter also experience the other decision, as described in many-worlds theory (see chapter 8)? I observed that when the coiling wire of the toy is extended, it seems straight, much as the Earth seems flat when we are hiking a trail. When both are seen from another viewpoint, or physically explained, we can believe that the Earth is round, the wire is coiled, and time folds back upon itself. Several questions arise from this: When does the fold occur? Is it after each life? Or can it happen at any time? Are these physics questions or philosophical or spiritual ones?

Currently in psychology, investigation of the subconscious is receiving more time and space in books and media. Hypnosis has become recognized as a medical modality for stress-reduction and to relieve symptoms due to the subconscious reaction to another noncurrent, past or future event. Through the conscious mind working with the subconscious via self-hypnosis or meditation, stress can be controlled and reduced. The only time the body is entirely free of stress is after death. Even in meditation, there is some tension or stress, because there is effort, however slight, to refrain from sleeping or falling over. Because more and more individuals are practicing meditation and self-hypnosis, the conscious and the subconscious dimensions of human awareness are drawing closer together. Barbour, along with many philosophers, states that there is no time, only Now(s). The conscious and the subconscious split in the mind of humanity is becoming one again. When the conscious and unconscious parts of a being can act and think in unison, it follows that one can more readily rejoin the pre-Bang state. What happens next? What can we expect? The possibilities are explored in the final chapter.

# Chapter 11

# Regression for a Better World

As I followed the beginnings of regression work, which have been entwined with theories of time and the evolution of quantum research, I realized how many remarkable ideas had emerged at the beginning of the twentieth century.

1. **Politics.** The revolutions in Russia started in 1905 and came to a head with the Bolshevik uprising in 1917. The resulting socialistic philosophies were discussed in the United States as US troops rushed to contain the conflict. The suffrage movement in the United States began to secure women's right to vote. Equality for women and minorities, however, was not discussed in polite company.

2. **Psychology.** Breuer was working with Pappenheim to develop a method of using regression as therapy. Sigmund Freud was exploring the subconscious as the controlling force behind the conscious. He found that the mind has a part to play in physical symptoms.

3. **Science.** Albert Einstein was overturning Isaac Newton's physics of absolute time. Quantum mechanics and various string theories came along to explain the subatomic world and conceptions of time. Wilhelm Conrad Roentgen's discovery of X-rays in 1895 changed the method of diagnostics.

4. **Religion.** Mary Baker Eddy started a religion based on the beliefs that the mind controls the body and that by changing the mind you can change the body. Various New Thought religions, as they came to be known, taught variations of these ideas. Eastern religions were introduced to the West via G. I. Gurdjieff (the Fourth Way), Helen Blavatsky (Theosophy), and Paramahansa Yogananda (Self-Realization Fellowship) among others. Later, while in self-induced trances, Edgar Cayce and Arthur Young expounded on the physical, mental, and emotional status of inquirers and their families.

Now at the beginning of the twenty-first century, we may review the latest trends in revolutionary thought:

1. **Politics.** Russia had a quiet revolution and is starting to flex muscles to bring back together her family. Socialism is publically discussed in the United States. Women are running for major positions on major political tickets in the United States. A person from an ethnic minority won the Presidency of the United States. Equality is openly argued and aggressively pursued by women as well as by religious, racial, and political minorities.

2. **Psychology.** Visits to a mental health practitioner, psychologist, psychiatrist, or hypnotherapist are as acceptable as visits to a physical health practitioner, medical doctor, chiropractor, and the like. The mind is seen as the controlling aspect of the physical. Clearing up of the past is a critical part of psychological treatments, achieved by various means, including regression work by medical professionals as well as hypnotherapists (depending on state regulations).

3. **Religion.** New Thought religions are competing in the spiritual marketplace for the same customers as conventional religions. Their message is clear: Love one another; love is

all there is. Control your mind, control your body, control your life—all is one. The difference among the various groups is in their theology, such as their view and prescribed manner of worshipping God, which is another topic and not the focus of this book.

4. **Science.** Quantum theory brings to the general population the ideas that an event is affected by an observer, that all time is now, and that all matter in the universe is part of each of us. Researchers are demonstrating that time is an independent structure. Electronics have made us instantly connected by the push of a few buttons on a cell phone or computer.

5. **Medicine.** Specialization has become widespread: Barbers cut hair, dentists pull teeth, and surgeons operate. After World War II, the American Psychiatric Association created its own diagnostic symptom manual based on the Veterans Administration's manual (DSM-I). The DSM-I included Gross Stress Reaction. The reference to stress was dropped in the DSM-II, however. It reappeared after the Vietnam War, in the DSM-III. In the DSM-IV, the term became Acute Stress Disorder. The DSMs are used to standardize diagnosis and treatment. For example, insurance companies assume that a condition does not exist if it is not in the DSM, making collection for treatment impossible. Today meditation and hypnosis are accepted medical treatments for stress. Many other alternative treatments—for example, chiropractic, acupuncture, and supplementation of certain nutrients and vitamins—are still being researched and have yet to be accepted by the medical profession.

What scientific developments will emerge in the twenty-first century? How will human trends continue to evolve, and what will be the place of regression work? Notice that at this time I use the term *regression* work in the place of *past-life* work. It seems to me from the research that all time is truly happening right now. It is just not in our immediate awareness. When we travel or journey into other time periods, we visit other layers (dimensions?) of now. We are journeying within ourselves to the events that have cost us part of ourselves, or that have kept an emotion or feeling hostage to other noncurrent events. The work of regressionists is to lead a client to those inner memories of events and places in order for emotions to be released—sometimes with abreaction. As a result, a client often changes his or her mind about the interpretation of such events and brings that conflicted part present to complete the person's entire being—right in the regressionist's office.

## What Does This Mean?

The following are my thoughts about what might be possible if all this is true:

1. **Politics.** People who are whole and complete within don't have the need or the tendency to feel that they have to acquire others' property. They feel equal to all, realizing we are all doing the best we can with what we have. Each being on Earth has a purpose. Could this mean the end to war?

2. **Psychology.** Psychological treatments and physical treatments will be integrated with what is now known as alternative or complementary medicine, which will become mainstream. It will be commonly acknowledged that other-dimensional events have an impact on one's current body.

3. **Science.** New theories will evolve from quantum theories. New technologies will be developed to tap into the abundant energies in the universe for practical use in daily activities. Expansion of time will encourage travel not limited to Earth. We will realize that we are connected and we are the same.

4. **Science and religion.** These will come closer together. When anger, greed, and fear decrease, the need for organized and unorganized religion will change, but it will not be eliminated. Perhaps religion will be based on various theologies or beliefs in God (by whatever name It or That is called). A single theory will develop that explains the workings of both the subatomic and the macroscopic (visible) worlds. Penrose, for example, is getting close with his planned experiment as discussed in chapter 7.

Psychiatrists, psychologists, social workers, and those working with alternative therapies will help bring the subconscious to conscious awareness, so multiple dimensions of consciousness can act as one, allowing persons to become whole and complete. When individuals become complete within themselves, they will recognize the wholeness of everyone else. When this happens, most if not all problems that are based on divisions will cease to be. *We will be as one!* All will collapse into the *oneness,* which is difficult for me to imagine.

To repeat, it is necessary for the regressionist to believe in only a successful outcome. And the client needs to allow for only this possibility. Research in hypnosis, and NLP in particular (see chapter 1), has shown that the choice of words is important. We also need further research on what affects the outcome of sessions, such as the beliefs of the regressionist and the words going through his or her mind. We have anecdotal evidence, but formal study would be more helpful.

This researcher suggests that new studies in the regression field will reveal the difference between formal, induced inductions and informal inductions, in which the client slides easily into an appropriate hypnotic state suitable for regression work. The continued research in physics will close the gap between the laws of the quantum, submicroscopic world and the larger visible worlds. The concept of folding time, or time folding back upon itself, could ultimately explain how the future affects the past and present, as well as how the past affects the future.

Most people currently consider the Earth to be round. However, those driving on the freeway see only a straight, flat section of it. Likewise, most people looking forward see only a straight, flat line—perhaps a timeline. If people were to look at the freeway or timeline from a higher viewpoint, they might view the actual curvature within its reality. Or time could be something else that we have not yet named.

# Comments

While researching and writing this book, I have come to insights that some might find difficult to agree with. However, mounting evidence shows that we exist in a multilayered world, where reality is not just black and white. The following possibilities, even probabilities, demonstrate how much there is yet to uncover about the mystery of life.

1.  For years I thought regression was a solution in and of itself. After thousands of sessions for a multitude of reasons, I noticed that just the process of regression would bring wholeness to an individual. However, simply being aware of the cause of a symptom or worrisome behavior might not be enough to provide a remedy, although this works in some cases. Likewise, it might seem that the cause is an event, when in reality, the individual's *perception* of the event is the critical factor. Regression is a powerful way to uncover new perceptions for immediate positive change.

    I at one time also thought that if a client had a troublesome symptom, formal regression was the only way for the client to become whole. By *formal* regression, I mean purposeful, therapeutic, and given by a qualified, trained regressionist. However, many religions have programs dealing with forgiveness and reparation that lead to wholeness. Meditation and prayer are also helpful. Because problems can be caused by abreacting (reacting to a past situation instead of a current one), the Buddhist practices found in vipassana, or insight meditation,[378] are also useful.

2. It was only after I had been doing regressions for years that I found the benefit of taking clients to a positive experience. I had a client who had had a series of negative, hurtful lifetimes of poverty, illness, and betrayal. For a balance, before the client left, I directed her to a lifetime of health, love, family, and wealth (having more than enough for the family and to share with others). She went to a life in a mansion with children and a loving husband, and she died in old age in her chair on her front porch. As she left my office, my client said she would not take life, love, and abundance for granted again. Since then, I usually make it my intention that the last regression for a client is a positive lifetime—past or future.

Sometimes I have taken clients to where they were once whole, and they see what happened to undo this. Maybe it was a choice they made that caused the difference. They learn that they can remake the choice.

3. "There is no such thing as a past life. We live one life." These statements are frequently made whenever I speak publically about past lives. I feel that my research can help resolve this dilemma. In the greater scope of reality, the third dimension, our material world, is a very small place. It is within this dimension that reincarnation takes place. Our "life," in its entire scope, is greater than most realize and encompasses many dimensions, simultaneously. I believe that for each of us life started when we first differentiated, and it will end when we recombine, making it essentially one total lifetime for all. What we have been and will be is the topic of another book.

4. Some people believe that formal hypnosis is important, perhaps necessary, for memory recall in a systematic way. Lipton and others have said that memories of generations are hidden in each cell of your body. You contain your entire history through all timespace. Just relax and let yourself recall. Formal hypnosis with a full induction, however, does help.

5. Some believe that all causes of all problems are in a previous reality. However, the cause can be in this lifetime—a childhood incident, a prenatal event, a past generation—or even from a future life. There may be a hint of the cause during the initial interview with the client, or there may not be. This is where training really helps the regressionist.

6. Have you heard that time is fixed and consistent? It appears to me that the existence of time is limited to the third dimension, the material world where most of us live while we are awake. During sleep time, we experience the dream state in which there is a sequence of events. Those who are aware of lucid dreaming are able to consciously repeat a segment and change an action to effect a better ending. The dream takes place in no-time during dream states, which can be only several minutes by a clock. There is current research into future events having results in the present.

7. *Live in the Moment* (2004) by Julie Clark Robinson and *The Power of Now* (2004) by Eckhart Tolle are interesting books, but the authors' suggestions are sometimes difficult to practice. In my experience with my clients releasing negative emotions by changing perceptions (reframing) of a former event that might still be lingering in the background helps the client live more fully in the present. It may also help to know that the persons involved did what they thought best at the time. You might do the practices in these books by

yourself or with the aid of someone else, such as a therapist or regressionist.

8. It is said that you can't escape karma. Karma is usually understood as a reaction or result of an action. You might not be able to escape, but you can temper karma. As in a classroom, you can learn from what you hear, see, or read in a book—or you can experience firsthand, as in a laboratory. You learn life lessons in the same way. Eventually a karmic situation is presented again as a test, so you can prove you have learned what you needed to learn.

It can take a lifetime of effort to become whole, and you can spend a modest fortune in therapy. If all clients considered therapy a shortcut to becoming whole, most regressionists and therapists would have a fortune. In the past it was possible to be whole without a therapist, or regressionist. Also in the past, a spiritual guide was often available in the person of a priest, elder, or shaman, for example. From what I have observed, however, most people do not have wholeness as a goal.

I would say most of my clients have already lived out their karma, or at least the karma they chose to work on in this lifetime. When they were experiencing their karma, they somehow learned survival behavior. This behavior became a habit that is no longer useful. Once a client realizes the cause of a behavior and releases the emotional charge, the behavior no longer is automatic. Many phobias, but not all, are the result of habitual abreaction. For example, a fear of cats can be traced to being fatally bitten by a large cat in another timespace. In this lifetime, the client may cry at the sight of even a kitten. Once the event is relived, the client starts to enjoy the company of cats.

Being whole and staying whole may appear to be a condition reserved for the saints—or impossible. That is a challenge we all have. I don't believe it is impossible, because some people have done it. Meditation, prayer, and regression help. It would take more time to explain than I have in this book, but I include some resources for those who wish to learn more.

# Summary

I trust that readers have benefited from the twofold purpose of this book. For regressionists, it gives more information on the use of techniques to help their clients. In addition, it gives more background about the ultimate purpose of regression—not only to reveal the past but also to integrate and resolve the negative or unwanted results of past events. To this end, the chapters present the scientific background and purpose for regression sessions. For other readers, especially those interested in personal growth and evolution, the book provides the background for regression and the purpose for delving into past events and attempting to resolve difficult memories or troublesome situations.

It is not always necessary to uncover specific events to move forward leaving some past event behind. For example, I had one client who, during the initial interview, revealed hurtful incidents in her past. The interview took up most of the allotted time, and not wanting her to leave without some experience, I led her through a session. We went to a past event in her current life that would have her experience a moment, before the events had started, when she had felt confident, successful, and positive about herself. She saw herself trying to walk and experiencing frustration. Next, she picked herself up, stood by herself, and took the first step, then the second. She felt the self-confidence she had forgotten and experienced the success she deserved.

I suggested that she replace any feelings of failure or lack of confidence with vivid memories, actual feelings, of strength and perseverance. I also suggested she remember those feelings and bring them forward to a successful outcome. "How many times did you fall before you walked by yourself?" I asked. "Continue past the present to a time in the future where you might feel overwhelmed by circumstances and might not 'feel worthy' (her words during the interview)." I asked her to tell me what was happening. She looked surprised as she told me about being a manager. A couple of years later, I saw her again. Not only was she a manager, but she was also overseeing the entire public operation of a well-known business.

What she did with my guidance, you, the reader, can do also. I gave her permission to go into her past and use her imagination to visualize what it was like before the negative events. All events serve a purpose. At some time the purpose is over. This assumes that you don't need or you have already incorporated those lessons. Thus, you are not required to continually relive those events. As you have read, all events could be occurring at the same time, simultaneously—the good as well as the not so good. By remembering and bringing the good, positive events to the forefront, you are acting to replace negative memories.

If you are having trouble letting go of the bad events when they come to mind, ask an event what it had to teach you and how it has affected your present. If you still have trouble, then a visit to a therapist might help. Not all therapists or regressionist do all that is mentioned in the first part of this book. Not all of the techniques are needed, and other techniques might be more useful in your situation. That is something to be discussed at your first appointment.

The last question to be answered is whether there is life between lives or before birth. There is strict belief on both sides. Most people believe something because somebody once told them it was so. Their belief is not necessarily based on firm scientific fact. Furthermore, as you realize, science has changed its mind on several issues in the past and probably will again. This explanation may answer some questions and present a way to resolve any conflict about contradictory perspectives. If in doubt about your beliefs, check with a minister, priest, or physicist whom you trust.

# Appendix A

# History of Hypnosis: Highlights

Genesis 2:21    The Lord God puts Adam in a sleep and takes a rib.

2000 BC         Unknown start of meditation, possibly by hunter-gatherer societies sitting around a fire or later in the religious practices of Tantra that date back five thousand years. The earliest written records date to 2000 BC, in Hindu Vedantism.

1000 BC         Ebers Papyrus, an Egyptian medical papyrus, is the first written record of hypnosis.

1526            Paracelsus uses magnets for healing.

1725            Father Maximilian Hell uses magnets for healing work.

1773            Franz Mesmer theorizes that healing comes from the animal magnetism of the conductor.

1778            Mesmer uses baquets (jars with rods sticking out) to cure many people at one time.

1784            The Academy of Science in France investigates Mesmer's treatment and says it is the imagination of the patient that causes changes, not animal magnetism.

Late 1700s      Marquis de Chastenet de Puysegur learns mesmerism from Mesmer. When his client goes into a deep sleep, Puysegur calls it somnambulism, and when the client answers questions lucidly, he calls it lucid sleep.

| | |
|---|---|
| 1797 | Abbe Faria develops autosuggestion while in d'If prison. |
| 1807-1885 | Andries Hoek uses magnetic treatment (mesmerism). |
| 1813 | Abbe Faria postulates that everything comes from within a person's mind, not the animal magnetism of the conductor. His method uses focused concentration and expectation. |
| 1815 | Napoleon is overthrown. |
| 1830 | Antoine Despine uses animal magnetism with his patients. |
| 1836 | Antoine Despine's patient, Estelle, gives her own diagnosis and treatment. |
| 1842 | James Braid investigates mesmerism and renames it hypnotism. Instead of a sleep state, it is considered focused concentration under the control of the client. Braid unsuccessfully tries to change the term hypnotism to monoideaism. |
| 1845 | James Esdaile uses hypnosis in surgery in India, in the style of Mesmer. Chloroform gradually replaces the use of hypnosis in surgery. In World War I, when chloroform was not available, hypnosis was used. |
| 1885 (circa) | Jean-Martin Charcot, a direct student of Mesmer and coworker with Joseph Breuer, teaches Sigmund Freud hypnosis-mesmerism. |
| 1847 | The Catholic Church states that the use of hypnosis for health reasons by trained professionals is permitted. |
| 1859-1947 | Pierre Janet is the first to describe the relationship of the mystery of somnambulism to hypnosis. |
| 1885-1900 | Sigmund Freud briefly uses hypnosis. (The explanation is in the text.) |
| 1882 | Breuer is the first to use the cathartic method to cure hysteria. |
| 1883 | Albert de Rochas begins past-life regressions. |

| | |
|---|---|
| 1891 | Freud is working with Breuer. |
| 1907-1912 | Carl Jung works with Freud. |
| 1903-1904 | Rudolf Steiner publishes a series of essays on experiencing one's own karma and previous incarnation. These are republished in the book *Knowledge of the Higher Worlds and Its Attainment* in 1909, 1910, and again in 2011. |
| 1911 | Albert de Rochas writes a book about his regressions. |
| 1914 | During World War I, hypnosis is applied in the field to control pain and blood loss. |
| 1920 | Milton Erickson starts moving from using direct suggestion to a permissive approach. |
| 1927 | Paul Brunton describes a technique that will allow individuals to discover their own past lives through a daily practice of reviewing the day backward, event by event, hour by hour. This is similar to R. Steiner's method of improving intuition and spiritual development. |
| 1930s | Hitler uses hypnosis to train his soldiers. |
| 1932 | Johannes Schultz develops Autogenic Training. |
| 1950-1960s | Meditation becomes popular in the West. |
| 1950s | Stanislav Grof pioneers the concept of rebirthing. |
| 1950s | L. Ron Hubbard starts a movement called Dianetics, later to be called Scientology. |
| 1958 | The American Medical Association approves hypnosis. |
| Late 1960s | Meditation starts to gain popularity in the West. |
| Early 1970s | Denys Kelsey uses hypnosis to move clients backward chronologically. |
| 1970s | Harry Arons develops the Arons Scale, to measure depth of trance, and pioneers the use of hypnosis in criminal investigations. |

*Barbara H. Pomar*

| Early 1970s | Jacqueline Parkhurst writes an article about the Christos Technique, a regression method. |
| 1976 | Marcia Moore publishes *Hypersentience: Exploring Your Past Lifetime.* |
| 1977 | Jose Silva publishes *The Silva Mind Control Method.* |
| 1970-1980 | Milton Erickson develops informal and instant hypnotic induction methods. |
| 1979 | First past-life regression conference is held at University of California, Irvine. |
| 1996 | Michael Newton publishes *Life Between Life: Hypnotherapy for Spiritual Regression.* |
| 1996 | The American Association of Pastlife Regression Therapists (AAPRT) changes its name to International Association for Regression Research and Therapists, Inc. (IARRT). |
| 2003 | Division 30 of the American Psychological Association (which deals with hypnosis) offers the following new official definition of hypnosis, but it is not widely accepted: |

Hypnosis typically involves an introduction to the procedure during which the subject is told that suggestions for imaginative experiences will be presented. The hypnotic induction is an extended initial suggestion for using one's imagination, and may contain further elaborations of the introduction. A hypnotic procedure is used to encourage and evaluate responses to suggestions. When using hypnosis, one person (the subject) is guided by another (the hypnotist) to respond to suggestions for changes in subjective experience, alterations in perception, sensation, emotion, thought or behavior.[1]

206

This definition is not well supported, partly because (1) there are other methods of achieving a hypnotic trance besides a formal induction, as already mentioned, and (2) there are other reasons to use hypnosis, such as to elicit information in regressions.

2004     The first World Congress of Regression Therapists (WCRT) is held in Amsterdam, the Netherlands.

Note:

[1] J. P. Green,     "Forging Ahead: The 2003 APA Division 30 Definition of Hypnosis," pp. 259-264.

# Appendix B

# Spirit Releasement

Early in my regression career, I found many clients would review a past life that had no relationship to their current life. When I checked for the possibility of an attachment and released the attachment, the relevancy of the session became clear.

## The Dying Process

Many books have been written about the dying process. Elisabeth Kubler-Ross in *Death and Dying* (1997) covers the subject very well. Basically, actual death is painless and relatively quick, according to her book. Most people are afraid of what leads up to death. As the spirit leaves the body, it is drawn into what has been identified as light, or it is lifted upward. A nonphysical being often helps, such as an angel, a deceased spouse, a family member or loved one, even a pet may help and greet the person on the other side. From there, the spirit starts to experience whatever it expects to. Eventually it is led to a place of healing and preparation for the next experience.

Sometimes a spirit or soul is really afraid of what might happen—hell, for example—or it just does not want to leave the physical world because of sensory attachments, including alcohol and drugs, or emotional attachments, such as a parent not wanting to leave the family. Occasionally, if the death is unexpected and tragic, such as in an accident or an explosion, the soul might continue to attempt to experience life. These bodiless spirits will look for another way to exist. They have two choices: either continue to float around or enter another body.

Those that float around usually remain near the scene of their death, their body, or a favorite place. Prayers for the deceased help tremendously. I understand each religion has its own prayer for the dead. When visiting hospitals, grave sites, or battle grounds, I ask any souls that are hanging around to gather together and look for a cool, pure-white light. I tell them that they have family and friends waiting. I say, for example, "Go to them. Somebody, a being, perhaps an angel, will help you and direct you there. Just feel yourself rising up. Go with God, Allah, or your own name for Great Spirit."

Those with an addiction before death often choose to enter a body that has easy access to their addiction of choice. If they had a sudden death, such as an accident, they might attach to the nearest live body. Another scenario happens when after death a parent's or child's soul does not want to leave its family. That spirit hangs around so closely that it joins a family member in his or her body. Sometimes, if a soul attaches to a child, she may feel she needs help and asks for this. Yet another floating spirit may try to help by joining the child to better communicate. Later, once the child grows up and can make her own choices, it forgets how to leave.

## Releasing the Attachment

The following is a typical procedure for the regressionist to follow (In the dialogue sections, "Client" replaces the name of your client):

I.   Identify attachment.

    A.   The client may have a tendency to speak in the third person, for example, "(Client's name) is not cooperating" or "Client does not want to do this."

B. Use the *mirror process* to access the unconscious mind. The client may see a different person or a different kind of dress in the mirror.

C. The client may say someone else is in control (the boss) or that it is a struggle to do what he or she wants to do. He may say, "It seems something always is stopping me from—"

D. Ask a direct question to the client's unconscious mind, such as: "Is there someone or something else inside Client that is not Client?"

II. Ask to speak to the being or entity. It might never have had a human or physical body.

A. Remember that your clients are your clients. They need to give you permission to speak to their guests. You might say, "May I talk to the image/being in the mirror?" or "Would you relay, verbatim, exactly what the image/being is saying, or what you sense the being is saying?"

B. Introduce yourself and ask the client to relay whatever his guest or hitchhiker says or thinks.

   i. "I am called Barbara, and as you know, Client has asked me for help. What may I call you?"

   ii. The being with the client usually gives a name. If none is forthcoming, then ask, "May I call you (an identifying feature your client has given you—Mr. Blue, for example)?" The being usually agrees or gives an alternate name.

III. Create a separation between your client and the guest/s (there may be more than one).

    A. "Mr. Blue, how long have you been with Client?" The being usually responds, "A long time." The response could also be a particular incident, a specific time, or a certain age. Occasionally, the answer is "Forever." I don't accept that as a final response.

    B. If it is "A long time," ask if the being was present when the client was a child, or was it with the person when he or she was born. Occasionally the hitchhiker may have been with the client for many lifetimes.

    C. If the answer is "Forever," then I ask, "Did you have your own body?"; "What do you remember about that life?"; "What happened to that body?"; "How did you come to join with Client?" It is possible that the client has a multiple personality disorder. If you get confusing answers, then you would bring the client back to normal awareness and refer to an appropriate psychologist.

This process of questioning separates the hitchhiker from the client. It lets both know that there was a time when they were different and had different existences. In some cases, the attachment might not have had a physical life before, only an existence.

IV. Create a desire in the attachment to leave. Ask permission of the client for the attachment to leave.

    A. "What is your purpose with Client?" Usually it is positive. Occasionally, it is negative.

    B. If it's positive, ask the following:

"When did you start helping Client?"; "Are you still helping Client?"

i.  Usually, the visitor joins at a time of stress (physical, mental, or emotional) when the client has asked for help of any kind.

ii.  Ask your client, "Do you still need the help of your visitor?" The best response is "No! Sometimes the client may be uncertain. Then counseling techniques are needed to boost the person's confidence in handling situations or in getting expert assistance. Just because the current visitor does not have its own body does not mean the being is an expert. The being's knowledge is from its own past lessons, which may be limited. If it were an expert, the being would probably be in its own body, not hitching a ride in someone else's body.

iii.  Ask the visitor, "What does Client do for you?"

iv.  "Are you happy with Client all the time?" Usually the answer is "No.". "What does Client do to make you *not* happy?" This could be almost anything.

v.  "Would you like to be in a place where you would always be happy and could eventually have your own body to experience?" It is also a good idea to include the things your client does that make the being happy. This could include things the hitchhiker misses in not having a physical body in which to experience them fully.

Keep asking questions and describing the place on the other side of the light, which will have the things that the being currently misses. In the afterdeath experience, the first things experienced are those that are missed or expected. These objects are in that dimension and are experienced as physical by the being in that dimension. The regressionist is creating positive expectations, something the spirit can go toward and be able to have or experience where it is now.

C. If it is a negative purpose:

i. Ask the visitor, "Why would you want to harm or cause harm to your host?"

ii. Ask the visitor, "Who told you to do that?" Usually the answer is very hesitant and slow in coming. Sometimes the answer is "The devil" or "My boss." Ask for a description. The hitchhiker often explains that its boss is a not-so-nice or evil spirit. The next step is separation of the controlling spirit (the boss of the visitor) from the client.

iii. Ask the visitor, "What will happen when your spirit boss finds out that you have been discovered?" The answer usually includes torture, pain, or whatever punishment that could be given.

iv. Solve the being's problem. Tell the being, "I have a way out for you." Describe the process and what it may find on the other side. Describe the assistance that is available and the others that have been waiting for the being.

Get permission from your client for the being to leave. "Is it okay for it/them to leave?" After all, it is the client's guest you are asking to leave.

V. When the attachment is ready and the client is ready, ask the attachment if there are any more beings. Ask the attachment to look around. "Can you take the others with you so they can leave at the same time?" Sometimes the attachment doesn't want to take others even when it says there are more. Then you might have to do one at a time.

VI. Describe the ideal scenario of what normally happens after a spirit's body dies.

   A. Describe the light as a gentle, soft, warm, pure White Light that will take the hitchhiker to a place of healing and kindness. If the spirit had a negative purpose, it might not think it is worthy of love and respect quite yet. Then ask it to look inside and see a light, which could be quite small but still there. Tell it this small light is the spark of love that is inside every being. (Keep it brief and to the point. This is not to be a therapeutic session.) Suggest that it let this spark join in the Light.

   B. Say to the attachment, "Look for a White Light that is coming down. Perhaps it is in a corner. Do you see it? Go over to it. Feel it. When you are ready, step into the light. Feel yourself gently rising up. Soon you might notice another being, perhaps an angel or other nonphysical being that is there to help and guide you. Soon you will see someone waiting for you. Someone patiently or impatiently is waiting for your arrival. Do you recognize the being? As it is leading you to a place of healing, can you send love and light to your former host for what this person has done for you? Go with love and light."

   C. Say to the attachment, "If there is difficulty, call the angels. Ask Client to ask these nonphysical beings to help and guide you to a place of safety, healing, and love."

VII. Look for others.

    A.  Say to the client, "Look, again, into the mirror and describe what you see." Repeat the process until the mirror reflects your client in present time.

VIII. Afterward, caution the client that he might feel grief or sadness, such as when a friend has died or moved away. Tell the person that such feelings are natural and to be kind to himself for the next day or so.

According to the time allotted for the session, the regressionist might proceed with what had been scheduled before the attachment was discovered, or an appointment can be scheduled for another time.

# Appendix C

# Past-Life Recall

There are many reasons that people may want information from their pasts. This appendix is not intended for therapeutic change. This is a basic outline of what I use when a client wants to review a past life for information or self-knowledge. It was developed as I read, took classes, and talked to other regressionists. It especially reflects the work of Henry Bolduc, author, teacher, and trainer in the self-help profession, who has given permission to use his technique.[1] Feel free to adjust the wording to fit the situation and your language preference. The following is only an outline of a past-life information-gathering session. A full explanation would fill a book.

## I. INTRODUCTION

The client needs to have information from the regressionist to have confidence in the regressionist. The regressionist needs some basic information from the client to better connect with the client. This is commonly known as the *intake*. You can complete forms beforehand and review them together. This is also where the client and regressionist agree upon the purpose of the session.

## II. INDUCTION

When accessing a client's past life for information, a formal induction is helpful. The preferred induction of the hypnotherapist can be used.

## III. BRIDGING TO THE MEMORY

Once the regressionist takes the client to the desired level that he or she deems necessary, then a bridge is used to deepen the hypnotic state.

A. "Focus your attention on the inside of your forehead."

B. "Imagine a path that will lead to a past life that reflects on the current life, or a past life in which you were healthy, wealthy, and had a good family life," or whatever purpose you and the client have agreed upon."

C. "Continue on the path. You will soon see a blue mist, like a fog."

D. "Enter the fog. It is amazingly comfortable. Go through the fog."

E. "You are out of the fog."

## IV. ACCLIMATING TO THAT TIMESPACE

At first, ask simple, multiple-choice questions. Get a description of the person you meet and the surrounding environment.

A. "Look down at your feet. What do you see?" Continue in this way to the head to get a description of the person's body, including age and sex.

B. "Look around you. Are you inside or outside?"

C.  If it is dark, ask the client to go before it is dark and describe what is there. The regressionist needs to use his imagination to form the necessary questions.

D.  "Are you standing or sitting? On what?" This provides more information about the setting.

E.  "How old are you? Give the first number that comes to mind."

F.  "What is the name of your town or village, or the nearest town or village? What year is it? Give the first number that comes to mind." If you hear a young age, these last questions might have to wait for an older age.

## V. GETTING THE STORY

Gradually switch from simple multiple-choice to open-ended questions, such as:
"What do you have in your hands?"
"What is happening around you?"
"Then what happens?"

Ask questions about who is there, what the client is eating, who is cooking, or who cooked the meal. You can also ask what is being discussed or what the father is doing to provide a living for the family.

A.  Process the most significant event.

  1.  "Go to the most important, most significant event in that lifetime." After getting the information, you might say to the client, "Go before the event to the initial event that led to that event." (Calling the event by an appropriate name)

2. "What is happening?"

3. "Why is this event significant?" or "What is the significance of this event?" (if it's not already apparent)

B. Process the next significant event.

1. "Go to another significant event."
This is treated the same way.

C. Process another significant event. The three events give a good idea about that lifetime.

1. "Go to another significant event."
This is treated the same way.

## VI. PROCESSING THE DEATH EXPERIENCE (and sealing off that life as being completed)

A. Get details about what happened to cause the death.

1. "Where are you? What are you doing?"

2. "What is happening to your body? How old are you? (If young) What caused this?"

B. Life review.

1. "What was the best part of this life?"

2. "What would you have done differently? What has been left unfinished?"

C. Go through the death and beyond.

1. "Continue through the death, leaving all sickness, illness, and pain behind in that body."

2. "Look back over the life you have just completed. What did you learn in that experience?"

3. "Continue through into a light or tunnel."

4. "Then what happens?"

## VII.   RECONNECTING TO PRESENT

A.   "It is time to come back to the present."

B.   "I will count back to one from ten. When I reach one, you will be fully alert, fully aware."

## VIII.   PROCESSING THE SESSION

A.   Discuss with the client what happened. Accept the client's viewpoint.

B.   It is often beneficial for the client to write down what he or she remembers of the session, because the experience may start to fade from memory. You may record the session and give a copy to the client. However, I have often found that the tape does not adequately record the entire event. That is, the client experiences more than the recording can capture.

# Comments

If a client wants to explore the between-life state more deeply or in fuller detail, then it is good to plan another session. Begin by going through a past-life session briefly. This could be a past life that the client has already recalled. Review chapter 6 for Michael Newton's preferred entry into the between-life period. Briefly review a significant event and the death in that lifetime.

The client's unconscious mind will usually block any memories that would be harmful to him or her. The regressionist should respect any memory blocks. The session is not meant to be therapeutic, unless the regressionist has the training to handle abreactions and the client has given permission to enter therapeutic areas.

Note:

[1] There is a notice on Bolduc's website (http://www. henrybolduc. com) that gives permission to download and use Henry's books and materials from his website without charge for personal, professional, or educational reasons. This tribute can also be found on his website:

> Henry, our loving friend, teacher, and mentor passed away on Saturday, July 9, 2011. He was surrounded by his friends and family during his final days—but we all hated to see him go.

> One of his favorite quotes, from Edgar Cayce, was: "Just be kind and patient." Henry was indeed a kind, patient, and a very generous soul. The world was a better place when he was among us.

> Henry Bolduc was a certified hypnotherapist with forty-five years of experience in past-life exploration and research.

> His goal with his website was to share experiences, ideas, and writings . . . to assist you on your way through the great adventure called *life*. On henrybolduc.com, you will find material that is not available anywhere else.

# Notes

## Introduction
## Chapter One

1.  Sigmund Freud and Josef Breuer, *The Complete Psychological Works of Sigmund Freud, Vol. II, Studies on Hysteria,* trans. by J. Strachey (London: The Harth Press, Limited, 1955).

2.  Hugh Everett III, Relative State Formulation of Quantum Mechanics.

3.  Julian Barbour, *The End of Time: The Next Revolution in Physics* (New York: Oxford University Press, 1990).

4.  Roger Penrose, *The Road to Reality: A Complete Guide to the Laws of the Universe* (New York: Vantage Books, 2004).

## Chapter One

5.  Bruce Lipton, *Biology of Belief* (Carlsbad, CA: Hay House, 2007).

6.  Lipton, *Biology of Belief,* 2007.

7.  Tad James and W. Woodsmall, *Time Line Therapy and the Basics of Personality* (Capitola, CA: Meta Publications, 1988).

## Chapter Two

8.  Mikowski and Einstein originally used *time-space* to describe the continuum between time and space. As the term became more widely and generally used, it morphed into *timespace* (no hyphen) during the end of the twentieth century. In this paper, I use *time-space* initially. Then, when I discuss developments that occur near the end of the twentieth century, *timespace* is used. The usage changed gradually as *timespace* was acknowledged to be one concept.

9.  J. P. Green, A. F. Barabasz, D. Barrett, and G. H. Montgomery, Forging Ahead: The 2003 APA Division 30 Definition of Hypnosis.

10 James Braid, Magic, Mesmerism, Hypnotism, Etc., Historically and Physiologically Considered.

11 *Holy Bible*, Revised Standard Version.

12 Kim Grant, The History of Hypnosis. Retrieved July 5, 2011 from www.kimgranthypnotist.com-/historyofhypnosis.

13 Henri Ellenberger, *The Discovery of the Unconscious: The History and Evolution of Dynamic Psychiatry* (New York: Basic Books, 1970).

14 Hans TenDam, *Exploring Reincarnation: The Classic Guide to the Evidence for Past-Life Experiences* (London: Rider, division of Random House Publishing, 2003).

15 Ellenberger, *The Discovery of the Unconscious*.

16 David Stafford-Clark, *What Freud Really Said* (New York: Random House, 1965), p. 47.

17 Joanne McKeown, Visions as Illness and Inspiration: Young Estelle. http://www.nacfla.ne/UP_JournalFiles-/JCFL%202006%20 29-43%20McKeown.pdf.

18 Ellenberger, *The Discovery of the Unconscious*.

19 Adam Crabtree, Multiple Personality before Eve. Retrieved July 3, 2011 from www.joannecrabtree.com-/psychotherapyarts/ multiplepersonalitiesbeforeeve.

20 Crabtree, Multiple Personality before Eve.

21 Ellenberger, *The Discovery of the Unconscious*.

22 Michael Holt, Marquis Chastenet de Puységur. http://www.docmagi. com/hypnosis/marquis-chastenet-de-puysegur-1751-1825/.

23 Ellenberger, *The Discovery of the Unconscious*.

24 TenDam, *Exploring Reincarnation,* p. 134.

25 TenDam, *Exploring Reincarnation*, p. 135.

26 Luis de Santa Rita Vas, Abbe Faria, www.geni.com/projects/ abbe-faria.

27 Vas, The Amazing Abbe Faria. Goanet-News, December 17, 2005.

28 A. G. Warrier, *108 Upanishads, Bhavana Upanishad* (2002).

29 Vas, The Amazing Abbe Faria.

30 Ellenberger, *The Discovery of the Unconscious*.

31 Vas, The Amazing Abbe Faria.

32 TenDam, *Exploring Reincarnation*.

33    George Meek, *A Guide to Spiritual & Magnetic Healing & Psychic Surgery in the Philippines* (Manila, Philippines: Christian Travel Service, 1998).

34    Meek, *A Guide to Spiritual & Magnetic Healing & Psychic Surgery in the Philippines.*

35    Pepito works with Christian Travel Center in Manila, Philippines, which is managed by Doris Almeda. Their last (family) names are not available. Contact: PO Box 2887, Manila, Philippines.

36    OnnoVan der Hart, The Hypnotherapy of Dr. Andries Hoek: Uncovering Hypnotherapy Before Janet, Breuer, and Freud, *American Journal of Clinical Hypnosis*, 29(4) April 1987: pp. 264-71.

37    James Braid, Mr. Braid on Hypnotism, *The Lancet*, Vol. 45, no. 1135, (May 1845): pp. 627-628.

38    Michael Holt, James Braid. http://www.docmagi.com/hypnosis/james-braid.

39    James Braid, Magic, Mesmerism, Hypnotism, Etc., Historically and Physiologically Considered.

40    Maurice Tinterow, *Foundations of Hypnosis* (London: Charles C. Thomas Publishers, 1970), p. 321.

41    Tinterow, *Foundations of Hypnosis*, p. 321.

42    Alan Gauld, *A History of Hypnotism* (Cambridge: Cambridge University Press, 1992), p. 257.

43    David Stafford-Clark, *What Freud Really Said* (New York: Random House, 1965).

44    Stafford-Clark, *What Freud Really Said.*

45    John Haule, Pierre Janet and Dissociation: The First Transference Theory and Its Origins in Hypnosis, p. 86.

46    Sigmund Freud, The Complete Psychological Works of Sigmund Freud, Vol II.

47    Ernest Jones, *The Life and Work of Signumd Freud* (New York: Basic Books, 1953).

48    Sigmund Freud and Josef Breuer, *The Complete Psychological Works of Sigmund Freud, Vol. II, Studies on Hysteria*, trans. by J. Strachey (London: The Harth Press, Limited, 1955).

49    Sigmund Freud, *The Basic Writings of Sigmund Freud*, trans. by A. A. Brill (New York: Random House, 1955).

50  Freud, *The Basic Writings of Sigmund Freud.*
51  Stafford-Clark, *What Freud Really Said.*
52  Stafford-Clark, *What Freud Really Said,* p. 50.
53  Freud, *The Basic Writings of Sigmund Freud,* p.17
54  Freud, *The History of the Psychoanalytic Movement,* p. 901.
55  Freud, *The Basic Writings of Sigmund Freud.*
56  Sigmund Freud, *The History of the Psychoanalytic Movement and Other Papers* (New York: Collier Books, 1963).
57  Sigmund Freud, *An Autobiographical Study: Inhibitions, Sypmtoms and Anxiety, Lay Analysis and Other Works, 1925-1926,* SE. Vol. XX, trans. by J. Strachey (London: The Hogarth Press, 1959) p. 19.
58  Stafford-Clark, *What Freud Really Said,* pp. 52-53.
59  Freud, *The History of the Psychoanalytic Movement,* p. 903.
60  Freud, *The History of the Psychoanalytic Movement,* p. 903.
61  Freud, *An Autobiographical Study: Inhibitions.* p. 17.
62  Freud, *An Autobiographical Study: Inhibitions.* p. 27.
63  Freud, *The History of the Psychoanalytic Movement and Other Papers.*
64  Mary Biaggio, Survey of Psychologists' Perspectives on Cartharsis.
65  Biaggio, A Survey of Psychologists' Perspectives on Cartharsis.
66  Jackson, Catharsis and a Reaction.
67  Hull, Psychological Treatment of Birth Trauma with Age Regression and its Relationship to Chemical Dependency.
68  Beck, *Cognitive Therapy of Depression.*
69  Biaggio, A Survey of Psychologists Perspectives on Cartharsis.
70  S. W. Jackson, Catharsis and a Reaction in the History of Psychological Healing.
71  William Kroger, William and M. Yapko, *Clinical and Experimental Hypnosis in Medicine, Dentistry, and Psychology; In Medicine, Dentistry, and Psychology,* Edition 2 (Philadelphia: Lippincott Williams & Wilkins, 1997), p. 92.
72  Frank Valente, History of Hypnosis. www.hypnoticadvancements.com.history.htm.
73  Ronald Havens and Catherine Walters, *Hypnotherapy Scripts: A Neo-Ericksonian Approach to Persuasive Healing* (New York: Brunner/Mazel Publishers, 2002).

[74] Pope Pius XII, Allocution to Doctors on the Moral Problems of Analgesia, as presented to the Catholic Association of Doctors, Nurses, and Health Professionals in Asia, 1957.

## Chapter Three

[75] Morris Netherton and Nancy Shiffrin, *Past Lives Therapy* (New York: Wm. Morrow & Co., 1978), p. 2.

[76] Ellen Bass and Laura Davis, *The Courage to Heal: Women Healing from Sexual Abuse* (New York: Harper & Row, 1988).

[77] K. McGowan, Out of the Past. *Discover Science, Technology and the Future.* July/August.

[78] Elizabeth Loftus and K. Ketcham, *The Myth of Repressed Memory* (New York: St. Martin's Press, 1994).

[79] William Baldwin, *Regression Therapy, Spirit Releasement Therapy: Technique Manual* (2nd Edition) (Terra Alta, WV: Headline Books, 1992).

[80] Alan Parkin, *Memory and Amnesia* (Cambridge: Basil Blackwell, 1987).

[81] Nicola Jones, Babies' Musical Memories Formed in Womb.

[82] P. G. Hepper, Fetal Memory: Does it Exist? What Does it Do?

[83] Lipton, Bruce. *Biology of Belief,* 2008.

[84] McDougall, An Experiment for the Testing of the Hypothesis of Lamarck; Crew, A Repetition of McDougall's Lamarckian Experiment; Agar, Fourth (Final) Report on a Test of McDougall's Lamarckian Experiment on the Training of Rats; Bryan, Age Regression before Birth.

[85] LaVonne Stiffler, Adoptees and Birth Parents Connected by Design: Surprising Synchronicities in Histories of Union/Loss/Reunion.

[86] Stiffler, Adoptees and Birth Parents Connected by Design.

[87] Lipton, Bruce. *Biology of Belief,* 2008.

[88] Stiffler, Adoptees and Birth Parents Connected by Design.

[89] Robert Waterland and Randy Jirtle, Transposable Elements: Targets for Early Nutritional Effects on Epigenetic Gene Regulation.

[90] Carl Jung, *Memories, Dreams and Reflections,* trans. by R. and C. Winston (New York: Vintage Books, 1989), p. 138.

[91] William James, *The Will to Believe and Human Mortality* (New York: Dover, 1956).

[92] James, *The Will to Believe and Human Mortality,* 1956.

93  William McDougall, *The Group Mind* (2nd Edition) (Salem, New Hampshire: Ayer Publications, 1972).

94  J. B. Rine and William McDougall, Third Report on a Lamarckian Experiment.

95  Rine, Third Report on a Lamarckian Experiment, p. 223.

96  William McDougall, Fourth Report on a Lamarckian Experiment.

97  W. Agar, F. Drummond, O. Tiegs, and M. Gunson. Fourth (Final) Report on a Test of McDougall's Lamarckian Experiment on the Training of Rats.

98  Rupert Sheldrake, *New Science of Life: The Hypothesis of Formative Causation.* Los Angeles: Tharcher, 1981.

99  Jung, *Memories, Dreams, and Reflections*; Sheldrake, *A New Science of Life;* Rosen, Empirical Study of Associations.

100  Agar, Fourth (Final) Report; McDougall, An Experiment for the Testing of the Hypothesis of Lamarck.

101  Marc Mishkind, Test for Morphic Resonance in Behavioral Responses to Multiple Choice Stimuli.

102  Sheldrake, *A New Science of Life.*

103  Elizabeth Loftus, The Reality of Repressed Memories; Loftus, *The Myth of Repressed Memory.*

104  Michael Bernstein, *The Search for Bridey Murphy* (Revised Edition). (New York: Pocket Books, 1965).

105  Baldwin, *Regression Therapy and Spirit Releasement Therapy.*

106  *The Light.* Many near-death experiencers have reported following or being attracted to a light after the event that precipitated the experience.

107  IARRT, International Association of Regression Research and Therapies, PO Box 20151, Riverside, CA 92516; http://www.iarrt.org.

108  Barbra Pomar, *Past Life Therapy: Origins and Sources*, Master's thesis. (University of Salisbury, Maryland, 2005).

109  F. Helmont, *Two Hundred Queries Moderately Propounded Concerning the Doctorine of the Revolution of Human Souls and Its Comformity to the Truths of Christianity. Translated by Rob Kettlmel* (London: University Microfilms International, 1684); G. Keith, *Truth and Innocency Defended Against Calumny and Defamation in a Late Report Spread Abroad Concerning the Revolution of Humane Souls* (Philadelphia: William Bradford on University Microfilm International, 1692).

110   Ian Stevenson, *Cases of the Reincarnation Type, Vol. 4: Twelve cases in Thailand and Burma* (Charlottesville, VA: University Press of Virginia, 1985); *Twenty Cases Suggestive of Reincarnation* (Charlottesville: University Press of Virginia, 1974).

111   Janet Cunningham, *A Tribe Returned* (Crest Park, CA: Deep Forest Press, 1994); Edith Fiore, *You Have Been Here Before* (New York: Putnam Publishing Group, 1978); Marge Rieder, *Mission to Millboro* (Nevada City, CA: Blue Dolphin Press, 1993); Chet Snow, *Mass Dreams of the Future* (New York: McGraw Hill, 1992).

112   Stevenson. 1985, *Cases of the Reincarnation Type,* Vol. 4; Stevenson, *Cases of the Reincarnation Type,* Vol. 2: *Ten Cases in Sri Lanka.* (Charlottesville, VA: University Press of Virginia, 1978); Stevenson, The Explanatory Value of the Idea of Reincarnation. *Journal of Nervous and Mental Disease* Vol. 164(5); Stevenson, *Twenty Cases Suggestive of Reincarnation.*

113   A. Mills, E. Haraldsson, and H. Keil. Replication Studies of Cases Suggestive of Reincarnation by Three Independent Investigators.

114   Mills, Replication Studies of Cases Suggestive of Reincarnation.

115   Stevenson, The Explanatory Value of the Idea of Reincarnation.

116   Nicholas Spanos, E. Menary, J. Gabora, S. Dubreuil, and B. Dewhirst, 1991. Secondary Identity Enactments During Hypnotic Past-Life Regression: A Sociocognitive Perspective.

117   W. P. Hull, Psychological Treatment of Birth Trauma with Age Regression and its Relationship to Chemical Dependency.

118   Ormond McGill, *The Many Lives of Alan Lee,* p. 15.

119   McGill, *The Many Lives of Alan Lee.*

120   Rieder, *Mission to Millboro.*

121   Cunningham, *A Tribe Returned.*

122   John Kihlstrom, Hypnosis, Delayed Recall, and the Principles of Memory.

123   Alan Parkin, *Memory and Amnesia (*Cambridge: Basil Blackwell, 1987).

124   K. Nash, What, if Anything, is Regressed About Hypnotic Age Regression? A Review of the Empirical Literature.

125   Loftus, The Reality of Repressed Memories; K. Nelson, The Psychological and Social Origins of Autobiographical Memory; J. Usher, J. and U. Neisser, Childhood Amnesia and the Beginnings of Memory for Four Early Life Events.

126 Fiore, *You Have Been Here Before*; Bruce Goldberg, *Past Lives, Future Lives* (New York: Ballantine Books, 1988); Helen Wambach and Lee, *The Wambach Method and Manual for Past Life Recall*; Stevenson,The Explanatory Value of the Idea of Reincarnation; Brian L.Weiss, *Many Lives, Many Masters: The True Story of a Prominent Psychiatrist, His Young Patient, and the Past-Life Therapy That Changed Both Their Lives* (New York: Simon & Schuster, 1988).

127 Marcia Moore, *Hypersentience: Exploring Your Past Lifetime* (New York: Crown Publishers, 1976).

128 Netherton, *Pastlives Therapy*; James, *Time Line Therapy*; Roger Woolger, *Other Lives, Other Selves* (New York: Bantam Books/ Doubleday, 1987) and Imaginal Techniques in Past-Life Therapy.

129 Stanislav Grof, Brief History of Transpersonal Psychology. http://www.stainislavgrof.com/articles.

130 K. R. Bryd, The Narrative Reconstructions of Incest Survivors.

131 Wambach, *The Wambach Method*.

132 Wambach, *The Wambach Method*; Stevenson, *Twenty Cases Suggestive of Reincarnation*; Snow, *Mass Dreams of the Future*; Rieder, *Mission to Millboro*; Cunningham, *A Tribe Returned*.

133 Wambach, *The Wambach Method*.

**Chapter Four**
134 Biaggio, A Survey of Psychologists' Perspectives on Cartharsis.

135 Stafford-Clark, *What Freud Really Said*, pp. 53-54.

136 Freud, *The History of the Psychoanalytic Movement*.

137 E. James Lieberman, (n.d.) Biography. http://www.ottorank.com).

138 TenDam, *Exploring Reincarnation*.

139 TenDam, *Exploring Reincarnation*, p. 134.

140 Grof, *A Brief History of Transpersonal Psychology*.

141 Paul Brunton, *A Hermit in the Himalayas* (New York: E. P. Dutton and Company, 2004).

142 Winafred Lucas, *Regression Therapy: a Handbook for Professionals* (Crest Park, CA: Deep Forest Press, 1993).

143 Jess Stern,. *The Sleeping Prophet*. (New York: Random House, 1967).

144 L. Ron Hubbard, *Dianetics: The Modern Science of Mental Health* (Los Angeles, CA: Bridge Publications, 2007).

[145] Denys Kelsey and J. Grant, *Many Lifetimes* (Alpharetta, GA: Ariel Press, 1967).

[146] Alastair McIntosh, *Psychoenergetic Systems* Vol. 3 (United Kingdom: Gordon and Breach Science Publishers, 1979).

[147] McIntosh, *Psychoenergetic Systems,* Vol 3.

[148] Moore, *Hypersentience.*

[149] Wambach, *The Wambach Method*

[150] Snow, *Mass Dreams of the Future.*

[151] European Association of Regression Therapy, www.earth-association. org.

[152] TenDam, *Exploring Reincarnation*, pp.125-127.

[153] TenDam, *Exploring Reincarnation.*

[154] TenDam, *Exploring Reincarnation.*

**Chapter Five**

[155] Netherton, *Past Lives Therapy.*

[156] Fritz Perls, *The Gestalt Approach and Eye Witness to Therapy* (USA: Science and Behavior Books, 1973).

[157] A *walk-in* is a spirit or soul who has died and who makes an agreement with a living person whose life purpose is finished but whose body is still usable. The person may have a health crisis or accident as a way out, and the incoming soul does not have to go through birth and childhood and can begin his purpose immediately. The original person must have completed all her relationship ties and completed most of her obligations. The new soul agrees to honor current relationships and obligations as well as his new tasks.

[158] Woolger, *Other Lives, Other Selves,* p. 7.

[159] Woolger, *Other Lives, Other Selves,* p. 9.

[160] Woolger, *Other Lives, Other Selves,* p. 9.

[161] Woolger, *Other Lives, Other Selves,* p. 15.

[162] Woolger, *Other Lives, Other Selves,* p. 29.

[163] Woolger, *Other Lives, Other Selves,* pp. 39-40.

[164] Woolger, *Other Lives, Other Selves,* pp. 28-29.

[165] Woolger, *Other Lives, Other Selves,* p. 7.

[166] Hans TenDam, *Deep Healing: A Practical Outline of Past-Life Therapy* (Amsterdam: Tasso Publishing, 1996), p. 15.

167 TenDam, *Deep Healing*, p. 15.

168 TenDam, *Deep Healing*.

169 TenDam, *Deep Healing*.

170 Michael Newton, *Life Between Lives: Hypnotherapy for Spiritual Regression* (Woodbury, MN: Llwellyn Publications, 1996).

171 TenDam, *Deep Healing*, p. 17.

172 TenDam, *Deep Healing*, p. 18.

173 TenDam, *Deep Healing*.

174 Faith Waude and Adam Waude, (n.d.). Frequently Asked Questions about Hypnosis (Retrieved December 15, 2009, from www.hypnoticworld.com).

175 Irene Hickman, *Spirit Depossession* (Kirksville, Missouri: Hickman Systems, 1994).

176 Occasionally, a client will recognize himself at a younger age. This might indicate an event that has happened at the earlier time and kept a part of him at that age. Two things can be done: (1) Go to that time and process that event and bring the client to the current age, or (2) ask the younger person in the mirror to assist with the current problem or situation, and continue. Prior experience with psychological theories and training helps at this point.

177 Neale Donald Walsch, *Conversations with God, an Uncommon Dialogue* (London: Hodder & Stoughton, 1997); Helen Schucman, *A Course in Miracles* (New York: Foundation for Inner Peace, 1980).

178 James, *Time Line Therapy*.

179 Bernstein, *The Search for Bridey Murphy*.

**Chapter Six**

180 Keith Williams, (Retrieved April 16, 2010, from http://www.Near-death.com/experiences/paranormal04.html).

181 Raymond Moody, *Life after Life: The Investigaqtion of a Phenomenon—Survival of Bodily Death* (New York: MMB. Inc., 1975).

182 W. Y. Evans-Wentz, trans. *The Tibetan Book of the Dead* (New York: Oxford Unversity Press, 1960).

183 Williams, http://www.near-death.com/experiences/paranormal04.html.

184 Ruth Montgomery, *A World Beyond* (Greenwich, Connecticut: Fawcett Publications, 1971), p. 27.

185 Montgomery, *A World Beyond*, p. 62.

186 Montgomery, *A World Beyond*.

187 Montgomery, *A World Beyond*, p. 65.

188 Newton, *Life Between Lives*.

189 Newton, *Life Between Lives*, p. 53.

190 Newton, *Life Between Lives*, pp. 46-47.

191 Newton, *Life Between Lives*, p. 57.

192 Newton, *Life Between Lives*, p. 68.

193 Newton, *Life Between Lives*, p. 72.

194 Newton, *Life Between Lives*, p. 71.

195 Newton, *Life Between Lives*.

196 David Moore, Three in Four Americans Believe in Paranormal. http:// homesandiego.edu/~babe/logic/gallop-html).

197 Carol Bowman, *Return from Heaven: Beloved Relatives Reincarnated Within Your Family* (New York: Harper Torch, 2003).

198 TenDam, *Deep Healing*, p. 19.

199 Edgar Cayce, *The Official Edgar Cayce Readings* on DVD (Association for Research and Enlightenment, Virginia Beach, 2010). (826-8, 2000-3, 2879-1, 4035-1, 3161-1).

**Chapter Seven**

200 Sean Carroll, *From Eternity to Here* (New York: Penguin Group, 2010), p. 1.

201 St. Augustine, *The Confessions*, quoted in Carroll, *From Eternity to Here*, p. 9.

202 Buddhists have various divisions called schools. Christians have various divisions called sects.

203 Carroll, *From Eternity to Here*.

204 Michio Kaku, *Physics of the Impossible* (London: Penguin Books, 2008).

205 Stephen Hawking, *A Briefer History of Time* (New York: Random Dell, 2005), p. 20.

206 Hawking, *A Briefer History of Time*, 2008, p. 23.

207 Hawking, *A Briefer History of Time*, 2008, p. 23.

208 Hawking, *A Briefer History of Time*, 2008, p. 25.

209 Gary Zukav, *The Dancing Wu Li Masters: An Overview of the New Physics* (New York: Bantam Book, 1984).

210  Barbour, *The End of Time.*
211  Barbour, *The End of Time.*
212  Barbour, *The End of Time.*
213  Hawking, *A Briefer History of Time,* 2008, p. 28.
214  Hawking, *A Briefer History of Time,* 2008, p. 32.
215  Hawking, *A Briefer History of Time,* 2008.
216  Kaku, *Physics of the Impossible,* p. 223.
217  Brian Greene, *The Elegant Universe* (New York: Vintage Books, 2000), p. 49.
218  Brian Greene, *The Fabric of the Cosmos* (New York: Vintage Books, 2004), p. 139.
219  Hendrik Antoon Lorentz, *The Principle of Relativity: A Collection of Original Memoirs on the Special and General Theory of Relativity* (New York: Dover, 1952).
220  Hawking, *A Briefer History of Time,* 2008, p. 90.
221  Hawking, *A Briefer History of Time,* 2008, p. 103.
222  Zukav, *The Dancing Wu Li Masters.*
223  Barbour, *The End of Time.*

**Chapter Eight**
224  Kaku, *Physics of the Impossible,* p. 56.
225  Kaku, *Physics of the Impossible,* p. 187.
226  Folger, *How Can You Be in Two Places at Once,* p. 58.
227  Folger, *How Can You Be in Two Places at Once,* p. 58.
228  Charles Krauthammer, Gone in 60 Nanoseconds, *The Washington Post,* October 6, 2011.
229  Zukav, *The Dancing Wu Li Masters,* p. 86.
230  Roger Penrose, *The Emperor's New Mind* (Oxford:Oxford University Press,1989).
231  Max Born and Albert Einstein, *The Born-Einstein Letters.* (New York: Walker and Company, 1971), p. 9.
232  Zukav, *The Dancing Wu Li Masters.*
233  Greene, *The Elegant Universe,* 2003, p. 129.
234  Zukav, *The Dancing Wu Li Masters.*
235  Hawking, *A Briefer History of Time,* 2007.
236  Kaku, *Physics of the Impossible,* p. 241.

[237] Greene, *The Elegant Universe*, 2003.

[238] Greene, *The Elegant Universe*, 2000, p. 6.

[239] Hawking, *A Briefer History of Time*, 2008, p. 125.

[240] Hawking, *A Briefer History of Time*, 2008, p. 126.

[241] Hawking, *A Briefer History of Time*, 2008.

[242] Greene, *The Elegant Universe*, 2000, p. 135.

[243] Greene, *The Elegant Universe*, 2000, pp. 135-136.

[244] Greene, *The Elegant Universe*, 2000, p. 130.

[245] Greene, *The Elegant Universe*, 2000, p. 387.

[246] Greene, *The Elegant Universe*, 2000, p. 387.

[247] Kaku, *Physics of the Impossible*.

[248] Pais, *Subtle Is the Lord*, p. 332.

[249] Kaku, *Physics of the Impossible*.

[250] Kaku, *Physics of the Impossible*.

[251] Kaku, *Physics of the Impossible*.

[252] Kaku, *Physics of the Impossible*, p. 138.

[253] Kaku, *Physics of the Impossible*, p. 148.

[254] Kaku, *Physics of the Impossible*.

[255] Hawking, *A Briefer History of Time*, p. 128.

[256] Hawking, *A Briefer History of Time*, 2008.

[257] Greene, *The Elegant Universe*, 2000, p. 139.

[258] Greene, *The Elegant Universe*, 2000.

[259] Greene, *The Elegant Universe*, 2000, p. 379.

[260] Kaku, *Physics of the Impossible*, p. 239.

[261] This ambiguity is not often found in mathematical or scientific writings. None of the physics books I read provided a definition, although some noted that the term has never been officially defined. Does that mean science and mathematics are not as precise as we think they are?

[262] Greene, *The Fabric of the Cosmos*, p. 385.

[263] Greene, *The Fabric of the Cosmos*, p. 386.

[264] Greene, *The Fabric of the Cosmos*, p. 388.

[265] Hawking, *A Briefer History of Time*, p. 130.

[266] Hawking, *A Briefer History of Time*, p. 130.

[267] Everett III, Relative State Formulation of Quantum Mechanics.

[268] Barbour, *The End of Time*, p. 224.

269  Barbour, *The End of Time.*
270  Barbour, *The End of Time.*
271  Barbour, *The End of Time*, p. 299.
272  Barbour, *The End of Time.*
273  Barbour, *The End of Time.*
274  Barbour, *The End of Time*, p. 300.
275  Kaku, *Physics of the Impossible*, p. 244.
276  Kaku, *Physics of the Impossible*, p. 244.
277  Barbour, *The End of Time*, p. 25.
278  Barbour, *The End of Time.*
279  Kaku, *Physics of the Impossible.*
280  Barbour, *The End of Time*, p. 2.
281  Barbour, *The End of Time*, p. 2.
282  Barbour, *The End of Time*, p. 16.
283  Barbour, *The End of Time.*
284  Barbour, *The End of Time*, p. 18-19.
285  Barbour, *The End of Time*, p. 34.
286  Barbour, *The End of Time*, p. 50.
287  Barbour, *The End of Time*, p. 49.
288  Barbour, *The End of Time*, p. 50.
289  Walsch, *Conversations With God*, pp. 28-29.
290  Adam Frank, The Discover Interview, Max Tegmark *Discover Magazine*, June 2008, pp. 38-43.
291  Witt, *Our Undiscovered Universe: Introducing Null Physics* (Melbourne: Aridian Publishing Corporation, 2007), p. 37.
292  Witt, *Our Undiscovered Universe*, p. 37.
293  Witt, *Our Undiscovered Universe*, p. 73.
294  Witt, *Our Undiscovered Universe.*
295  Witt, *Our Undiscovered Universe*, p. 80.
296  Witt, *Our Undiscovered Universe*, p. 83.
297  Witt, *Our Undiscovered Universe*, p. 84.
298  Witt, *Our Undiscovered Universe*, p. 84.
299  Witt, *Our Undiscovered Universe*, p. 86.
300  Witt, *Our Undiscovered Universe.*
301  Witt, *Our Undiscovered Universe*, p. 87.
302  Witt, *Our Undiscovered Universe*, p. 91.

303 Witt, *Our Undiscovered Universe*, p. 90.

304 Michel Serres, *Conversations on Science, Culture and Time*, p. 65.

305 Roger Penrose, *The Road to Reality: A Complete Guide to the Laws of the Universe* (New York: Vantage Books, 2004), p. 409.

306 Penrose, *The Road to Reality*, p. 409.

307 Donald Reed, Torsion Field Research, p. 22.

308 Steven Cullidane, (n.d.) Folded Time. http://www.finitegeometry.org/sc/dth/diamondtheory.html.

309 Sean Carroll, New Rules for Time Travel, p. 76.

310 Carroll, New Rules for Time Travel, p. 76.

311 Greene, *The Elegant Universe*, p. 6.

312 Kaku, *Physics of the Impossible*, p. 233.

313 Greene, *The Elegant Universe*.

314 Barbour, *The End of Time*.

315 Barbour, *The End of Time*, p. 2.

316 Barbour, *The End of Time*, p. 16.

317 Barbour, *The End of Time*.

318 Barbour, *The End of Time*, p. 50.

319 Although I was in attendance, I did not keep detailed notes on the statistical significance of the findings. I do remember that the significance was greater than chance, but not by much. It was enough to warrant further research, however.

## Chapter Nine

320 Barbour, *The End of Time*, p. 16.

321 Barbour, *The End of Time*.

322 Lorentz, *The Principle of Relativity*.

323 McDougall, *An Experiment for the Testing of the Hypothesis of Lamarck*.

324 Freud, *An Autobiographical Study*.

325 Lipton, *Biology of Belief*, 2008.

326 Pomar, *Past Life Therapy*.

327 Kaku, *Physics of the Impossible*.

328 Hawking, *A Briefer History of Time*.

329 Greene, *The Elegant Universe*, 2000, p. 136.

330 Greene, *The Elegant Universe*, 2000, p. 6.

331 Greene, *The Elegant Universe*, 2000, p. 6.

332 Greene, *The Elegant Universe*, 2000, p. 6.

333 Everett III, Relative State Formulation of Quantum Mechanics.

334 Barbour, *The End of Time*.

335 Barbour, *The End of Time*.

336 Loftus, *The Reality of Repressed Memories*; Loftus, *The Repressed Memory Controversy*; Loftus, *The Myth of Repressed Memory*.

337 20 Barbour, *The End of Time*, p. 2.

338 Barbour, *The End of Time*.

339 Barbour, *The End of Time*.

340 Barbour, *The End of Time*, p. 50.

341 Loftus, *The Myth of Repressed Memory*.

342 Barbour, *The End of Time*, p. 50.

343 Barbour, *The End of Time*, p. 50.

344 Frank, The Discover Interview, Max Tegmark, pp. 38-43.

345 R. Kuhn, (n.d.) What is Space-Time? (Max Tegmark). http://www.closetotruth.com-/videoprofiles/whatisspace-time-max-tegmark.

346 Witt, *Our Undiscovered Universe*. p. 37.

347 Witt, *Our Undiscovered Universe*, p. 73.

348 Witt, *Our Undiscovered Universe*, p. 80.

349 Witt, *Our Undiscovered Universe*, p. 83.

350 Witt, *Our Undiscovered Universe*, p. 86.

351 *Time capsule* is the way Barbour refers to complex Nows or what Franz Perls called *gestalt*. It is a conglomeration of all the sense perceptions, thoughts, and emotions in a specific instant or Now.

352 Lipton, *Biology of Belief*, 2008.

353 Newton, *Life Between Lives*.

## Chapter Ten

354 Witt, *Our Undiscovered Universe*.

355 Carroll, *From Eternity to Here*.

356 Carroll, *From Eternity to Here*, p. 350.

357 Zeeya Merali, Back From the Future. *Discover Magazine* Apr 2010.

358 Conscious-Unconscious Split: These words are capitalized to indicate that this term refers to part of the First Cause, which some call God/Goddess, for example. We know that it is possible for some to control heart rate, stop or reduce blood flow in the event of an operation or

accident, or control other things that are under the direction of the autonomic nervous system. There also is the possibility that this type of control was a natural part of our original being, maybe even before the original separation.

359   Pomar, *Past Life Therapy.*

360   Pomar, *Past Life Therapy.*

361   Jose Silva, *The Silva Mind Control Method* (New York: Simon & Schuster, 1977).

362   Paramahansa Yogananda, *Autobiography of a Yogi* (Los Angeles: Self-Realization Fellowship, 1988).

363   Norman Vincent Peale, *The Power of Positive Thinking* (New York: Prentice Hall, 1952).

364   Stern, *The Sleeping Prophet.*

365   Sigmund Freud, *Dream Psychology for Beginners*, trans. by M.D. Elder (New York: The James A. McCann Company, 1920), Kindle Edition location 33-36.

366   Freud, *Dream Psychology for Beginners*, location 30-36.

367   Jung, *Memories, Dreams, and Reflections*, p. 161.

368   Lipton, *Biology of Belief*, 2008.

369   These words are quoted directly from Pam's session. The current word in use could be *rape.*

370   The speed of light experiment: In the spring of 2011, there was in experiment in Switzerland that used the super collider to send a neutrino from one end of the collider to the other. It arrived much faster than expected—six nanoseconds faster than the speed of light. Subsequent articles noted that the mathematics had been checked and rechecked, but there could be a fault in the experiment design. From Krauthammer, Gone in 60 Nanoseconds. On November 18, 2011 Jason Palmer, a science and technology reporter for the BBC news wrote about repeated experiments that reached the same conclusions.

371   Everett III, Relative State Formulation of Quantum Mechanics.

372   Richard Bach, *One* (New York: Dell Publishing, 1989).

373   Merali, Back From the Future, p. 2.

374   Merali, Back From the Future, p. 2.

375   Stephen Hawking and Leonard Mlodinow, The (Elusive) Theory of Everything, p. 70.

376 Francis Pharcellus, Yes, Virginia, There Is a Santa Claus.

377 Barbour, *The End of Time*, p. 50.

## Chapter Eleven

378 In most meditation techniques, the key is to keep the mind focused on one thought or idea. This means ignoring all other thoughts. During insight meditation, however, you watch the thoughts as they arise. Then you follow each thought to its origin or end. The psychological benefit is that you can see how meaningless the troublesome thought really is. The meditative or spiritual benefit is that your logical mind becomes silent and thought-less. Once the logical mind becomes quiet, the higher mind can connect and receive insights from the unconscious and nonphysical (spiritual) realms. In my understanding, the unconscious has constant contact with the nonphysical. Find more information on insight meditation at: www.budsas.org/ebud/emed012.htm.

# Bibliography

Agar, W., F. Drummond, O. Tiegs, and M. Gunson. 1954. Fourth (Final) Report on a Test of McDougall's Lamarckian Experiment on the Training of Rats. *Journal of Experimental Biology* Vol. 31: 307-321.

Bach, Richard. *One.* New York: Dell publishing, 1989.

Baldwin, William. *Regression Therapy, Spirit Releasement Therapy: Technique Manual* (2nd Edition). Terra Alta, WV: Headline Books, 1992.

Barbour, Julian. *The End of Time: The Next Revolution in Physics.* New York: Oxford University Press, 1999.

Bass, Ellen, and Laura Davis. *The Courage to Heal: Women Healing from Sexual Abuse.* New York: Harper & Row, 1988.

Beck, A., A. Rush, B. Shaw, and G. Emery. *Cognitive Therapy of Depression.* New York: Gilford Press, 1983.

Bernstein, Michael. *The Search for Bridey Murphy* (Revised Edition). New York: Pocket Books, 1965.

Biaggio, Mary. 1987. A Survey of Psychologists' Perspectives on Cartharsis. *The Journal of Psychology* 121(3): 243-248.

Bolduc, Henry. (n.d.) *Adventures into Time.* Retrieved from www.henrybolduc.com (no longer available).

Born, Max, and Albert Einstein. *The Born-Einstein Letters.* New York: Walker and Company, 1971.

Bowman, Carol. *Return from Heaven: Beloved Relatives Reincarnated Within Your Family.* New York: HarperTorch, 2003.

Braid, James. October 5, 1844, to March 29, 1845. Magic, Mesmerism, Hypnotism, Etc., Historically and Physiologically Considered. *Medical Times* Vol. 11: 203-304, 224-227, 296-299, 399-400, 439-441. Retrieved from http://wehypnosis.com/19/magic-mesmerism-hypnotism-historically-considered-james-braid.

———. Mr. Braid on Hypnotism. May 1845. *The Lancet* Vol. 45, no. 1135: 627-628.

Brennan, B. *William James.* New York: Twayne, 1968.

Brunton, Paul. *A Hermit in the Himalayas.* New York: E. P. Dutton and Company, 2004. Available from www.archive.org/details/AHermitintheHimalayas.

Bryan, W. J. 1974. Age Regression Before Birth. *Journal of American Institute of Hypnosis* Vol. 15(2): 35-37.

Bryd, K. R. 1994. The Narrative Reconstrutions of Incest Survivors. *American Psychologist* Vol. 49(5): 439-440.

Carroll, Sean. *From Eternity to Here.* New York: Penguin Group, 2010.

———. 2010. The New Rules of Time-Travel. *Discover Magazine* March: 43, 76.

Cayce, Edgar. *The Official Edgar Cayce Readings DVD*, Association for Research and Enlightenment, Virginia Beach, 2010.

Crabtree, Adam. Multiple Personalities Before Eve. Retrieved July 3, 2011 from www.joannecrabtree.com/psychotherapyarts/ multiplepersonalitiesbeforeeve.

Crew, F. 1936. A Repetition of McDougall's Lamarckian Experiment. *Journal of Genetics* Vol. 33: 16-101.

Cullidane, Steven. (n.d.) Folded Time. Retrieved on April 18, 2010, from http://www.finitegeometry.org/sc/dth/diamondtheory.html.

Cunningham, Janet. *A Tribe Returned.* Crest Park, CA: Deep Forest Press, 1994.

Ellenberger, Henri. *The Discovery of the Unconscious: The History and Evolution of Dynamic Psychiatry.* New York: Basic Books, 1970.

Evans-Wentz, W. Y. translator. *The Tibetan Book of the Dead.* New York: Oxford Unversity Press, 1960.

Everett III, Hugh. 1957. Relative State Formulation of Quantum Mechanics. *Reviews of Modern Physics* Vol. 29(3): 452-462. Retrieved June 4, 2011, from www.prola.aps.org.

Fiore, Edith. *The Unquiet Dead.* New York: Doubleday, 1987.

———. *You Have Been Here Before.* New York: Putnam Publishing Group, 1978.

Folger, Tim. 2010. How Can You be in Two Places at Once? Discover Presents Extreme Universe. *Discover Magazine* Winter: 57-61.

Frank, A. 2008. The Discover Interview, Max Tegmark. *Discover Magazine.* June: 38-43.

Freud, Sigmund. *The History of the Psychoanalytic Movement and Other Papers.* New York: Collier Books, 1963.

————. *An Autobiographical Study: Inhibitions, Symptoms and Anxiety, Lay Analysis and Other Works 1925-1926,* SE. Vol. XX, translated by J. Strachey. London: The Hogarth Press, 1959.

————. *The Basic Writings of Sigmund Freud,* translated by A. A. Brill. New York: Random House, 1955.

————. *Dream Psychology for Beginners,* translated by M. D. Elder. New York: The James A. McCann Company, Kindle Edition, 1920.

Freud, Sigmund, and Josef Breuer. *The Complete Psychological Works of Sigmund Freud,* Vol. II, *Studies on Hysteria,* translated by J. Strachey. London: The Harth Press, Limited, 1955.

Gauld, Alan. *A History of Hypnotism.* Cambridge: Cambridge University Press, 1992.

Goldberg, Bruce. *Past Lives, Future Lives.* New York: Ballantine Books, 1988.

Grant, Kim. The History of Hypnosis. Retrieved July 5, 2011 from www.kimgranthypnotist.com/historyofhypnosis.

Green, J. P., A. F. Barabasz, D. Barrett, and G. H. Montgomery. 2005. Forging Ahead: The 2003 APA Division 30 Definition of Hypnosis. *International Journal of Clinical and Experimental Hypnosis, 53*: 259-264.

Greene, Brian. *The Elegant Universe.* New York: Vintage Books, 2000.

————. *The Elegant Universe.* New York: Norton & Company, 2003.

————. *The Fabric of the Cosmos.* New York: Vintage Books, 2004.

Grof, Stanislav. Brief History of Transpersonal Psychology. Retrieved 14 March, 2010, from www.stainislavgrof.com/articles.

Van der Hart, Onno. 1987. The Hypnotherapy of Dr. Andries Hoek: Uncovering Hypnotherapy Before Janet, Breuer, and Freud. *American Journal of Clinical Hypnosis*, 29(4) April: 264-71.

Haule, John. 1986. Pierre Janet and Dissociation: The First Transference Theory and Its Origins in Hypnosis. *American Journal of Clinical Hypnosis* 29(2) October: pp. 86-94.

Havens, Ronald, and Catherine Walters. *Hypnotherapy Scripts: A Neo-Ericksonian Approach to Persuasive Healing.* New York: Brunner/Mazel Publishers, 2002.

Hawking, Stephen. *A Briefer History of Time.* New York: Random Dell, 2005.

Hawking, Stephen and Leonard Mlodinow. 2010. The (Elusive) Theory of Everything. *Scientific American.* October Vol. 303(4): 69-71.

Helmont, F. translated by Rob Kettlmel. *Two Hundred Queries Moderately Propounded Concerning the Doctrine of the Revolution of Human Souls and Its Comformity to the Truths of Christianity.* London: University Microfilms International, 1684.

Hepper, P. G. 1996. Fetal Memory: Does it Exist? What Does it Do? *Acta Paediatr Supplement* 416:16-20. Retrieved from http://www.cirp.org/library/psych/hepper1.

Hickman, Irene. *Spirit Depossession.* Kirksville, MO: Hickman Systems, 1994.

Hill, Napoleon. *Think and Grow Rich.* New York: Random House, 1937.

*Holy Bible,* Revised Standard Version. New York: Thomas Nelson and Sons, 1952.

Holt, Michael. James Braid. Retrieved April 18, 2009, from www. docmagi.com/hypnosis/james-braid.

———. Marquis Chastenet de Puysegur. Retrieved July 3, 2011 from www.docmagi.com/hypnosis/marquis-chastenet-de-puysegur-1751-1825/.

Holmes, Richard. Reincarnation FAQ. Retrieved August 21, 2011 from http://webspace.webring.om/people/mr/richard_holmes/reincarnation/faq.htm#a

Hubbard, L. Ron. *Dianetics: The Modern Science of Mental Health.* Los Angeles, CA: Bridge Publications, 2007.

Hull, W. P. 1986. Psychological reatment of Birth Trauma with Age Regression and its Relationship to Chemical Dependency. *Pre-and Perinatal Psychology* 1(2): 111-134.

Jackson, S. W. 1994. Catharsis and a Reaction in the History of Psychological Healing. *Psychiatric Clinics of North America,* 17(3): 471-491.

James, Tad, and W. Woodsmall. *Time Line Therapy and the Basics of Personality.* Capitola, CA: Meta Publications, 1988.

James, William. *The Will to Believe and Human Mortality.* New York: Dover, 1956.

Jones, Ernest. *The Life and Work of Sigmund Freud.* New York: Basic Books, 1953.

Jones, Nicola. 2001. Babies' Musical Memories Formed in Womb. *New Scientist.* July 11. Retrieved from www.newscientist.com/article/dn994-babbies-musical-memories-formed-in-womb.hmtl.

Jung, Carl. *Memories, Dreams, and Reflections,* translated by R. and C. Winston. New York: Vintage Books, 1989.

Kaku, Michio. *Physics of the Impossible.* London: Penguin Books, 2008.

Keith, G. *Truth and Innocency Defended Against Calumny and Defamation in a Late Report Spread Abroad Concerning the Revolution of Humane Souls.* 1692. Philadelphia: William Bradford on University Microfilm International.

Kelsey, Denys, and J. Grant. *Many Lifetimes.* Alpharetta, GA: Ariel Press, 1967.

Kihlstrom, John. 1994. Hypnosis, Delayed Recall, and the Principles of Memory. *The International Journal of Clinical and Experimental Hypnosis,* Vol. 42(4): 337-345.

Krauthammer, Charles. Gone in 60 Nanoseconds. *The Washington Post,* October 6, 2011. www.washingtonpost.com/opinions/ gone-in-60-nanoseconds/2011/10/01/gIQAfIRE

Kroger, William, and M.Yapko. *Clinical and Experimental Hypnosis in Medicine, Dentistry, and Psychology* Edition 2. Philadelphia: Lippincott Williams & Wilkins, 1997.

Kuhn, R. (n.d.) What is Space-Time? (Max Tegmark). September 25, 2010, from http://www.closetotruth.com/videoprofiles/ whatisspace-time-max-tegmark.

Lama, Dalai. *The Universe in a Single Atom.* New York: Morgan Books (Random House), 2005.

Lieberman, E. James. (n.d.) Biography. November 14, 2010, from http://www.ottorank.com.

Lipton, Bruce. *Biology of Belief.* Carlsbad, CA: Hay House, 2007.

———. *Biology of Belief.* Carlsbad, CA: Hay House, 2008.

Loftus, Elizabeth. 1993. The Reality of Repressed Memories. *American Psychologist* Vol. 48: 518-517.

Loftus, Elizabeth and K. Ketcham. *The Myth of Repressed Memory.* New York: St. Martin's Press, 1994.

Lorentz, Hendrik Antoon. *The Principle of Relativity: A Collection of Original Memoirs on the Special and General Theory of Relativity.* New York: Dover, 1952.

Lucas, Winafred. *Regression Therapy: A Handbook for Professionals.* Crest Park, CA: Deep Forest Press, 1993.

McCloskey, Fr. Pat. Confession Helps in Many Ways, *St. Anthony Messenger.* March 2000. Retrieved from: http://www.americancatholic.org/messenger/mar2000/wiseman.asp

McDougall, William. 1927. An Experiment for the Testing of the Hypothesis of Lamarck. *British Journal of Psychology* Vol. 17: 267-304.

———. 1938. Fourth Report on a Lamarckian Experiment. *British Journal of Psychology* Vol. 28: 321-345.

———. *The Group Mind* (2nd Edition). Salem, NH: Ayer Publications, 1972.

McGill, Ormond. *The Many Lives of Alan Lee.* Available from National Guild of Hypnotists, Box 308, Merrimack, NH 03054, 1988.

McGowan, K. Out of the Past. *Discover Magazine for Science, Technology and the Future.* July/August 2009.

McIntosh, Alastair. *Psychoenergetic Systems* Vol. 3. United Kingdom: Gorden and Breach Science Publishers, 1979. Retrieved August 14, 2009, from http://www.alastairmcintosh.com.

McKeown, Joanne. Visions as Illness and Inspiration: Young Estelle. Retrieved July 3, 2011 from www.nacfla.net/UP_JournalFiles/ JCFL%202006%2029-43%20McKeown.pdf.

Meek, George. *A Guide to Spiritual & Magnetic Healing & Psychic Surgery in the Philippines.* Manila, Philippines: Christian Travel Service, 1998.

Merali, Zeeya. Back from the Future. *Discover Magazine.* Retrieved from http://discovermagazine.com/2010/apr/01-back-from-the-future; published online August 26, 2010.

Mills, A., E. Haraldsson, and H. Keil. 1994. Replication Studies of Cases Suggestive of Reincarnation by Three Independent Investigators. *The Journal of the American Society for Psychical Research,* Vol. 8: 207-219.

Mishkind, Marc. 1993. Test for Morphic Resonance in Behavioral Responses to Multiple Choice Stimuli. *Journal of Analytical Psychology* Vol. 38: 257-271.

Moody, Raymond. *Coming Back.* New York: Bantam Books, 1991.

———. *Life after Life: The Investigation of a Phenomenon—Survival of Bodily Death.* New York: MMB. Inc., 1975. It was republished in 2001 as *Life After Life: The Investigation of a Phenomenon—Survival of Bodily Death,* by Raymond Moody and Elisabeth Kubler-Ross.

Moore, C. (n.d.) Dr. Helen Wambach and Reincarnation. Retrieved August 8, 2009, from http://www.carolmoore.net/articles/helenwambach.

Moore, David, Three in Four Americans Believe in Paranormal. Retrieved August 21, 2011 from http://homesandiego.edu/~babe/logic/gallop-html.

Moore, Marcia. *Hypersentience: Exploring Your Past Lifetime.* New York: Crown Publishers, 1976.

Montgomery, Ruth. *A World Beyond.* Greenwich, CT: Fawcett Publications, 1971.

Nash, K. 1987. What, if Anything, is Regressed About Hypnotic Age Regression? A Review of the Empirical Literature. *Psychological Bulletin* 102(1): 42-52.

Nelson, K. 1993. The Psychological and Social Origins of Autobiographical Memory. *Psychological Science,* Vol. 4: 7-14.

Netherton, Morris, and Nancy Shiffrin. *Past Lives Therapy.* New York: Wm. Morrow & Co., 1978.

Newton, Michael. *Life Between Lives: Hypnotherapy for Spiritual Regression.* Woodbury, MN: Llwellyn Publications, 1996.

Nobel Peace Prize, retrieved from www.nobelprize.org/nobel_prizes/physics/laureates.

Pais, A. *Subtle is the Lord.* New York: Oxford University Press, 1982.

Palmer, Jason Neutrino Experiment Repeat at Cern Finds Same Result. BBC News. 18 November 2011, http://www.bbc.co.uk/go/em/fr/-/news/science-environment-15791236.

Parkin, Alan. *Memory and Amnesia.* Cambridge: Basil Blackwell, 1987.

Peale, Norman Vincent. *The Power of Positive Thinking.* New York: Prentice Hall, 1952.

Penrose, Roger. *Emperor's New Mind.* Oxford: Oxford University Press, 1990.

———. *The Road to Reality: A Complete Guide to the Laws of the Universe.* New York: Vantage Books, 2004.

Perls, Fritz. *The Gestalt Approach and Eye Witness to Therapy.* USA: Science and Behavior Books, 1973.

Pharcellus, Francis. 1897. Yes, Virginia There Is a Santa Claus. *The Sun Newspaper.* (September 21, 1897). Retrieved from http;// wwwnewseum.org/yesvirginia.

Pius XII, Pope. 1957. Allocution to Doctors on the Moral Problems of Analgesia, as presented to the Catholic Association of Doctors, Nurses and Health Professionals in Asia. http://*www.acim-asia. com/documents/allocutiontodoctorsonthemoralproblemsofanalgesia.*

Pomar, Barbara. *Past Life Therapy: Origins and Sources.* Master's thesis. University of Salisbury, Maryland, 2005.

Reed, Donald. 1998. Torsion Field Research. *New Energy News* Vol. 6 (1) May, 22-4. Online version at www.padrak.com/ine/ nen_6_1_.

Rieder, Marge. *Mission to Millboro.* Nevada City, CA: Blue Dolphin Press, 1993.

Rine, J., and William McDougall. 1933. Third Report on a Lamarckian Experiment. *British Journal of Psychology* Vol. 24: 213-235.

De Rochas, Alberto. *Les Vies Successives.* Paris: Chacornac, 1911, reprinted 1924.

Rosen, D. 1991. Empirical Study of Associations Between Symbols and Their Meaning: Evidence of Collective Unconscious (Archetypal) Memory. *Journal of Analytical Psychology* Vol. 36(2): 2122-2228.

Schucman, Helen. *Course in Miracles.* New York: Foundation for Inner Peace, 1980.

Serres, Michel, and Bruno Latour. *Conversations on Science, Culture and Time,* translated by Roxanne Lapidus. Ann Arbor: The University of Michigan Press, 1995.

Sheldrake, Rupert. *A New Science of Life: The Hypothesis of Formative Causation.* Los Angeles: Tharcher, 1981.

Silva, Jose. *The Silva Mind Control Method.* New York: Simon & Schuster, 1977.

Smith, David L. *Approaching Psychoanalysis.* London: Karma Books, 1999.

Snow, Chet. *Mass Dreams of the Future.* New York: McGraw Hill, 1992.

Spanos, Nicholas, E. Menary, J. Gabora, S. Dubreuil, and B. Dewhirst. 1991. Secondary Identity Enactments During Hypnotic Past-Life Regression: A Sociocognitive Perspective. *Journal of Personality and Social Psychology* Vol. 61(2): 308-320.

Stafford-Clark, David. *What Freud Really Said.* New York: Random House, 1965.

Steiner, Rudolf. *Knowledge of the Higher Worlds and its Attainment.* First published in 1909. books.google.com/books?isbn=1855842556.

Stern, Jess. *The Sleeping Prophet.* New York: Random House, 1967.

Stevenson, Ian. *Cases of the Reincarnation Type,* Vol. 4: *Twelve cases in Thailand and Burma.* Charlottesville, VA: University Press of Virginia, 1985.

———. *Cases of the Reincarnation Type,* Vol. 2: *Ten Cases in Sri Lanka.* Charlottesville, VA: University Press of Virginia, 1978.

———. 1977. The Explanatory Value of the Idea of Reincarnation. *Journal of Nervous and Mental Disease* Vol. 164(5): 304-326.

———. *Twenty Cases Suggestive of Reincarnation.* Charlottesville: University Press of Virginia, 1974.

———. 1966. Twenty Cases Suggestive of Reincarnation. *Proceedings of the American Society for Psychical Research* Vol. 25.

Stiffler, LaVonne. 1993. Adoptees and Birth Parents Connected by Design: Surprising Synchronicities in Histories of Union/Loss/Reunion. *Pre- and Perinatal Psychology* Vol. 7(4): 267-286.

TenDam, Hans. *Exploring Reincarnation: The Classic Guide to the Evidence for Past Life Experiences.* London: Rider, division of Random House Publishing, 2003.

———. *Deep Healing, A Practical Outline of Past-Life Therapy.* Amsterdam: Tasso Publishing, 1996.

Tinterow, Maurice. *Foundations of Hypnosis.* London: Charles C. Thomas Publishers, 1970.

Usher, J., and U. Neisser. 1993. Childhood Amnesia and the Beginnings of Memory for Four Early Life Events. *Journal of Experimental Psychology: General* Vol. 122: 155-165.

Vas, L. The Amazing Abbe Faria. Goanet-News, December 17, 2005. http://www.mail-archhive.com/goanet-news@goanet. org/msg00089.html.

Valente, Frank. History of Hypnosis. www.hypnoticadvancements. com.history.htm.

Walsch, Neale Donald. *Conversations with God, an Uncommon Dialogue.* London: Hodder & Stoughton, 1997.

Wambach, Helen, and L. Lee. 1978. *The Wambach Method and Manual for Past Life Recall.* Available from IART, PO Box 20151, Riverside, CA 92516.

Warrier, A. G. 2002. *108 Upanishads, Bhavana Upanishad.* Retrieved from Vedanta Spiritual Library. www.celexel.org/108upanishads/ ramarahasya.html.

Waterland, Robert, and Randy Jirtle. 2003. Transposable Elements: Targets for Early Nutritional Effects on Epigenetic Gene Regulation. *Molecular and Cellular Biology* Vol. 23 (15): 5293-5300.

Waude, Faith, and Adam Waude. (n.d.) Frequestly Asked Questions About Hypnosis. Retrieved December 15, 2009, from www. hypnoticworld.com.

Weiss, Brian. L. *Many Lives, Many Masters: The True Story of a Prominent Psychiatrist, His Young Patient, and the Past-Life Therapy that Changed Both Their Lives.* New York: Simon & Schuster, 1988.

———. *Through Time into Healing.* New York: Simon & Schuster, 1992.

Williams, Keith. 2010. Retrieved April 16, 2010, from http://www. Near-death.com.

Witt, Terence. *Our Undiscovered Universe: Introducing Null Physics.* Melbourne: Aridian Publishing Corporation, 2007.

Woolger, Roger. *Other Lives, Other Selves.* New York: Bantam Books/ Doubleday, 1987.

————. 1986. Imaginal Techniques in Past-Life Therapy. *Journal of Regression Therapy* Vol. I(1).

Yogananda, Paramahansa. *Autobiography of a Yogi.* Los Angeles: Self-Realization Fellowship, 1988.

Zukav, Gary. *The Dancing Wu Li Masters: An Overview of the New Physics.* New York: Bantam Books, 1984.

**ORGANIZATIONS:** This is not a comprehensive list of all the regression organizations.

Brazil

ABTR: Brazilian Association of Regression Therapy, www. abtrterapiaregresiva.blogspot.com * www.abtrbrasil.org * president, as of 2011, Idalino Almeida

India

ARRR: Association for Regression and Reincarnation Research, www.global.org * www.lifeuniversityglobal.org

Europe

EARTh: European Association of Regression Therapists, www.

*Barbara H. Pomar*

United States

IARRT: International Association of Regression and Research
Therapies, www.iarrt.org.

IBRT: International Board of Regression Therapists, www.ibrt.org.

# Index

# About the Author

Having been raised a Roman Catholic, Dr. Pomar had a poor view of reincarnation. As part of a military family, however, she learned there was more than one way of looking at most questions. She did not have to agree, but Dr. Pomar was advised not to disagree—at least openly.

After reading Edgar Cayce and Paramahansa Yogananda, she researched and learned how to access past lives by using guided imagery and through meditation techniques—what she found out later, in 1976, was a light state of hypnosis. While in Maryland, she started Edgar Cayce study groups and taught meditation. Someone asked if she knew of anyone who conducted past-life regression sessions. That started her in a different area of work. Hearing that Morris Netherton was giving past-life training workshops in Baltimore, she started her training in regression therapy. Since then, she has received her certification in hypnosis, a master's degree in psychology, and eventually a doctorate in clinical hypnotherapy. Having over thirty-five years of regression experience, she has regressed more than 5,000 individuals, either one on one or in groups.

While in Maryland, Dr. Pomar taught classes in meditation, dream interpretation, and past lives/reincarnation at the University of Delaware and Delaware Technical College. She also taught in Delaware and Maryland, as well as at the Association of Research and Enlightenment in Virginia. In addition, she was president of the Delmarva Ski Club and vice-president of the Wicomico County Republican Committee.

Currently Dr. Pomar, her husband Craig, and their cairn terrier, George, are snowbirds residing in Fairbanks, Alaska. When temperatures get cool they will migrate south to Rancho Mirage, California. She teaches meditation during the Fairbanks Summer Arts Festival for two weeks and volunteers as a docent at the Bear Gallery. While in California, Barbara can often be found on the golf course. She volunteers by teaching meditation at the Stroke Recovery Center and is on the board of directors of the Palm Springs Opera Guild of the Desert.

# Cover—About the Artist

The cover is an oil painting titled *Koyukukiatatna* by Spelman Evans Downer. The painting has been hanging our house since 1994. I chose this painting as it depicts time as it meanders, folding back and forth. Downer is a professional visual artist and art educator and has been a landscape painter since 1977. He has exhibited internationally and nationally from Alaska to New York City to California. Currently, he is an art instructor at Copper Mountain College in Joshua Tree, California. Downer permanently resides in Southern California's Mohave Desert in Yucca Valley. In summers when not rafting the Yukon and other Alaskan rivers, he can be found at his studio and Gallery Turquoise on the banks of the Kenai River in Cooper Landing in Alaska. His work can be viewed on-line at www.spelmanevansdowner.com.